IP'91 40.55

40—
‾‾‾
RS

D1602873

ECONOMIC AND POLITICAL INCENTIVES TO PETROLEUM EXPLORATION

Developments in the Asia–Pacific Region

Edited by
Jeremiah D. Lambert
Fereidun Fesharaki

INTERNATIONAL LAW INSTITUTE
Washington, D.C.

Distributed by arrangement with

University Press of America, Inc.
4720 Boston Way
Lanham, MD 20706

3 Henrietta Street
London WC2E 8LU England

International Law Institute
888 16th Street, N.W.
Washington, D.C. 20006

Library of Congress Cataloging–in–Publication Data

Economic and political incentives to petroleum exploration : Developments in the
Asia–Pacific region / edited by Jeremiah D. Lambert, Fereidun Fesharaki.
p.   cm.
Includes bibliographies.
1. Petroleum—Pacific Area—Prospecting—Finance—International cooperation.
2. Petroleum—East Asia—Prospecting—Finance—International cooperation.
3. Investments—Taxation.   4. Tax incentives.   I. Lambert, Jeremiah D., 1934–
II. Fesharaki, Fereidun.   III. International Law Institute (Washington, D.C.)
HD9578.P162E29   1989   338.2'3282'095—dc20   89–34648 CIP

ISBN 0–935328–57–2 (alk. paper)

The paper used in this publication meets the minimum requirements of American
National Standard for Information Sciences—Permanence of Paper for Printed
Library Materials, ANSI Z39.48—1984.

Table of Contents

Preface*

The world oil market is undergoing extreme change characterized by transient oversupply and price volatility. For the time being, the balance of power between producing and consuming nations has shifted, although great uncertainty exists as to the future availability and flow of oil.

Whatever the near-term price of oil, most observers agree that it will become less abundant and more expensive in the 1990's, resulting in an increased reliance on other forms of energy. Although forecasts differ greatly based on projections of economic growth, OPEC disunity, and prevailing prices, there remains little doubt that demand will eventually outstrip supply. In order to understand the workings of the oil market generally, it has proved useful to assess the principal sources and patterns of demand within a regional context.

The Asian-Pacific region, which includes both net producers and consumers of oil, is expected to increase its demand for petroleum products at a greater rate than any other part of the world over the next two decades. Indonesia, an OPEC member, as well as Malaysia, Brunei, and China (Beijing)**, will remain or become significant suppliers of oil, but the region as a whole will continue to depend on the Middle East for most of its oil imports. Regional growth is expected to occur in the context of significant changes in financing arrangements, public and private sector responsibilities, geopolitical relationships, and marketing and downstream operations.

In order to address these issues, the International Law Institute and the Resource Systems Institute of the East-West Center organized and sponsored a conference held in Honolulu, Hawaii, in the summer of 1986, which examined the impact of OPEC disunity on the Asian-Pacific region, identified innovative financing arrangements available to countries during the cyclical downturn, assessed the prospects of increased private sector involvement in petroleum activities, focused on the role of the multilateral institutions in the promotion of this objective, and discussed the problems and potential of instituting joint development arrangements in areas of overlapping maritime claims.

The conference, co-chaired by Jeremiah D. Lambert, a partner in Kirkpatrick & Lockhart (Washington, D.C.) and formerly a Trustee of the International Law Institute, and Dr. Fereidun Fesharaki, Leader of the Energy Pro-

---

* The Editors wish to express their appreciation to Matthew Hensley, formerly of the International Law Institute staff, and Heather L. Martley, a legal assistant at Kirkpatrick & Lockhart, Washington, D.C., for their invaluable help in preparing this book for publication.

** The term agreed upon by both China (Beijing) and China (Taipei) for international comparisons.

gram at the Resource Systems Institute, was attended by international petroleum professionals representing international organizations, oil corporations, energy law firms, state-owned enterprises, financial institutions and research organizations.

Papers presented at the conference are set forth here in the order in which they were discussed together with additional papers whose genesis was either a result of discussion at the conference or whose contents are of immediate relevance to the theme of the conference.

An Overview of Economic and Political Incentives to Petroleum Exploration

*by Jeremiah D. Lambert**

" . . . [T]he question of energy and oil supply is really in the hands of governments. If governments want more oil, they will aid rather than hinder oilmen in achieving greater levels of production. Once the oilman sees he is receiving some consideration, being given a fair chance to profit after risking his capital at staggering odds, he will respond. He always has and always will. It's in the nature of the breed.

"But if governments levy excessive taxes, pass restrictive legislation and otherwise make the petroleum industry a target and a whipping boy—the future will only grow darker. It's an old saying that oilmen scare easily. They become very frightened, indeed, when after being called upon to make multimillion and even billion dollar expenditures on 50-to-1 shots, they suspect that governments will not permit them a fair return for their risk and efforts. They'd much rather put their capital into savings banks. That would at least be a safe bet, even if it failed to produce a single additional barrel of oil."

J. Paul Getty, "As I See It," Prentice-Hall 1976, pp. 215–16.

I.

By 1986, when the crude oil market collapsed, the oil industry had already sustained its fifth year of recession. The free fall in oil prices thus followed a long period of stagnation, coupled with high oil prices, during which OPEC's market share eroded from 30 million to 16 million barrels per day.[1] Ultimately, OPEC could not administer production in a shrinking market, and prices fell as each OPEC member sought to maximize revenues without regard to previously agreed allocations.

The impact of oil's price collapse has reshaped many private sector economic decisions. Utilities in industrialized countries have been induced to switch from coal or gas to oil. High-cost oil producers have shut in or abandoned

---

*A. B., Princeton University; LL.B., Yale Law School. Mr. Lambert, a partner in Kirkpatrick & Lockhart, Washington, D.C., and a trustee of the International Law Institute from 1983 through 1988, served as co-chair of the conference on "Overcoming Obstacles to Regional Cooperation," jointly sponsored by the East-West Center and the International Law Institute in Honolulu on June 30-July 1, 1986.

wells, and exploration and development expenditures have been slashed, notably in the United States.

Plunging oil prices have had a similar negative effect on exploration and development worldwide, but with less impact in certain oil prospective countries. Thus, despite extreme price uncertainty, the budgeted expenditures of major oil companies for international exploration and development declined by less than 5% in 1987 compared with 1986, and much of that decline can be attributed to non-U.S. companies.[2] It is a fair inference that overseas drilling economics in recent years have grown relatively more attractive than domestic economics, as some host governments—particularly those in developing countries—have begun to redistribute the costs, risks, and benefits of oil exploration and development. In shifting their exploration and production emphasis outside the U.S., major domestic companies may therefore be responding, in part, to improvements in tax, concession, and similar institutional arrangements obtainable overseas.

Governments, it is clear, are reassessing the way they do business to attract investment in the face of adverse industry conditions. The U.K. has eased its tax regime for North Sea producers; Australia is considering a comparable move to encourage production; Canada has eliminated its Federal Petroleum and Gas Revenue Tax; and developing countries, including those with only incipient petroleum production, have in certain instances improved historic participation terms in order to make exploration feasible notwithstanding an uncertain market. Industry observers have even discerned an international market for petroleum work rights.

Whether such a market truly exists, except in contemplation of theoretical economists and editorial writers, remains to be proven. What seems little in doubt, however, is that developing countries, including those with petroleum resources, have had to cope over the past five years with an increasing scarcity of external capital. Between 1981 and 1984, for example, commercial bank lending to developing countries fell from $87 billion to $16 billion—a massive drop.[3] With foreign direct investment also in decline, many developing countries, and particularly those in the Asian-Pacific Region, have sought ways of increasing inflows of risk capital, including capital for petroleum exploration and development.

In most developing countries, direct investment finances less than 2–3 per cent of total investment, although the share was much larger in the 1950's and the 1960's.[4] The key to enhancing direct investment lies in the economic policies that are most conducive to productive foreign investment are those that have been followed by a number of Asian-Pacific countries. While the impact of specific policies on the incidence of foreign direct investment is certainly debatable, the choice of country location does reflect both incentives and, on the downside, performance requirements.[5]

That the balance is tipping toward incentives in many developing countries suggests a global trend away from hostility toward multinational corporations, accompanied by host government realization that foreign private investment can promote industrialization and generate jobs, foreign exchange, and tax revenues, not to mention the transfer of indispensable technology.

In many countries abandonment of socialist economics has been specific and noticeable: Turkey has discarded protectionism, as well as export controls, and has proposed free-trade zones as an encouragement to foreign investment. Algeria has adopted a new investment code that guarantees repatriation of profits. China had avidly pursued free-market policies, resulting in $4.6 billion in foreign investment since 1979.[6]

Nowhere do these policy considerations assume more complex dimensions than with respect to unevenly distributed petroleum resources whose recoverability is a function of volatile market factors rooted in OPEC administration as well as worldwide demand for oil. The decision to invest presupposes the existence of an accessible oil prospective area and oil prices that justify the risk undertaken.

Oil price forecasting is notoriously risky, although longtime price rises seem plausible in view of predicted growth in oil demand and overall declines in non-OPEC supply. Since individual countries cannot control these factors, however, the quest for development of petroleum resources must focus on appropriate contractual and fiscal arrangements, the existence of necessary infrastructure, and the avoidance of undue political risk. While these factors will not attract investment if commodity prices plummet, they are at least in principle manageable concerns.

II.

Recent scholarly analysis (see, e.g., Broadman, "Incentives and Constraints on Exploratory Drilling for Petroleum in Developing Countries," 10 Ann. Rev. Energy 217 (1985)) views the institutional arrangements between host government and foreign oil company—including contracts and taxes—as a prime means of allocating risk and reward.[7]

Contracts commonly include concessions, production-sharing contracts, service contracts (both risk and non-risk), and joint ventures. Broadly speaking, those arrangements may be summarized as follows:

– A traditional concession is in effect a government lease permitting a foreign oil company to explore in a specific geographic area and requiring it to provide all the capital required. The company then markets the oil produced and pays the government a royalty per barrel. Recent concession agreements accord only limited property rights and impose operational constraints. Exploration risk is borne by the company.

– A production-sharing contract, like a concession, requires the company to provide all exploration and development capital required but permits its recovery of investment and operating costs through ownership of a share of the oil produced, called "cost oil." The balance of oil produced, "profit oil" as opposed to "cost oil," is then divided between the government and the company by agreement. If an exploration project yields commercial production, production-sharing should compensate the company in accordance with the risk it assumed, which includes all the cost risk and a proportionate share of the geologic and revenue risk.

- Service contracts contemplate payment of a fee for exploration and development services, either in cash or oil. Under nonrisk contracts the company is paid a flat fee for exploration services, regardless of the commercial outcome of its performance and a flat fee per barrel for development services. Risk contracts require the contractor to bear all exploration outlays but provide incentive compensation if a commercial discovery is made.

- Joint ventures between the foreign company and the government as equity partners usually require the company to assume exploration risks, thereafter permitting all exploration costs to be recovered by the company before splitting later production in accordance with the parties' equity interests.

Rational contractual arrangements must therefore address and allocate an array of risks, including those related to the geology of the prospective area; the costs of exploration, development, and operation; and, of course, the imponderable impact of fluctuating oil prices on project revenues. At the exploration stage, nonrecovery of costs is the dominant private sector risk consideration, replaced at the development stage by the risk that anticipated project revenues will be taxed away or otherwise eroded.

Over recent years governments have tended to shift from passive concession arrangements in which risk is borne by the foreign company to greater participation in both the benefits and risks of oil projects, with corresponding influence over project management and operations and greater ownership rights in crude oil. The form of contractual agreements chosen is in this connection less important than the substantive question of allocating control, risk, and revenue-sharing, which can be equally addressed by means of concession/investment agreements, service contracts, joint venture arrangements or hybrid combinations thereof. Contractual arrangements that accommodate corporate needs—through seismic options, flexible work programs, and enhanced economic inducements—can serve to maintain exploration momentum in a period of industry recession.

III.

Like contractual arrangements, tax regimes can have a profound effect on petroleum exploration and development. Three typical taxation schemes in developing countries include signature bonuses, royalties, and profit taxes.

- A signature bonus is essentially a lump sum payment made to the government when an exploration contract is initiated, often when exploration rights are obtained through competitive bidding or negotiation.

- Under a royalty system, the government receives cash when commercial production begins as a function of revenue, not profits, thus allocating development risk primarily to the company.

- Profit taxes are determined by profits, not gross revenues, deferring tax burden until later in the project cycle and sharing risks more evenly between the government and the company. A "resource rent" profit tax subjects the company's net income to a higher rate of tax when the rate of return on the project exceeds a predetermined level, whether through production or price increases, thus capturing windfalls. Most tax systems do not adequately take account of the economics of scale related to oil field size and as a result effectively discourage development of small, high-cost fields.

In recent years, encouraged by oil prices elevated above historic levels, developing countries have been able to extract higher tax yields but have done so "less by applying higher tax rates than by moving from specific to *ad valorem* taxes, recovering tax holidays, decreasing percentage depletion allowances, and scrutinizing the transfer prices governing transactions between foreign oil company exploration affiliates and their parent companies."[8] Starting in the early 1980's, however, such countries have been compelled to rethink fiscal policy to maintain petroleum exploration and development.

Seen from the perspective of the economist, signature bonuses, requiring *ex ante* cash outlays, are regressive; royalties are in principle also regressive (but can be made proportional to field size); production-based taxes may serve as incentives for development by facilitating company realization of superprofits from large-field production; while resource rent taxes fulfill the ideal of progressivity by providing a specified rate of return and reduced exposure to risk, at the same time permitting quicker cost recovery on smaller fields and capturing windfalls for the host country.[9]

Theoretical considerations aside, liberalization of fiscal terms can be seen as an inevitable response to the recent global change in the economics of oil exploration and development. The dramatic increase in oil prices during the late 1970's and early 1980's invited governments to increase revenues, without rendering company operations unprofitable, through tax and quasi-tax increases. In today's lower price world, however, the surplus for taxation has substantially diminished and has not been offset by capital cost reductions.

As a consequence, the fiscal structure presently necessary for oil field development, particularly of marginal, smaller prospects in less developed countries, is likely to forego heavy front-end payments, such as contract and production bonuses, and fixed levies in the form of royalties and large production payments. As a further inducement, it will also permit accelerated recovery of expenditures incurred, thus delaying payment of taxes and production-sharing, while increasing the cost oil percentage to 100% in the year an expenditure is incurred and permitting losses to be carried forward without limitation.

IV.

It should not be assumed that mere tinkering with rates and terms will call forth the petroleum genie from his place of repose. Real world considerations are apt to be more complex.

As we have seen, traditional sources of petroleum finance—including private companies' self-generated cashflow, bank loans, and equity investment—have been virtually withdrawn in the wake of oil price decline and uncertainty about less developed country creditworthiness. Both domestically and internationally, energy loans have subjected commercial banks to huge losses, while loans from multinational institutions such as the World Bank can best be regarded as seed money, not an ultimate source of alternative finance.

It is not surprising, therefore, that attention has focused on alternative financing techniques as a means of encouraging private sector finance, without which the international petroleum industry may well overcontract, thereby setting the stage for a further round of price escalations should OPEC regain economic dominance.[10]

Such techniques include:

- Co-financing arrangements associating public and private sector financial institutions, and including World Bank, Inter-American Development Bank, and Asian Development Bank.

- Countertrade, in which oil is bartered for industrial goods, agricultural commodities, military equipment, or construction of facilities and is also used to co-finance specific projects or to provide payment in kind to project suppliers.

- Advanced payment facilities involving pre-export finance.

- Petroleum-backed securities or debt obligations collateralized by an oil-producing country's contract to deliver crude oil to a creditworthy international oil company.

However promising they may be in principle, it is not clear that such techniques can be expected to mobilize significant amounts of capital in the face of lenders' continued credit concerns and oil price uncertainty. What they do signify, however, is that financial and contractual terms shaped by experience with large, low-cost oil fields in mideastern OPEC countries must be adapted to the requirements of marginal fields under radically changed economic conditions.

V.

As major oil companies move petroleum dollars out of the U.S. and Canada in favor of less developed country exploration, they will necessarily pay attention to offshore prospective areas, particularly in the Asian-Pacific region, where overlapping sovereign claims could—barring successful joint development—constitute a political and legal hazard to private investors.[11] Such overlapping claim areas exist in the Gulf of Thailand, the Timor Strait, the Gulf of Tonkin, the Natuna Sea, and offshore Brunei, among other locations.

Given the relatively greater risk associated with offshore drilling and the uncertainty posed by lower oil prices, it might be thought that governments would have little incentive to pursue complicated joint development schemes. In fact, the opposite has been true for Indonesia and Australia with respect to overlapping claims in the Timor Strait; and the glacial pace of joint development efforts suggests the virtue of long-range planning, even in the face of oversupply and low prices, based on precedental joint development agreements including those between Thailand and Malaysia, South Korea and Japan, Saudi Arabia and Kuwait, and Iceland and Norway).

Such agreements typically define the extent of the disputed area and prescribe contractual regime, selection and supervision of operators, financial and tax arrangements, functions of the joint management body, and duration of the joint accord. They may also address what system of civil and even criminal law will apply to joint development areas. In any event, the array of legal, economic, jurisprudential, and governmental problems posed by joint development is formidable, and only the Saudi Arabia-Kuwait agreement has yet resulted in successful exploration and development. Nonetheless, joint development may provide the only practicable means of resolving otherwise irreconcilable differences between sovereigns' inconsistent claims to disputed offshore areas. The pursuit of such difficult government-to-government negotiations, although blunted by lower oil prices, may be the indispensable predicate for eventual recovery of valuable petroleum resources.

VI.

Although contractual, tax, and governmental incentives in less developed countries may be devised to attract foreign investment, they can at the outside only marginally dent the impact of worldwide oil economics, which have been decisively shaped by OPEC's need to increase production as a means of regaining market share. As OPEC production rises, oil prices tend to drop toward the marginal cost of production, and much high cost non-OPEC oil is forced from the market. As a result, non-communist, non-OPEC oil production declined in 1986 after having increased for 10 consecutive years.[12] Although both OPEC production and oil prices may now have stabilized, further price uncertainty—and corresponding investor diffidence—are both predictable.

Ultimately, the fate of many non-OPEC oil economies will reside with OPEC and its ability—thought problematic by many—to regain control of the marketplace by curtailing production. OPEC's collapse suggests more than momen tary disarray and implicates instead a stagnant worldwide market for oil coupled with the displacement of multinational oil companies as market intermediaries capable of cutting production more or less equally in all countries when actual demand fails to match projected levels of consumption.[13] Such structural changes have led to dissipation of the once orderly, regulated market in oil wehre volumes moved through established channels in favor of a volatile commodity market, driven by players' reliance on spot and futures contracts.

To attract capital for oil and gas exploration in today's market, as the following papers show, will require retrenchment from statist intervention, favorable contractual terms, rational fiscal regimes, innovative financing techniques, and regional cooperation. If those efforts are not vigorously pursued by Asian-Pacific countries, the region's overall dependence on Middle Eastern oil supplies will continue, and development of indigenous resources will be suppressed.

Footnotes

[1] *Oil & Gas Journal,* March 9, 1987, pp. 13–15. A price-cutting OPEC move to regain market share boosted 1986 demand for OPEC oil by 12.6% to just over 18 million barrels per day.

[2] *Oil & Gas Journal,* January 19, 1987, pp. 28–29.

[3] Ryrie, "Increasing the Flow of Risk Capital to Developing Countries," The Royal Bank of Scotland Review, Number 150, June 1986, p.5.

[4] *Id.* at pp. 7–8.

[5] See generally Carpio, "Promoting Private Sector Petroleum Investments in LDC's: A World Bank Objective," *Infra.*

[6] See Bordewich, "The Lessons of Bhopal," *The Atlantic,* March 1987, p.32.

[7] See also Walde, "Investment Policies in the International Petroleum Industry: Responses to the Current Crises," *Infra, Passim.*

[8] Broadman, *op. cit.,* pp. 232–33.

[9] *Ibid.*

[10] See Morse, "Innovative Financing of Petroleum Projects: Options During the Cyclical Downturn," *Infra, Passim.*

[11] See generally Valencia, "Joint Development of Petroleum Resources in Overlapping Claim Areas," *Infra, Passim.*

[12] *Oil & Gas Journal,* March 9, 1987, pp. 13–14.

[13] See Verleger, "Too Many Booths at the Oil Bazaar," *Oil and Gas Investor,* Volume 6, Number 7, February 1987, pp. 16–18.

Investment Policies in the International Petroleum Industry: Responses to the Current Crisis

by Thomas Walde

With declining oil prices, interest in investment in petroleum exploration projects in less-developed countries has slackened. As capital becomes scarce and competition among countries increases, companies generally look for investment opportunities having higher yield and lower risk profiles. In order to attract investment in petroleum projects, countries will thus be forced to reevaluate their legislative, contractual, and financial policies to accomodate the current market environment. The author examines a comprehensive range of policy responses to the current crisis available to host governments and assesses the impact of technical cooperation on energy investment policies.

The world's petroleum industry is currently undergoing a change that, from the perspective of the last 15 years at least, appears fundamental. While other commodities, and in particular non-fuel minerals (iron ore, copper, nickel, bauxite, tin, coal, uranium et al.) have since 1982 entered into a lasting price depression to levels, in real prices, close to those seen during the Great Depression of the 1930s, petroleum appeared largely unaffected. In fact, it appeared, and was widely believed, that petroleum was exempt from market forces and the cyclical movements affecting the prices of mineral commodities. OPEC was supposed to be able to control both prices and production. However, this has changed, first gradually, and, in the course of 1986, with increasing, utterly unexpected speed and dramatic effects: Oil prices which reached 36 US$ and above after 1979, have plummeted (by July 1986) below the 10 US$ benchmark. In real, inflation-adjusted terms (in 1972 US$), these oil prices have fallen from US$ 16 in 1981 to about $5 in 1986; this level is not much above the 3-5 US$ average (in real, 1972 terms) of the oil prices averaged over a period from 1901 to 1979.[3] The reasons for this decline seem to lie basically in a large excess of current production over demand and in the loss of OPEC in maintaining price control. OPEC's decreasing influence is due to the declining demand brought about by the oil price hikes in the past and by the simultaneously occurring substantial growth of oil production in non-OPEC countries.[4] A, though controversial, facet of OPEC strategy currently seems to be to maintain production and thus drive out higher-cost producers with the reduced price, thus aiming at restoring the market share for OPEC countries.

Predicting future oil prices is eminently important for the industry, but highly speculative and, as demonstrates the past, very likely to produce a prog-

9

nosis widely off the mark.[5] Should OPEC be unable to reassert its market power by imposing and negotiating (with non-OPEC producers) large cuts in production, then prices could fall, according to standard economic theory, to the costs of the marginal producers; such costs are estimated to be around 5-6 US$ (in current terms)[6]. The price-setting power by producing countries has been seriously eroded in the past year by the emergence of spot and futures markets for petroleum independent of producers. While spot and futures markets to a large extent deal mainly with "paper oil", many contracts even for "wet" oil are linked to the spot market.[7] The erosion of official posted prices started with invisible discounts offered through countertrade arrangements and continued in 1986 through the expansion of netback pricing, a mechanism whereby the price for crude is determined by the price realized after sale of refined products; here, the producer assumes the risk of price volatility for refined products for quite some time after delivery of crude. It is estimated by many that a lasting decline of oil prices will after several years lead to an increase in demand, and also to some decline in production. While already operating production capacities are unlikely to close down and shut in oil even at today's prices[8], new exploration and development, particularly in high-cost and high-risk areas will be severely curtailed: Debt-loaded companies have no cash flow available for exploration and development, banks are unwilling to finance such activities, and even large and well-positioned international oil companies may prefer to purchase reserves at a discount price from failing companies instead of exploring and developing new reserves.

The implications of a continued period of low oil prices are already becoming visible: New exploration and development is heavily curtailed[9], financing difficult to obtain, be it from banks or, for state enterprises, from government resources. While oil-importing countries benefit, oil producing countries—and their banks and suppliers—suffer; lending to oil producing countries on the strength of their petroleum assets is likely to dry up, while repayment of existing debt is currently unlikely. On the other hand, oil importing countries will have much more leeway in handling their foreign debt. Petroleum enterprises—both private and public—are forced to reduce their operating, investment and overhead costs in a massive way: All companies are reporting a reduction of staff and of exploration expenditures, a scale-down of new projects and a re-assessment of current and planned operations. Governments which expected a steady resource flow from petroleum companies face the possibility of a serious decrease of such flows, or even the claim for subsidies by state petroleum companies. This, in turn, is provoking a more critical appraisal of performance and expenditures by state petroleum companies which have built up visibly costly operations based on their state monopoly over petroleum in times of high prices[10]. In the following, the report will survey changes that have already taken place in the last years as response to the gradual erosion of the petroleum price and as a reaction of non-oil producing countries to obtain development of smaller, more marginal oilfields and changes that are currently taking place or likely to take place if the oil price does not rebound to previous high levels. As the response of governments and industry is in the very process of being formulated in a situation of high uncertainty and price volatility, it is naturally difficult to portray the current evolution with full precision. The dramatic price decline of 1986 has as yet not been reflected in legislation and contracts, but is likely to make an impact in 1986 and in subsequent years.

INVESTMENT POLICIES IN THE PETROLEUM INDUSTRY

Petroleum Legislation

Petroleum legislation is the basic instrument employed by governments to regulate the exploration for and development of petroleum.[11] While petroleum was traditionally governed by the general mining law—and still is in some countries—, the worldwide tendency is to recognize the role of petroleum as the world's most important mineral by separate petroleum laws. Most mining and petroleum laws by now attribute ownership and full dominion over petroleum (and other energy minerals, such as coal, natural gas, uranium and geothermal energy) to the state, with, basically, the exception of the US; here, ownership of land includes subsurface minerals.[12] While petroleum laws and regulations covering petroleum operations and contracts with (foreign or national) contractors in very much detail and without flexibility for negotiations are found, in particular in Latin America[13], the current trend is characterized by very short, framework-type petroleum laws. These laws basically set forth the major principles, assign petroleum to the state and authorize government agencies, often state petroleum companies, to negotiate petroleum development agreements. These agreements, and some subsidiary petroleum regulations, constitute the hard core of the legal regime applicable to petroleum activities.

The current trend towards new petroleum laws is heavily influenced by the extensive petroleum promotion program of the World Bank[14]. In over 33 countries, mainly non-oil producing developing countries, the Bank is financing petroleum promotion projects to encourage private investment in petroleum exploration. These projects include, in general, the preparation of an information package of geological data, including some seismic and other geophysical work; the emphasis, however, is on the formulation of a petroleum law, petroleum regulations and a petroleum model agreement attractive to foreign investors. In addition, under the program the Bank finances promotion activities and direct legal advice in negotiations. While the Bank officially disclaims responsibility since the mentioned activities are in principle executed by advisers and consulting firms contracted directly by the government, and Bank's loan procedures, its emphasis on a continuous policy dialogue and the attention it enjoys from borrowers seem to ensure that the Bank's respective current policies and philosophies are reflected in these petroleum law packages. Reportedly, as of

July 1986, over 50 new exploration contracts have been signed subsequent to completion of the mentioned petroleum promotion projects.

A noteworthy feature of these modern petroleum laws is the relationship between the petroleum law as such and specific contracts. While, given the state ownership of petroleum in the ground, one might expect the petroleum law to be the exclusive legal instrument governing operations, the US-type of all-encompassing petroleum contract appears to have become the main instrument for regulating specific petroleum development operations.[15] This legal form does not break up individual entitlements for the prospection, exploration drilling and extraction phase (as is done by traditional mining law instruments such as prospection, exploration and exploration title/concession), but provides a single legal title for all phases of petroleum development; it assures, from the beginning of prospection, to the company its rights throughout the sequence of phases up to and through exploitation.

While some laws define in detail, and with much rigidity, the permissible scope of such contracts (e.g., the 1979 Decreto-Ley 22774 in Peru), most more recent laws (e.g., Zambia, 1985; Ethiopia, 1986, Proclamation 295) give broad powers to the government to negotiate petroleum agreements. While the main issues for contracts are mentioned, the competent government authorities possess considerable discretion in negotiating specific terms under the umbrella of the general and broad directives of the petroleum law. This approach allows the government to adjust its terms to the changing and volatile world market for petroleum contracts and to the specific risks and benefits of the acreage it can offer, to learn and increase its negotiating capabilities and to evolve terms over time[16].

PETROLEUM DEVELOPMENT AGREEMENTS: RESPONSE TO THE DECLINING OIL PRICE

Constraints and Competition of Governments in New Petroleum Contracts

With the declining oil price, the negotiating power of countries offering acreage for petroleum activities decreases by necessity: The world market for petroleum rights is converted from a seller's to a buyer's market, capital is more scarce, competition among countries increases and the revenues available for sharing between government and contractor shrink, often, particularly in the class of higher-cost deposits, dramatically close to zero. Companies look out primarily for high-yield, low-risk operations, preferably with lower capital costs and high and immediate pay-back. The volatility of the price dampens interest in investment and financing. The most attractive deposits are those where the geological risk is very small and where exploration expenditures and thus risk is borne or shared by the government, as is the case of companies with operations in major producing countries; here, by way of tax deductibility of incremental investment and exploration or even by way of tax credit[17] for exploration, the government assumes all or a major share (in case of high marginal tax rates reaching up to 90% of net income almost all) of high-risk exploration expenditures. International agencies, such as the International Finance Corporation[18] tend to follow this strategy. The implication of these developments in the current world environment is that countries have to reduce their expectations, as generated by the 1979–82 boom in petroleum prices, substantially, that it is much more difficult to attract petroleum investment and that marginal deposits are not very likely to find investors. Particular attention should be paid to the fact that petroleum-importing developing countries without current production or large proven reserves are facing almost insurmountable obstacles in finding access to new petroleum exploration from public or private sources. Many of the risk-taking smaller oil companies, but also several of the larger, heavily leveraged international oil companies previously attracted to unexplored acreage by the expectations of eventual high rewards have either gone out of business, are selling assets to stave off bankruptcy and are in general unwilling and financially incapable of continuing the exploration intensity seen from 1980 to 1983.

The full implications of such behavior are still difficult to precisely discern. Should after a prolonged slump oil prices pick up in the early 1990s, then oil importing countries would be hit quite hard, since given the 6–10 year lag between exploration and production, it would not be possible to re-start exploration in time to reduce the then likely import burden. Also, the reduced number of players in petroleum would make it relatively costly to attract and execute petroleum exploration projects. The choices for governments in this difficult situation are basically the following:

Governments may postpone action, hope for a petroleum price increase and a better bargaining position; a prolonged decline, with a following steep increase in prices in the early 1990s would make this a risky strategy, as governments would then be forced to import at a high price, until a new exploration efforts bears fruit after several years;

Governments may decide to strengthen state enterprise activities, exploit the greatly reduced costs for petroleum services and carry out risk exploration directly or by non-risk taking service contractors. Such a contrarian strategy would bank on the expectation that oil prices would rise steeply in the 1990s or earlier. It assumes considerable risk-taking by governments and availability of risk capital (mostly in foreign exchange), management and technical capabilities. While such policy appears feasible in theory and interesting as a longer-term speculation, most indications are that governments will not take such strategy, as given the indebtedness of countries and the intense competition for both local and foreign funds, no additional local or foreign exchange funds will be available. In fact, current indications are that governments are forced to reduce the availability of exploration and developments funds for state enterprises;

Governments may after assessment of the relative value of their acreage in the international exploration market decide to pursue a strategy of vigorous investment promotion. This implies considerable incentives (see infra). It would also be advisable to negotiate for maximum flexibility to take into account the possibility of a further decrease, but also of an increase in petroleum prices. In other words: The current volatility of oil prices must be responded to by an extremely flexible contractual arrangement.

These strategies, naturally, may also be combined in some way or other. In addition, given the uncertainty of future prices, a sound policy would be to keep domestic petroleum demand under control. The risk, and particularly in developing countries with domestic petroleum supply at subsidized prices, is that available reserves will be fast depleted, no new exploration will take place an an upturn in prices will imply importation of oil at high prices. It appears that in several countries, particularly in Southeast Asia, governments are already responding to the decline by imposing additional taxes on petroleum consumption, thus minimizing the stimulus to consumption provided by the lower price.

Forms of Contract

The question of the form of petroleum contract has been highly overrated in the laymen's, diplomatic and political debate and it has thus overshadowed the more important questions of key functions and real substance. The various forms, and many single-issue mechanisms of agreements upgraded to a specific new form[19], have been frequently described in previous reports by the United Nations[20]. Currently, the major forms such as concession/investment agreement, service contracts and joint venture agreements coexist in an endless number of hybrid combinations. The basic functions of an agreement—control, risk, revenue-sharing—are largely independent from the form chosen; a slight tendency can be said to be implied in concession/investment agreements in favor of investor management and risk assumption and in service agreements towards government influence on decision-making and assumption of risk. Some petroleum laws prescribe a specific form, but most new laws tend to leave the choice open to government agencies empowered to negotiate. The form is mostly dependent on the legal tradition and on precedent in a particular country.

Companies have found no problem in adapting whatever form is preferred to their specific interests. It was once believed that there was a natural transition from concession over joint venture to service contract. However, the fact that a real service contract would imply government equity financing, government management capability and government assumption of geological, technical and price risk has led under the impact of the current situation to; the extinction of such real service contracts—as contrasted to mere service contract labels[21]. Given the current situation, one can expect all currently used forms to survive, as the main adjustments occurring are adjustments more of substance than of form. However, a slight trend in favor of joint ventures with production-sharing mechanisms and a revival of concession agreements with no government participation can be expected, as the willingness and ability of governments to assume risks and contribute funds appears severely curtailed.[22]

Exploration Requirements

The petroleum price boom in the early 1980s meant an intense competition by companies for available acreage; the expectation of ever rising oil prices translated into the willingness to speed up exploration, assume stringent and high minimum exploration requirements, expressed in monetary value and work programmes (e.g., minimum lines of seismic; minimum footage of exploration drilling), to relinquish acreage held under exclusive rights rather fast and to accept development obligations based on the invest-now-or-go-away principle. Having reserves was considered the key and commerciality was assumed to exist in most cases of discovery. Given the present scenario, such extensive exploration and development obligations are likely to disappear, except in cases of low geological risk (e.g., acreage adjacent to large oilfields with known geology) and likelihood for large, low-cost oilfields.

Exploration terms are likely to be differentiated according to geological risk, likely cost and production structures and competition among companies. In the large case of acreage considered more marginal, in non-oil producing countries and in areas without already existing infrastructure (e.g. pipelines, docking facilities et al.), one can expect and already perceive more extended exploration terms (10–12 years instead of 6–8 years), reduced minimum requirements, more time given to appraise discoveries and to develop oilfields considered commercial, to wait for the establishment of pipelines and a slow-down of the rhythm of mandatory relinquishment. Recent agreements do rarely contain the develop-now-or-go-away method, with the discovery reverting to the national oil company. Also, the often seen requirement to spend within the exploration period a minimum amount (often several tens of millions of US$), regardless of the geological results and, in the case of non-compliance, pay the non-expended amount, secured by an unconditional performance bond, is giving way to a more gradual, incremental phasing of exploration activities and obligations. For example, the minimum requirement is now often stipulated for each phase of exploration activity; the company may then decide whether to withdraw or to assume the rights and obligations of the next phase. The "seismic option", allowing a company to carry out a seismic survey and then decide if it wishes to continue by farming-out and obtaining the requisite financing for drilling or to withdraw is becoming more popular. Smaller companies, a major source for smaller countries and more marginal operations, are as a rule unable to obtain the necessary financing and bank guarantees to assume bond-secured extensive minimum requirements. The same applies to larger, but highly leveraged international oil companies. Given the current volatility of the price and the industry conditions, exploration is hence becoming a more careful, gradual and incremental activity.

Financial Terms, Revenue-Sharing and Remuneration

The increase of the oil price up to 10–15 times the cost of production of the main low-cost production capacities in 1980 has produced a huge potential for increasing governmental revenues without making the operations unprofitable to the companies. The division of the additional surplus created by the oil price increases is what the large number of fiscal renegotiations, taking of government participation, nationalizations plus subsequent service/management arrangement, imposition of additional taxes and quasi-tax levies (additional petroleum royalties, taxes, export taxes, bonuses, production-sharing) basically was about. The marginal government take in major producing countries exceeded sometimes 90% of the price of a barrel of oil. "Caps" were placed on realized prices beyond which all sales revenue would accrue to government[23]. With an oil price shrinking in real terms from 16 US\$ (1972 prices) in 1981 to about 5 US\$ (in 1972 prices) in 1986 (July), the scope for revenue-sharing has diminished to often close to zero, while companies will still only continue to operate or to invest with an expectation to earn around 15%, in real terms, return on capital, with adjustment to political, geological, technical and commercial risk[24]. In addition, the popularity of the classical Mideastern fiscal regime based on high oil prices and large, low-cost oilfields has proven prohibitive for the more marginal oilfields discovered and likely to be discovered in non-oil producing developing countries. Such marginal fields are not capable of generating sufficient cash flow to pay large signature, discovery and production bonuses, support a rigid production-sharing percentage independent of profitability and large payments based on production rather than on profits or profitability.

Governments that currently wish to attract investment—instead of waiting out for a more propitious time in oil prices, with the risks inherent in such a temporizing strategy—are accordingly realizing that while the price for investment capital has not much lowered, the surplus available for taxation has greatly diminished. Lower royalties, abolishment of the ring-fence clause, elimination of front-end bonuses, reduced government shares in production-sharing and the disappearance of many additional supplemental and special surtaxes are hence a feature of contracts since 1983/84; this trend is accelerating and is likely to become more prominent if the oil price should further decline or maintain roughly current levels[25].

Quite apart from the implications of a smaller profit-pie to share in, the current situation calls for and imposes a new concept of flexibility in oil taxation. Oil development agreements in the 1970s have been greatly influenced by the contract paradigm developed for large, low-cost oilfields in mainly Mideastern OPEC countries. This contract model was based on a very large and rigidly structured government take. It is being replaced by new concepts more responsive to the price volatility and to more marginal oilfields. This evolution towards contractual flexibility was apparent already in petroleum agreements of non-oil producing countries in the last years and is now reaching countries with middle-to-high-cost oil production. In fact, it might also be applicable to large oil producing countries where new oilfields are likely to be smaller, high-cost or where development can only occur after heavy infrastructure investment. Such flexibility is particularly called for in view of the current uncertainty: While current conditions require a low-tax regime, a future rise in oil prices will inevitably result in a new wave of renegotiations and imposition of additional taxes; negotiating a flexible and responsive fiscal regime at present means also taking into account the possibility, but not certainty of a price increase a few years hence. Typical features of such new petroleum agreements—they might be labelled "incentive agreements"—is the formulation of production-sharing mechanisms where the shares are conditioned by the volume of daily production; while the government would take low shares in the case of low-production, production in excess of specified thresholds will trigger a larger government share for the excess portion. Royalties in some agreements are reduced or eliminated altogether, while in others such royalties are reduced for the first years or their percentage linked to price levels. Government participation in the form of large equity shares carried by the contractor throughout high-risk exploration are also likely to be reduced, and their exercise may be on more commercial conditions.

The resource-rent (or additional-profits) tax concept[26] where all or part of taxation is triggered after the investor has recovered his investment and a specified internal rate of return, has been incorporated in the past in several petroleum model agreements prepared under the World Bank exploration promotion program (e.g. in Equatorial Guinea; Guyana et. al.), but also in Australia (offshore petroleum development), Papua New Guinea, Cayman, Tanzania and other countries. While support from the World Bank for this model has diminished, it is still a very worthwhile mechanism to consider, as the mechanism spares marginal deposits and is only triggered in case of high profitability after full, IRR increased recovery of total investment. It is probably more suitable for relatively large and less risky operations to respond flexibly to the price uncertainty, but may be less adequate for high-risk unknown acreage, where the possibility of very high profits is a motivation to undertake high-risk investment[27]; also, it appears more acceptable to large companies and to non-US companies[28].

Probably one of the most powerful incentives to encourage oil exploration by basically only delaying, but not reducing the government's share is through accelerated recovery. This method increases the net present value in the investor's cash flow calculation, it accelerates repayment of loans and it can greatly contribute to the reduction of the political risk perception by minimizing the time during which the investment is exposed to such risk. While the normal accounting method would be to write off expenditures over the life-span of the assets purchased or created, accelerated recovery lets the contractor write off much faster, thus delaying payment of taxes and production-sharing. In a production-sharing system, the essential variable is the cost oil percentage; in primarily income-tax based systems the comparable key function is the percentage allowed for depreciation and amortization. While rates of 30–40% of cost oil, respective amortization, were customary, new petroleum incentive agreements provide for cost recovery at 100% in the year the expenditure is incurred, with unlimited loss carry forward[29].

The fiscal methods discussed require a rather sophisticated tax administration, with full knowledge of international industry practices and effective control over inputs (costs) and outputs (production volume and sales receipts). Some countries have gone radically away from these tax concepts: Major petroleum producing countries (e.g. Libya and Nigeria) pay the contractor a fixed profit element of about US$ 2 per bpd, irrespective of petroleum prices. Thereby, they fully assume any risk or benefit associated with costs and prices. This approach, approaching the method of regulating power utilities in many countries where a fixed profit is guaranteed, can be attractive to a company selling its services to a government, but will not induce much risk-taking. Also, the more the available surplus shrinks, the more will it be difficult for these countries to pay the fixed fee to the contractor. Other countries, basically non-oil producing countries, have taken the contrasting approach of simplifying to a maximum any petroleum tax by replacing all taxes, participations and levies by one simple production-sharing percentage meant to be promotional (e.g. Togo)[30]. In such an arrangement, not much different from the first petroleum concessions signed in earlier days, the government takes no risk, but only monitors production and to some extent marketing. It is a regime which seeks to attract investment at any price to high-risk acreage.

Development Obligations and Transfer of Technology

Most petroleum agreements signed in the last decade provide for obligations to employ and train citizens of the host country, purchase supplies and services on the national market, transfer technologies to the national petroleum company, establish and support national refineries and other downstream facilities and use local transportation[31]. Given the surplus available in petroleum operations, these obligations were often negotiated to mean rather specific obligations for the company to incur expenditures it would not incur for pure business reasons. As such, they constitute, apart from an expression of good will and an attempt to re-orient the operations to the extent commercially feasible to the national economy, an additional cost element. As the margins available for revenue-sharing diminish, these obligations tend to be increasingly limited to what is commercially feasible for the company without generating additional costs. Thus, while development and technology obligations have not lost their role completely, they are likely to diminish with respect to their financial implications; given the current financial squeeze, governments prefer to obtain the revenues that are available directly rather than see them spent for specific purposes related to the petroleum operations.

Petroleum Financing

As traditional sources of petroleum finance—self-generated cash-flow by private and public petroleum companies, bank loans, equity investment through farm-out—dry out, much interest is directed towards the search for innovative financing techniques which are expected to fill the gap created by the withdrawal of traditional sources[32]. Petrobonds, i.e. bonds issued by producer/producer countries with interest/debt service linked to petroleum prices[33], countertrade financing, increased use of suppliers' credits, conversion of payment claims by oil services contractors into equity or longer-term loans, a revolving fund for exploration, equity-like non-recourse financing (possibly under Islamic banking principles) and increased financing by multi-lateral institutions through co-financing to lengthen private-debt maturities and reduce political risk have been urged as possible solutions.

It is not certain if such innovations will, by the sheer force of imagination, be able to overcome the basic cause of financing reluctance, i.e. the fact that private banks are currently losing billions of US$ on petroleum loans[34] and that with the decrease of oil prices and the perceptions of uncertainty energy lending is viewed as an extremely risky business. Petrobonds imply a speculation in future oil prices, and such speculation can be carried out in the international commodity futures exchanges without the political risk involved in government bonds linked to oil prices[35]. Oil service companies are currently desperate to obtain business, but their financial structure scarcely enables them to carry out new contracts without immediate payment in cash, while their ability to obtain new loans on the strength of such new contracts paid by equity is close to zero. Countertrade is practiced widely with petroleum products, but mostly on a spot basis and without more than short-term credit implications. In addition, countertrade involves deep discount to pay for the considerable profit margins taken by trading intermediaries and involves high negotiating costs for complex transactions, most of which do not materialize.

The proposed UN Revolving Fund for Natural Resources Exploration already exists, and it is authorized in principle to enter into petroleum exploration; however, due to absence of sufficient donations and unlikelihood of even a modest replenishment through successful discoveries, it is trying to survive modestly in the non-fuel metals exploration field. World Bank equity/loan financing through IEC (supra) is subject to a ceiling of 100 MM US$ over a four-year period and is concentrating on very promising prospects in oil producing countries; IFC participation is generally sought by companies not for the modest financial contribution, but to mitigate political risk factors. World Bank financing or co-financing is concentrated on exploration promotion projects and on infrastructure loans for larger projects; due to the current strategy of the Bank and in response to objections by the US petroleum industry[36], such lending is very much influenced by an interest to encourage private, not public investment in petroleum development. Little counter-cyclical elements can be perceived in multilateral energy lending which appear to diminish parallel to private bank lending, albeit with a time lag and at a slower pace. In sum, while the so-called innovative arrangements have to be tried out before an evaluation is possible, the mobilization only of marginal amounts can be expected in addition to what is currently available to finance operations that still are appraised as commercially attractive.

Natural Gas, Heavy Crude and Geothermal Development

The development of many energy minerals requiring high investment in infrastructure facilities mainly for domestic consumption is an important objective for countries desirous to diversity their energy sources, reduce local consumption of exportable petroleum and increase use of such domestic energy sources. The difficulty with this strategy is the absence of sufficient capital and technology required for the substantial investment in mainly infrastructure facilities (pipelines, refineries, power plants). Also, given that the market is domestic and no exportable product earning directly foreign exchange exists, it is difficult to encourage companies to invest into such types of energy development. In these cases, it is less the type of mineral which is making the difference, but the fact that demand will be mainly from a local market, payment in local currency and that considerable infrastructure investment is necessary. Petroleum discovered far from pipeline networks in volumes which do not justify the putting in place of a pipeline/transportation system, is not much different from non-exportable gas, geothermal energy or heavy crude mainly used for local consumption.

Earlier petroleum contracts left gas to the discretion of the contractor. Subsequently, obligations to prevent unnecessary waste of associated and non-associated natural gas were imposed. Often, the simplest solution is to treat non-associated natural gas under the same regime as oil; however, in these cases the fiscal regime and the time-limits feasible for petroleum will often prevent any gas development, but, even before, they will not encourage companies to take a serious interest in gas exploration. The next level device would be a general renegotiation clause which opens up the contractual regime for gas development in case of a gas discovery for new negotiations to adjust the contractual regime to what is reasonable and sufficiently attractive to develop gas. Even this method rarely provides sufficient attractiveness for a company to actively search for gas, as the terms will be renegotiated when the gas already has been discovered, e.g. when the company's position is not overly strong.

Gas incentives clauses have hence been designed in recent times with the objective to encourage a company to have a commercial interest in gas discovery and to make the very costly appraisal and development of gas deposits commercially interesting. One obstacle for this objective is that to justify the substantial infrastructure investment for gas, large deposits must be available and a reliable local market demand must have been created. Under Egypt's new gas incentive mechanism, discovered gas reserves will be pooled, EGPC will reimburse producers for recovery costs and buy the producer's equity-share of gas with crude supplies[37]. In other countries, in a similar vein, governments contribute towards the costs of gas appraisal and upstream and downstream facilities (e.g. Turkey, 1986) and provide a long-term gas purchase commitment for gas production (China, 1985). To encourage gas—but also geothermal energy, heavy crude and remote petroleum development without access to pipelines and export markets (e.g. the oil discoveries in Chad)—three issues are crucial:

> There must be a long-term commitment to take the output; in the case of a fledgling and yet to be developed local market, a long-term, government guarantee sales contract, coming close to a take-or-pay contract, has to assure reliability of demand.

> There must be a pricing mechanism which takes into account the monopsonistic role of the energy user and the absence of competing demand. For example, pricing can be on an energy equivalent/market price between gas (geothermal energy, heavy crude) on one side[38] and petroleum on the other side; another solution (used in a Union Oil/Philippines geothermal project) would be to adopt the pricing mechanism of regulated utilities and basing a price on total costs with a mark-up for allowed return. The later version is likely to produce energy at non-competitive prices once a fundamental change of the economic environment has taken place and may imperil the acceptance of power produced by consumers.

> To the extent investment is imported, payback has to be in foreign exchange, which is difficult to arrange, since, different from oil, no exportable production earning foreign exchange is available. If the energy produced replaces imports, it would seem easier to negotiate payment in foreign exchange. Sometimes (e.g. in Egypt or Argentina), payment in oil or other commodities can be arranged in a countertrade-like form. Merely paying in local currency will not interest a company having imported capital.

INTERNATIONAL COOPERATION FOR OFFSHORE PETROLEUM DEVELOPMENT

With the acceptance, de jure and de facto, of the rules of the UN Law of the Sea Convention relating to offshore jurisdiction (continental shelf and exclusive economic zone), most, if not all petroleum bearing tracts of the seas have been assigned to coastal states. There are three major issues of interest for petroleum development:

1. The delimitation of offshore jurisdiction between two or more adjacent states with competing claims;
2. The handling of petroleum deposits straddling the border of two or more states ("cross-border unitization"); and
3. The development of petroleum deposits underlying competing claims ("joint petroleum development").

A large number of boundary delimitation agreements have been concluded in the last decades. Several cases by the International Court of Justice and ad hoc arbitration tribunals have been issued dealing with the principles of delimitation, and sometimes determining a maritime boundary[39]. The knowledge or the perception of significant petroleum reserves in the disputed areas has, in general, been a factor making the resolution of the dispute more difficult.

Oilfields straddling boundaries are in general damaged if no coordinated and mutually planned development ("unitization") takes place. In national jurisdictions recognizing landownership over subsurface oil (e.g. US), unilateral operations and competitive drilling were prohibited in the laws of several states to prevent the loss of resources and the inefficiency of such uncoordinated extraction. The situation is more difficult with international cross-boundary oilfields. Apparently, while obligations to negotiate a cooperative arrangement for such situations can be said to exist, no definite prohibition on unilateral development after failure of negotiations to reach a settlement can be inferred under international law. However, there are several precedents where states have agreed to utilize a cross-boundary field[40]. Another approach followed by many governments is less intensive: There is no unitization, but an obligation to cooperate; the form and implications of such a duty to cooperate have still to materialize in the future[41].

To avoid border disputes several governments have negotiated arrangements for joint petroleum development in disputed areas so as to allow petroleum development before a definite settlement has been reached. Joint development arrangements have been concluded between Bahrain and Saudi Arabia, Japan and the Republic of Korea, Kuwait and Saudi Arabia (Neutral Zone), Saudi Arabia and Sudan (Red Sea), Malaysia and Thailand and Iceland and Norway[42]. Under such arrangements states agree to jointly manage exploration and exploitation and to share the petroleum found in the areas of overlapping claims. The first basic issue is management (Joint Authority/Joint Commission), including the issue if such joint authority has the power to issue licenses or just serves as a consultation mechanism between the authorities of the participating states. The second issue is if the disputed, jointly developed zone is to be split up into subzones (e.g. Iceland/Norway; Japan/Republic of Korea) which are managed basically by one state, or with preference to the operator nominated by one state) or if it is developed as an integral unit. The third issue is how to appoint the operator(s) for the operation(s), with the need to give proper attention to the operator(s) nominated by each state. The fourth issue is how to calculate and divide net revenues, and in particular to ensure that each state's fiscal authority is not used to obtain special advantages before the partitioning of the revenues. The last major issue is the application of law; either a new, specific system of law has to be created for the joint development area or some partitioning of the area into subzones subject to the respective national laws has to be agreed upon.

INTERNATIONAL ARRANGEMENTS FOR PETROLEUM AND MINERAL DEVELOPMENT

Within the United Nations, and since 1976, negotiations have been underway for a Code of Conduct on Transnational Corporations, an instrument that would have a bearing on petroleum and mineral investment in developing countries. So far, no agreement has been reached. The major unresolved issues relate to applicability of law, settlement of disputes, treatment of transnational corporations by host states and standards for nationalization and compensation[43].

The most conspicuous development has been the establishment, by the World Bank, of the *Multilateral Investment Guarantee Agency*[44]. After failures to set up a multilateral insurance system in the late 1960s, the new agency (MIGA) has been partly modelled on previous regional arrangements, such as the Inter-Arab Investment Guarantee Corporation. Its purpose is mainly to insure investment from abroad (including funds repatriated by nationals of the host country) against major political risks (straight and creeping nationalization, deprivation of control of, or substantial benefit from his investment, repudiation of government contracts in case of no access to a competent forum, unreasonable delays in courts of law, inability to enforce a final judicial or arbitral decision, armed conflict and civil unrest, non-convertibility risks). MIGA will focus on direct investment, but may expand coverage to other forms of industrial cooperation (licensing, transfer of technology, turn-key, management contacts). MIGA will only issue insurance coverage once the host government has approved such issuance; thus, governments have to accept insurance coverage—to which the arrangement is likely to prod them. Through reducing political risk perceptions, MIGA is seen by the Bank as a response to the World debt crisis and the decline in capital flows to developing countries. MIGA is hence to stipulate direct investment flows which have declined sharply in the first half of the 1980s. In addition, MIGA has a mandate to promote investment and provide advisory services on investment matters to developing countries.

As of July 7, 1986, 33 countries had signed, with 33% of the capital committed, thus paving the way for the preparatory commission. MIGA will become effective after ratification by only 20 countries. Signatory countries include Ecuador, Jordan, Senegal, Sierra Leone, Colombia, Tunisia, Republic of Korea, Turkey, St. Lucia, Grenada, Netherlands, Italy, Vanuatu, Zaire, Eq. Guinea, Saudi Arabia, Uruguay, United Kingdom, Chile, Canada, Morocco, Benin, St. Christopher/Nevis, Bolivia, Barbados, Cote d'Ivoire, Togo, Egypt, US, Cyprus, Pakistan, Indonesia and Switzerland. MIGA is structured with weighted voting, but with parity in principle between developing and developed countries. Its operations will be backed by an authorized capital of SDR 1 billion, most of which is not paid up, but subject to call if needed. MIGA will pay investors affected by insured political risk and, by subrogation, will then attempt to recover by direct negotiations with the respective countries.

At present, it is not yet possible to predict the scope of membership and action by MIGA. The fact that a major international arrangement for investment in developing countries has been established, is backed by the World Bank and linked to the World Bank affiliated International Centre for the Settlement of Investment Disputes (ICSID), is likely to have an impact. It is not clear to what extent MIGA will affect the current negotiations, interest in and the potential scope of the UN Code of Conduct for Transnational Corporations. Also, it is difficult to predict if the existence of MIGA will motivate investors to seek insurance from it and governments to join the MIGA-convention to positively affect their political risk rating and attractiveness to investment. Should a case of political risk materialize, governments would no longer deal directly with the investor, and not with the home state of the investor claiming diplomatic protection rights, but with MIGA as subrogee and hence indirectly with the World Bank.

TECHNICAL COOPERATION IN PETROLEUM AND MINERAL DEVELOPMENT

The Impact of the United Nations on Energy and Mineral Policies in Developing Countries

The impact of the United Nations, and its many suborganizations, on mineral and energy legislation in developing countries has been quite extensive, though it is very difficult to grasp in purely quantitative terms. While the World Bank, for example, impacts very directly through the "policy dialogue" it conducts in the context of loans to the energy sector and through the petroleum promotion loans for more than 33 non-oil producing countries with a legislation/contract component, the role of the UN is less based on financial leverage, and more on opinion-building, transfer of expertise and information and on the disinterested and objective expertise provided to governments on request in the discreet framework of its relatively less known technical cooperation agencies. This subsection focuses on the better known role of the political bodies of the United Nations in fostering a dialogue between government representatives, supported by technical secretariat papers resulting in mostly non-binding resolutions. The next subsections will deal with the nature and impact of technical cooperation activities.

The UN General Assembly, with its relevant suborgans (Economic and Social Council, Committee on Natural Resources, Commission on Transnational Corporations) and, to a lesser extent, the specialized agencies or semi-autonomous bodies served by their own legislative assemblies (UN Industrial Development Organization; UN Conference on Trade and Development) is constituted by the official representatives of all governments of the world, different from agencies, such as the World Bank group, which has a select membership group excluding mainly socialist countries. In this form, the UN also has a regional presence through its five regional economic commissions[45]; the regional economic commissions mostly have their own regional government representative bodies specialized in natural resources and energy[46]. All these conference bodies are basically a meeting ground for government representatives, on the higher level mainly diplomats, sometimes with specialized ministry representatives as advisers, in the more regional and specialized subcommittees more frequently for delegates from specialized government agencies, such as ministries of energy and mines, ministries of finance and economy, geological survey agencies and state petroleum and mineral enterprises. Their official purpose is to discuss and ultimately issue non-binding recommendations and to guide the work of the supportive secretariat services. There is relatively little direct linkage between the work and the output of such meetings—mainly, for the sake of finding consensus—rather general resolutions and specific national petroleum legislation, as compared to World Bank or UNDP financed advisory services directly related to the appraisal and preparation of legislation.

On the other hand, the indirect impact of such international committee work, particularly when the national experts and specialized ministries are brought together, on national legislation can not be underestimated: National experiences flow into the opinion-building process of a UN committee and conference, and secretariat services are intended to provide a comparative survey and an indication of trends and new methods[47]. The resolution will reflect, even if not too specific to accommodate diverse backgrounds and countries, a consensus. This consensus, and the inter-regional or regional experiences studied and discussed assist the national experts and government officials in evaluating their own laws, in setting new standards and in proposing, advocating and persuading their national constituency about what a suitable petroleum code could and should be. It is in particular the legitimizing effect of UN reports and resolutions in the national technical and political context which is the main channel of transmission of impacts from the UN scene to national policy-making. In addition to this more formal impact, there is the influence effected through the sharing of experiences, evaluations and new legislative mechanisms between government officials; formal UN committee work, but also the large number of UN expert group meetings and technical conferences provide a framework for a constant flow of communication from the selected experts to governments and between governments[48].

While it is difficult to pinpoint this impact in a quantitative way—and very little work seems to have been undertaken on the feed-back between UN resolutions and national legislation—we can observe a strong parallelism between the pertinent UN resolutions—mainly on permanent sovereignty over natural resources[49]. The principle of permanent sovereignty over natural resources is by now mostly incorporated into resolutions such as on the "New International Economic Order" and in the various negotiating texts of a prospective Code of Conduct on Transnational Corporations. Parallel to the growing emphasis on permanent sovereignty of states over natural resources—a not very well defined concept[50]—petroleum laws in the 1970s emphasized state ownership, exclusive state jurisdiction in cases of nationalization and set up state petroleum enterprises with a monopoly over petroleum rights and petroleum operations.

Cycles can be observed in the evolution of both political UN resolutions and national legislation. While up to the middle 1960s consensus tended to prevail, the 1970s were the age of confrontation between developing countries and foreign investors, supported by their home governments. The 1980s, again, witness a decline of interest and intensity of the debate in the UN fora, paralleled by the absence of significant nationalizations and a re-emphasis by governments on attraction, instead of on restriction, of foreign petroleum investment. If it is the UN system which encourages governments towards certain policies, or if its governments which move the UN debate to support their own policies, is an intractable question. It appears plausible that a certain feed-back between both the UN debate and national policies exist; this feed-back is slower in that the major UN fora (General Assembly and ECOSOC) are dominated by diplomats who, in general, and particularly in developing countries, are quite insulated from what is happening in their country's economy and in the current policy thinking in the ministries dealing with the energy and minerals sector[51].

The debate by international lawyers on the legal effects of General Assembly resolutions illustrates the difficulty in coming to grips with the persuasive, political, technical and legal impact of opinion-building and decision-making in the UN's political fora[52]. While it is easier to come to a consensus about the legal effect of such resolutions which are voted with unanimity and which tend to be repeated and reflect state practice, it is more difficult to evaluate the impact of repeated majority resolutions strongly objected to by important capital-exporting countries. These resolutions cannot be said to make new law, but they may be said to break old law, as they indicate that the majority group of newly established countries does not wish to be bound by international law concepts created before their time[53]. A flurry of arbitration cases rendered on petroleum contracts signed in the 1950s, broken in the 1970s and litigated in the late 1970s and 1980s, does not provide a much more clearer picture: While arbitrator J.R. Dupuy in the TEXACO v. Libya case considered all UN resolutions (except the unanimous Res. 1803 of 1961) as legally worthless, arbitrators S. Mahmassani, in LIAMCO v. Libya and P. Reuter, in Kuwait v. AMINOIL, found some legal effect in such resolutions, as indicating a growing state practice, as derogating the legal effect of traditional international law concepts and as criteria useful in interpreting these agreements and in clarifying international law concepts[54]. While we can not state the impact in any way to precision and clarity, it appears difficult to dispute on the other hand that in legislative practice, in the formulation of standards, expectations and criteria for petroleum legislation and contract negotiation, but also in the lofty realm of international law and arbitration, the UN resolutions as tediously negotiated by factional groupings of diplomats with little exposure to the industry in New York do not have a not negligible impact.

THE ROLE OF TECHNICAL COOPORATION ON ENERGY INVESTMENT POLICIES AND LAW

Technical cooporation in the field of petroleum and mineral legislation is rendered, within the UN system, by the UN Centre on Transnational Corporations[55], having a mandate to advise governments on matters of transnational corporations and being funded by UN regular programme and trust funds, and by UNDTCD, being financed from the UN regular programme of technical cooperation and, increasingly, by UNDP project funds and funds loaned to governments by multilateral development Banks. Advisory assistance is also rendered, to some extent, in this field by the Commonwealth Secretariat and, in a more limited way, through bilateral aid programmes.

A very important role in the area of petroleum and mineral legislation (including contract negotiations, investment consulting et al.), if, in numbers, not the most important role, is being played by international law firms and consulting firms specialized in these industries. While their advisory activities are sometimes paid directly by governments, international financial institutions, and, in the energy field, in particular the World Bank, are the main funding organizations. Basically, the World Bank gives a loan[56], and countries, in accordance with the Bank's procurement regulations, choose a consulting firm; in general, a short list is elaborated, generally with the advice of the Bank, a selection is made, generally with the consent of the Bank, and terms of reference are drawn up and negotiated, often with the informal assistance of Bank personnel. However, legally, it is a relationship exclusively between borrower and consulting contractor, and the Bank assumes no responsibility for the selection of the consultant or the output. The output is regularly reviewed by the government, with Bank assistance. It appears that most of the law/consulting firms are internationally operating law firms, particularly from Houston, Washington, New York, London and Paris. While these firms play a role in UN sponsored technical cooperation, their contribution is rather limited, mainly due to the standard fees for US law firm services which are not easily accommodated in the procedures of technical services recruitment by UN agencies[57].

No neutral and objective evaluation of these various forms of advisory assistance in the petroleum and mineral investment field has been carried out so far. Disinterestedness, both in commercial, ideological and political terms, a long involvement in developing countries as prime and exclusive client of advisory services and relative independence from a specific country or business context can be said to be the prime advantages of advisory services rendered through the UN system. These qualities may be of particular value when a politically and economically sensitive issue such as policy-making for foreign investment in natural resources and energy is at stake. An argument is often made that subcontracting or loan-financed consulting by international law firms tends to provide to countries high-quality, expeditious and well organized advice, with guarantees that such international law/consulting firms have their hands on the pulse of the industry and can thus help a country in correctly assessing current industry practices, constraints, interests and attitudes. UN assistance has been criticized for being too much oriented at a civil-service, bureaucratic approach tending to emphasize restrictions and controls and thus suggesting more obstacles than justified by a cost/benefit assessment; also, the tendency of the UN agencies to rely on inexpensive, retired and academically oriented experts, with little feed-back to industry, a time-lag in information on up-to-date developments and an overemphasis on quantitatively assessed one-shot advisory projects instead of a long-term involvement resulting in actual investment were mentioned in objections recently published[58].

UNDTCD and its predecessor, UNOTC, have been carrying out advisory missions on energy and mineral legislation since the late 1960s in basically all developing countries. Such advisory missions were generally of a short duration and were carried out by in-house interregional advisers, sometimes supported or complemented by ad-hoc consultants. From 1982 to 1984, 50 advisory missions were completed in the field of natural resources and energy. Such missions mainly provided an evaluation of existing legislation, a review of draft contracts and new legislation, and sometimes assistance for negotiations. A headquarters information system on legislation and contracts and a computerized roster of experts support these activities (for more details: E/C.7/1985/8).

In the last years, these activities have evolved, both in terms of intensity and quality: While in 1985 and 1986 (September) another 40 of such advisory projects were executed, a mere number count would not adequately reflect the evolution of substance and quality. The current, and evolving salient feature of DTCD investment advisory services in natural resources and energy is an emphasis on an interdisciplinary approach, integrating the in-house and external expertise available in fields such as petroleum and minerals economics/finance, engineering, geology and trading with expertise in the field of legislation. This interdisciplinary approach characteristic for DTCD investment advisory services is based on the close collaboration of headquarters and project technical staff in these disciplines and the close integration of DTCD-executed and UNDP-financed petroleum and mineral projects in the field with investment advisory services: Major and successfully executed projects that have resulted in investment of probably several tens of MM US$ have started with DTCD explorations and proceeded from discovery of gold over investment promotion to the negotiation of a major gold development agreement; similarly, in Ghana, a long-standing mineral engineering rehabilitation project for a state gold mining enterprise was followed-up and complemented by negotiations assistance resulting in a World-Bank financed management agreement resulting in investment up to about 100 MM $.

Continuity of cooperation with a government or even a specific government agency assures that advisory assistance is not geared at maximizing one-shot missions with little lasting effect. Most current advisory missions are a link in a chain of continuous assistance and, after some time, it becomes possible to continue the assistance from headquarters with reduced costs. For example, in a Caribbean country, DTCD assistance included the evaluation of petroleum indications, the preparation of a petroleum law and regulations, the negotiation for an exploration agreement, conducted in several sessions and, finally, advice on contract implementation monitoring and the review of a petroleum operating agreement.

The current trends indicate an increase of activities, though regular budget funds available for ad-hoc consultants have been cut as a consequence of the UN financial crisis. Such increase is basically due to a substantial increase, in percentage terms, of advisory assistance executed by DTCD with UNDP, European Community and, in the pipeline, World Bank funding. While in earlier years, the UN regular programme covered about 80% of advisory services of this nature, currently it appears that UNDP-funded projects have expanded by several multiples and would seem to cover about 70–80% of new investment advisory projects. It is estimated that a budget well exceeding 1 MM $, mainly from UNDP and World Bank sources, will be available in 1986/87 for funding investment advisory services in natural resources and energy. Also, cooperative arrangements with other agencies indicate a renewed usefulness of DTCD services in this field: On several occasions, advisory services have been carried out on the recommendation, and with the cooperation of international organizations as the Andean Pact, the European Community, the World Bank group and the UN regional economic commissions. Following such missions, an exploration agreement for coal involving an immediate investment over one MM $ was signed in an African country and a joint review of investment conditions for the natural resources sector in the ASEAN countries' group was undertaken. Linkages have also been strengthened with several national natural resources agencies and bilateral technical cooperation agencies. A close cooperative relationship exists at present between NRED/DTCD and the UN Revolving Fund (UNRFNRE); for example, UNRF assistance for a Latin American country in organizing gold investment promotion was carried out in close collabration between UNRFNRE and UNDTCD.

Currently, several larger UNDP-financed projects are about to start, mainly in French- and Portugese-speaking Africa, but also in Ethiopia. These projects will result in new petroleum and mineral legislation, in model contracts and training for international investment negotiations. The approach of these projects is based on the recognition that short-term training workshops and one-shot visits by experts without previous exposure to the country have proven of little use; accordingly, a new concept has been designed combining continuous assistance in negotiations, supported by the short-term visits of specialists in specific aspects of negotiations (e.g. industry experts; computer-supported financial analysis experts; petroleum exploration, reservoir engineering and refining experts); this continuous assistance to negotiations will be combined with a long-term, locally organized training programme for government officials. The objective is hence to establish a sequence of steps which will gradually build up local expertise and reduce the need for external expertise to high-level short-term specialists, using the machinery and the practical experience of actual negotiations as a training tool.

In projects designed to generate new petroleum and mineral laws, the emphasis is very much on a systematic preparatory analysis of other laws of the same type in other developing countries, and on a very close collaboration between local and external experts to accelerate a process of transferring the requisite expertise. This approach differs markedly from comparable projects where ready-made laws are prepared abroad, often with minor adaptations of an existing document, and then sent to the government for ready enactment.

Given the scarcity of investment, a distinct re-orientation of technical cooperation received by governments towards promotion of investment can be observed. In response, DTCD has pioneered an investment promotion model: Here, the mineral potential and the legal and administrative investment conditions are systematically surveyed and evaluated, investment opportunities are identified and publicized in the commercially attractive form of an investment prospectus, a suitable model agreement is drafted with the view of government benefit and acceptance by the industry groups targeted, and investment promotion and subsequent negotiations by the government are fully supported. This project, already in implementation in one South American country, is being adapted for comparable situations and needs.

In general, legislation and negotiation are considered the high points of investment activity. Much effort, talent and resources are invested. However, when the stage of implementation comes, interest wanes and the potential inherent in good legislation and well negotiated contracts is lost. Accordingly, new DTCD technical cooperation projects emphasize the contract implementation phase: Projects to strengthen government monitoring capabilities are likely, as evidence already demonstrates, to increase a relationship of constructive cooperation, as distrust borne out of ignorance and inexperience diminishes. Also, a contractor well supervised is likely to adhere to international standards of his industry and the provisions of law and contract. Effective monitoring hence both reduces unnecessary frictions and increases government benefits from a project well conceived and well implemented.

The advent of new governments and the current crisis, affecting equally state and private enterprises, is moving another concern of governments into the foreground of technical cooperation: Rehabilitation and restructuring of state enterprises, a review of investment conditions and more systematic decision-making on natural resources and energy policies. Two current projects concern these issues, and, with the continuation of the crisis in both petroleum and metals prices, an increase in requests of this nature can be expected. While recent DTCD-projects have concerned rehabilitation, for example the assistance resulting in a management contract for rehabilitation of the State Gold Mining Corporation in Ghana or assistance for rehabilitation of iron ore and diamond mines in Angola, there is a need for more systematic, in-depth, practical and conceptual thinking. Accordingly, in May 1986, DTCD convened with the government of Argentina an international conference on mineral development planning; in October 1987, DTCD organized with the government of Hungary an international conference on state enterprise. In addition, within the severe constraints imposed by the UN financial crisis, several technical studies on state enterprises and on project rehabilitation/restructuring have been commissioned in order to stimulate the search for effective and practical solutions to the problems faced by governments and state enterprises on account of the current crisis in the commodities sector.

Another new element in DTCD-advisory services is the gradual introduction of experts from developing countries with extensive and proven experience in several aspects of resource development (title management; small-scale gold mining promotion; legal issues) in advisory projects. While experts from developing countries are often handicapped by their limited access to information on new developments worldwide, state-of-the-art industry practices and up-to-date familiarity with the various petroleum and mineral industries, they can contribute a wealth of sensitivity and practical experience in the difficulties of organizing and managing mineral development in the context of a developing economy. Making such valuable expertise available to and acceptable in other countries has not always been easy. However, the concept currently employed aims at a continuous build-up and diversification of such experts that have proved successful, and intensive headquarters support particularly in areas where developing country experts have only a limited access to international expertise and exposure. The same applies to petroleum and mining law projects where considerable efforts have been expended to intensify the use of local experts and to combine local and external expertise; however, since the operational procedures and orientation of technical cooperation are geared towards bringing in external expertise, efforts to combine both local and external expertise have to surmount considerable obstacles and require much input of time.

Lastly, also in the field of petroleum and mineral investment policies, the increased use of electronic data processing, now available in relatively inexpensive, but powerful microcomputers, is proving an important tool to increase effectiveness and productivity. Given that the new generation of microcomputers has been introduced relatively recently, it is not easy to persuade professionals not having been trained during school in such devices, to perceive and accept the benefits of new techniques often considered threatening. Also, without intensive, and user-oriented intensive initial training, there is the risk that such facilities remain largely under-used. In the field of investment, the use of microcomputers tends to contribute much in the process of negotiations, when the financial impact of negotiating issues (e.g. different royalty, tax, participation rates) can be tested under different scenarios (e.g. petroleum/metals price, oilfield/deposit size; quality/grade; capital costs; production costs) within seconds, so that negotiations become more rational and less a matter of the rule-of-the-thumb. Also, it appears that the use of modern data-base management programmes can enhance the collection and the storage of petroleum/mining tiles, including the attached geological and technical information and make access very easy. Modern word processing and data transmission facilitates the technical support for negotiations and, in particular, these techniques can greatly cut down time and cost required for expensive expertise. It is, however, also a matter of generational adjustment and the productivity enhancement of well used microcomputers is being realized only gradually by a younger generation of experts, officials and bureaucratic administrators. A DTCD seminar on the application of EDP convened in cooperation with the government of Canada in October 1986 will accordingly include a session of the use of such techniques for investment and financial negotiations.

In countries with an already higher level of domestically available expertise and development (particularly South America and the Southeast Asian countries), interest and ability to effectively use microcomputers effectively is progressing rapidly. A new DTCD project to be financed with World Bank funds in Colombia is tended to develop a computerized model of decision-making to be able to appraise the direct financial and then more indirect economic effects of major contract options for coal investment in an effective, rapid and scientific way.

Footnotes

[1] The opinions expressed in this paper are those of the author and do not necessarily reflect those of the United Nations. The paper is prepared for conference presentation and will be revised and finalized subsequently.

[2] Dr. Iur. (Frankfurt), LL.M. (Harvard), Member of the Frankfurt bar.

[3] See Paul Mlotok, World Oil Markets—Back to the Future, a presentation to the July 1, 1986 Conference on Petroleum Exploration in Honolulu (East-West Center; ILI).

[4] OPEC production is currently (July 1986) at around 19MM barrels per day (bpd), i.e. x % of world oil production; non-OPEC oil production is at about x bpd, i.e. x % of world oil production.

[5] It is known that companies, governments and independent research services have been assuming a steadily growing (in real terms) oil price; investment and government decisions based on such assumptions (e.g. contracts, investment in exploration and development, financing by loans and equity, nationalizations et al.) have proven wrong and the financial risks assumed on the basis of such expectations have materialized into massive losses.

[6] See Robert Mabro, Director, Oxford Energy Institute, in Middle East Economic Survey 29:21, 3 March 1986; contribution to discussion at Honolulu 1986 petroleum conference by F. Gadar.

[7] It is estimated that about 1/3 of oil is sold directly on the spot market or at government prices linked to the spot market, another 50–55% is sold at prices linked to the spot market through mechanisms such as countertrade, netback pricing, toll processing or spot market formulas. Only 10–15% is currently sold on contract at official prices, see, F. Fesharaki, presentation to 1986 Honolulu petroleum seminar; Wall Street Journal, July 1, 1986.

[8] It is estimated that even 80% high-cost North Sea producers have operating costs under US$ 5, which would not make them shut-in oil before this price level is reached. The high-cost, low-production stripper wells in Texas, on the other hand, are already now being forced to close down current production, with, however, negligible effect on world supplies.

[9] Rig counts indicate a dramatic decrease of exploration activity particularly in the US (from 1800 rigs in operation in 1981 to about 400 in 1986) and a somewhat less pronounced decline in international exploration activity, Fesharaki, op.cit., July 1, 1986.

[10] A characteristic example is PETROPERU, the Peruvian state petroleum company. Under the current new government, decisions have been taken to reduce headquarters staff, which had grown from about 50 before nationalization of IPC in the late 1960s, to several thousands, to reduce exploration funds (from about 60 MM$ to about 15 MM$) and to relocate the enterprise to its operational center away from the capital.

[11] On petroleum law: Binn, Duval, Leleuch, Pertuzio, International Petroleum Exploration and Exploitation Agreements, Barrows, 1986; R. Brasseur, Le Droit des Hydrocarbures, 1976, Institut de Petrol.

[12] However, since public land (including offshore areas) constitutes the major part of land in the US, minerals on public land are owned by state and federal governments; thus, their development is also fully subject to government regulation, see Pertuzio, Instrumentos Juridicos para la Exploracion y Explotacion Petrolera Internacional, in: PETROPERU, Politica Petrolera, Lima Seminar of 1985, Vol. III.

[13] E.G. the Peruvian petroleum contracts law of 1979 or the respective laws in Argentina, Ecuador, Chile and other countries of the region.

[14] See the newest presentation of the program by the World Bank entitled "Promoting Private Sector Petroleum Investments in Developing Countries, A World Bank Objective," to the July 1, 1986 Honolulu Conference.

[15] The reason is probably the preponderance of US international oil companies as investors and their familiarity with the petroleum lease/contract as developed in the origin of the US petroleum industry, mainly in Texas.

[16] A well-established more rigid and precise framework has, on the other hand, advantages of standardization and reduces negotiating costs; it also increases public transparency. However, it makes adjustment to a changing environment more difficult. The best solution might be to start with a rather flexible approach, subsequently standardize most terms, but leave some essential terms (e.g., work programme and one major tax variable) open for negotiation and bidding, if required or desired.

[17] See P. van Meurs, Current Issues in the Economics of Offshore Petroleum Agreements, a consultant's report for the Natural Resources and Energy Division, UNDTCD, 1985 (to be published in: Natural Resources Forum). Peru, the law 23231 of 1981 provides existing producers with a tax credit for new exploration, i.e. the government de facto pays 100% of costs for new exploration; subsequently, in 1985, this law was abolished with retroactive effect by the new government.

[18] Compare an IFC statement to the 1986 Honolulu Conference which notes that IFC petroleum exploration support is unlikely in the deep offshore or frontier areas, and most likely focused in countries which are already hydrocarbon producers.

[19] Such as the "production-sharing contract," in reality either a concession-investment, service or joint-venture contract where the revenue-sharing/remuneration is at least partly effected in kind, either more like a production-based royalty (in older production-sharing arrangements) or basically as a net-income tax, as in the current version.

[20] E/C.7/1985/8 of 25 February 1985; E/C.7/1983/5 of 7 April 1983; UN, Alternative Arrangements for Petroleum Development, ST/CTC/43 of 1982. For a functional and substantive as compared to a formal and descriptive analysis see Thomas Walde, Mineral Investment Policies in the late 1980s, contribution to UNDTCD Conference on Mineral Development Planning, Buenos Aires, May 1986. See also UNDTCD/D-SE, Legal and Institutional Arrangements in Mineral Development.

[21] Most service/risk contracts in South America still imply assumption of all risks, full management and full financing by the contractor; this applies even to a recent "service contract" such as the Occidental/PETROPERU agreement of 1986, where the service fee is linked to a crude price basket. Nothing different applies to contracts

labelled "production-sharing/service" in Southeast Asia. Real service contracts are limited to a few major oil countries and to post-nationalization situations (1982).

[22] See the discussion by R. Sims, Government Ownership versus Regulation of Mining Enterprises in Less-Developed Countries, in: UN Natural Resources Forum, 9 (November 1985) 265.

[23] E.g. the windfall profits tax imposed by the Carter Administration in the US or the price cap imposed on oil production in Angola, for a survey see Barrows, World Petroleum Arrangements, 1985, for a financial/cash flow assessment see P. Van Meurs, op.cit. 1985.

[24] The incorporation of these risks into the investor's rate-of-return/cash flow/net present value calculus is demonstrated by V. Van Meurs, op.cit. (to be published soon in UN Natural Resources Forum); see also C. Blitzer et al., Oil Exploration in Developing Countries, in: UN Natural Resources Forum, 9 (1985, November) 293.

[25] A survey of most new petroleum agreements executed by the International Petroleum Institute (Barrows, New York) in July 1986 for NRED/DTCD confirms these findings.

[26] Discussed in detail in E/C.7/1985/8 at para. 9; see Thomas Walde, review of ESCAP (Garnaut/Emerson), Mining Taxation in the ESCAP Region, in: JCSID REVIEW, Foreign Investment Law Journal, 1 (1986) 233.

[27] For a critical examination of some in-built tendencies of the resource-rent tax mechanism, in particular the tendency to encourage unnecessary incremental investment and "gold-plating" in view of the high marginal tax rates of this tax see Van Meurs, op.cit., 1986. In some new model agreements, e.g. Kenya or Ethiopia, the resource-rent tax mechanism was dropped after original inclusion in the preparatory documentation.

[28] In US resource companies, the resource-rent tax is often mixed-up with the windfall profits tax enacted under the Carter Administration and hence disliked. Such attitude is due to ignorance of the basic difference on the two regimes: While the US windfall profits tax on oil did place a cap on profits generated by the oil price exceeding a specified level, the RRT places no cap on profits, but triggers an additional, mostly modest government take if the internal rate of return exceeds a specified level.

[29] E.g. in Ghana, Guatemala, Kenya and Liberia. Very high recovery is also inherent in countries where the resource-rent tax (additional profits tax) method is used as the exclusive or major tax mechanism, e.g. in Equatorial Guinea, as this tax is only triggered after full recovery. However, to provide during the recovery period some income to government, a royalty is usually included.

[30] The new petroleum agreement in Togo provides for a high oil share to the contractor in a production-sharing agreement. There is no tax, no royalty and no government participation.

[31] See T. Walde, Transnational Investment in the Natural Resources Industries, in: Law and Policy in International Business II (1979) 33–75; H. Zakaryia, Transfer of Technology under Petroleum Development Contracts, in: JWTL 16 (1982) 207; K. Khan, The Transfer of Technology and Petroleum Development in Developing Countries, in: Journal of Energy and Natural Resources Law 4 (1986) 10.

[32] See Edward Morse, Innovative Financing of Petroleum Projects: Options During the Cyclical Downturn, Presentation for 1986 Honolulu Conference, op.cit.; Z. Mikdashi, Oil Funding and International Financial Arrangements, in: UN Natural Resources Forum, 9 (1985, November) 283.

[33] Mexico, in 1983, reportedly, Chislett/Montagnon, Financial Times 29 April 1983, p. 21, issued petrobonds where principal and interest are linked to the price of Mexican

oil. A major international company reportedly also has recently issued bonds/ debentures linked to oil prices.

[34] E.g. the case study by M. Singer, Annals of Finance, The New Yorker, 1985.

[35] It may be recalled that in the 1930s many, if not most gold-denominated bonds— basically identical to the proposed petrobonds—were paid in domestic currency, with abrogation of the gold denomination.

[36] See National Petroleum Council, 1982, Third World Petroleum Development.

[37] Plan's Oilgram, November 7, 1985, p.2; Barrows, Study for NRED/DTCD, p. 50; as reported most recently (MEES 29:22, 10 March 1986), exploration will be subject to rules similar to oil, but the period for assessment, appraisal and production will be longer. Egypt will assume a take-or-pay obligation in a long-term sales contract (35 years). EGPC will bear the cost of transportation to the final consumer. The reference price for gas will be fuel oil (on a BTU equivalence basis) less 15% (5% for LPG).

[38] E.g. the 1982 Union Oil/Indonesia geothermal agreement; similarly, most modern long-term natural gas contracts, e.g. USSR/Western Europe; Algeria/Western Europe, have been based on an energy equivalent linked to the oil price, or, where possible, on an emerging market for natural gas directly, e.g. MEES 28:38 1 July 1985 (Algerian LNG price renegotiation, Algerian gas is indexed to a basket of crude, the indexation mechanism was adjusted to reach competitive parity with USSR exports.

[39] These remarks are based on an extensive study by I. Towsend-Gault, Offshore Petroleum Development: Legal Implication for NRED/DTCD, 1986; the main cases: North Sea Continental Shelf, Tunisia/Libya; Libya/Malta; Gulf of Maine (US/ Canada); Guinea/Guinea Bissau; France/UK. Some issues have been decided by conciliation, e.g. Beagle Channel (Chile/Argentina; Jan Mayen (Norway/Iceland).

[40] See UK/Norway Boundary Treaty of 1965, 1965 UKTS 71; the British and Norwegian consortia signed a series of agreements which unitized the Frigg gas field, these were confirmed, by an intergovernmental agreement in 1976, between Norway and the UK. There is a single unit for the field, with a single operator acting on behalf of all interested parties. Each state party receives a percentage of the proceeds according with the proportion of the deposit within its jurisdiction.

[41] E.g. the Iran/Saudi Arabia agreement of 1969, ST/LEG/SER.B/18, p. 403; 1. Townsend-Gault's cited report discusses in more detail many other agreements between states that have followed these two approaches and their implications. The UK/ Norway solution may hence also be adopted in the future in cases of cross-border oilfields where the parties have to find a suitable form of the treaty-mandated cooperation.

[42] See Townsend-Gault, op.cit.; M. Valencia, Joint Development of Petroleum Resources in Overlapping Claim Areas, Presentation to 1986 Honolulu Petroleum Conference; W. Onorato, Promoting Foreign Investment Through International Petroleum Joint Development Regimes, in: ICSID Review-Foreign Investment Law Journal, 1 (1986) 81. Negotiations are currently underway between Indonesia and Australia on joint offshore petroleum development in disputed areas.

[43] See the progress report by S. Asante, CTC-Reporter, No. 21, 1986, p. 11.

[44] See I. Shihata, Towards a Greater Depoliticization of Investment Disputes: The Roles of ICSID and MIGA, in: ICSID-REVIEW-Foreign Investment Law Journal, 1 (1986) 1.

[45] ESCAP in Bangkok for Asia and the Pacific; ECLAC, in Santiago de Chile for South America and the Caribbean; ECA in Addis Abbaba for Africa; ECWA in Baghdad for Western Asia (mainly Arab countries) and ECE in Geneva for the, East and West, European countries.

[46] ESCAP, in Bangkok, has some linkage to several regional bodies specialized in off-shore prospection and regional resource development.

[47] Compare such pertinent UN technical publications as UN, Alternative Arrangements for Petroleum Development, ST/CTC/43 of 1982; the biannual reports of the UN Secretary General on Permanent Sovereignty over Natural Resources (E/C.7/1985/8; E/C.7/1983/5; the reports on UN Conferences such as the one on State Petroleum Enterprises in Developing Countries (1980) or the continuous publication of relevant articles on petroleum laws and contracts in the UN edited Natural Resources Forum.

[48] For example, UNDTCD organized conferences on State Petroleum Enterprises in the Developing Countries (1978), on Petroleum Exploration in Developing Countries; UNDIESA organized recently, with UNDTCD support, meetings on petroleum contracts (1986 in New York), on exploration and legal issues (Athens, 1985), UNITAR organizes working groups on heavy crude legislation and on shallow petroleum deposits (1984). DTCD is regularly participating in petroleum law meetings, as by OAPEC, East/West Center, ILI and IDLI.

[49] There is a chain of resolutions from the early 1950s until now, with Res. 1803 of 1961 representing a last important expression of unanimity and thus perhaps a reflection of customary international law, while Res 3201 and 3202 (1974) (New International Economic Order) represent a majority view of the South/East coalition, with the US and the main Western countries objecting or abstaining, and thus at most a reflection of derogation of traditional international law principles, but not a creation of new ones.

[50] See R. Kempei, Nationale Verfuegung ueber natuerliche Ressoursen und die NWWO der Verreinten Nationen, 1976; K. Hossain (ed) Permanent Sovereignty over National Resources, 1984 (particularly S. Chowdhury); G. Elian, The Principle of Sovereignty over Natural Resources, 1979; K. Hossain (ed), Legal Aspects of the New International Economic Order, 1980 (particularly S. Asante, E. Jimenez de Arechaga and H. Zakariya).

[51] The organization of the diplomatic UN fora into factions, Developing Countries (group of 77), Western Countries, Eastern Countries also plays a role, with the Third World characterized by especially slow and more rhetorical decision-making, the Western countries by their rather static defensive position and Eastern countries by their tendency to support the Third World where no interest or money of theirs is at stake. All these factors restrict, but do not exclude, the feedback to national reality.

[52] See I. Seidl-Hohenveldern, International Economic Soft Law, in: Recueil des Cours, Vol. 163, 171; M. Silagi, Entwicklungsvoelkerrecht und Neue Weltwirtschaftsordnung, in: oesterreichische Ztscht. f. Oeff. Recht und Voelkerrecht, 32 (1982) 177; Sornarajah, Compensation for Expropriation, in: JWTL 13 (1979) 108; K. Hossain, (Ed) Permanent Sovereignty over Natural Resources in International Law. 1984, with, particular, the contributions by S. Chowdhury.

[53] An argument made by the writer: T. Walde, Contract Stability: Adaptation and Conflict Resolution, in: UN, Legal and Institutional Arrangements for Mineral Development, 1982, 163.

[54] This is an extremely brief remark and it would be worth going into the issue with more detail, on these arbitrations, see: T. Riad, Host Countries' Permanent Sovereignty over Natural Resources and Protection of Foreign Investors, in: Rev. Egypt. Droit Int'l 39 (1983) 35; idem, SJD Thesis, Harvard Law School, Sept. 1985 on: Applicable Law Governing Transnational Development Agreements.

[55] See R. Brown, Technical Assistance in Petroleum and Mining, in: CTC-Reporter, 21, 1986, 32.

[56] Most of the new petroleum law/model contract/promotion packages were financed by the standard petroleum promotion loan package developed by the Bank and ap-

plied in over 33 countries. It is estimated that in a large part of these loans a new petroleum law package is included and that average costs may be between 500.000—1 MM US $ for the total legal/financial package (law, model contract, promotion, advisory services, tax revision, financial modelling).

[57] However, subcontracting through UNOPE without involvement of UN in-house personnel with substantive professional expertise seems to rely more on the use of major international law and consulting firm that DTCD, where a preference exists for recruitment of individuals. It has been found that UNDTCD can, if absolutely necessary for high-level, short-term urgent advice, obtain comparable services at a substantial rebate.

[58] E.g. the US National Petroleum Council, Third World Petroleum Development, 1982, p. 25, concluding "The NPC does not believe that a need for this last type of activity on behalf of the UN (sc. UNCTC) exists. Competent and experienced private consultants and information sources in all these areas of expertise are readily available." See also: Petroleum Finance Company, Washington DC, 1985, Handbook for Government Officials and National Oil Companies.

Promoting Private Sector Petroleum Investments in Developing Countries: A World Bank Objective

by Denis T. Carpio

The World Bank and other multilateral institutions play a significant role in promoting private-sector petroleum investments in less-developed countries. The World Bank seeks to encourage private investments in the petroleum industry by eliminating barriers to entry, accelerating investment decisions, and assisting governments in the operation or divestiture of public enterprises. The author sees many developing countries following an "open door" policy as an inducement to private sector investments, very likely in the form of joint ventures between the public sector and foreign private companies.

Mr. Chairman, fellow participants, ladies and gentlemen: I wish to thank the International Law Institute and the East-West Center for inviting me to participate in this conference. It is a privilege to address this gathering and it is particularly timely to examine the impact of, and the challenges posed by, the unstable world petroleum industry to the developing countries in general, and the Asia/Pacific region in particular. This region has established a pivotal framework, and hopefully a tradition as well, for broadly based economic and commercial cooperation through the Association of South East Asian Nations (ASEAN). The region also has a long history of trading and commercial relationships among countries and includes significant petroleum exporters and importers. This background has led to a rather high degree of linkages among the petroleum sectors of these countries and has contributed, for example, to the emergence of Singapore as a major center for petroleum activities, particularly support services, in the region.

My presentation will deal with the World Bank's objective, and the approaches it utilizes to promote private sector petroleum investments in developing countries, as well as my own perceptions about the recent trends towards increased privatization—in its broadest sense—of the petroleum industry in these countries. Hopefully, this can set the stage for a discussion among the conference participants on the concepts, realities and future of privatization in the specific context of the petroleum industry in the Asia/Pacific Basin.

A FUNDAMENTAL WORLD BANK OBJECTIVE—TO PROMOTE PRIVATE SECTOR INVESTMENTS IN DEVELOPING COUNTRIES

It is widely known that the World Bank aims at promoting the economic development of the poor countries. But this is generally thought to be through public sector investments only. This is most unfortunate, because one of the most important World Bank objectives is to promote private sector investments in the developing countries.

There are four broad constraints to economic development: the first is the absence or a deficiency in overall government legislation, policies, institutions and regulations which generally inhibits investments in productive capacity or the efficient operation of existing capacity. These deficiencies discourage or seriously delay investments and reduce competitiveness. In particular, they are barriers to the entry of the private sector. The second is the lack of savings for investments, coupled with the inability to attract sufficient capital in-flow for investments, particularly foreign private capital, due to various political, economic and institutional reasons. The third is the lack of entrepreneurial, managerial and technological resources which reduces operating efficiency and competitiveness. These can only be overcome by a long-term industrialization process and by the import of these resources, primarily from foreign private companies, to help accelerate both the industrialization process as well as the adaptation process. And the fourth is the lack of facilities and institutional arrangements to promote trade and exports. In the context of the petroleum industry, the first three constraints are particularly serious and must be addressed if progress is to be achieved.

The policy dialogue between the World Bank and its borrowers, as well as a major portion of the Bank's lending operations, contain elements designed to improve the government's economic development policies and strategies, including its legislative and regulatory framework. Such improvements are necessary for the creation of an overall economic and business climate that encourages efficient investment operations including the participation of the private sector, and eventually, competition and growth. This is the most important and difficult aspect of the World Bank's work—yet it is also the least recognized and the least appreciated. It is also a rule that the Bank is uniquely qualified to undertake.

The private sector, for its part, can contribute much to the developing countries in the form of capital, particularly risk capital, in the form of entrepreneurial and managerial skills, and in the form of technological resources. Thus, the role of the private sector is, and has to be, critical to the economic development process of these countries. It is in recognition of this critical role for the private sector that the founders of the World Bank explicitly provided in Article 1 of the World Bank's Articles of Agreement that it is the Bank's purpose "to assist the reconstruction and development of territories of members by facilitating the investment of capital for productive purposes . . . " and . . . "to promote private foreign investment by means of guarantees or participations in loans and other investments by private investors. . . ." In pursuit of this mandate, the Bank has, since its inception, undertaken several major initiatives to provide the institutional capability as well as the operating policies and instruments, to promote private sector investments in developing countries. Three particularly landmark initiatives involving institutional capabilities were: first, the establishment of the International Finance Corporation (IFC) in 1956 to provide direct equity investments as well as loans without government guarantees for private sector sponsored or operated projects; secondly the establishment of the International Centre for Settlement of Investment Disputes (ICSID) in 1965 to provide a framework for arbitration between governments and foreign investors; and thirdly, the initiative currently underway of establishing the Multilateral Investment Guarantee Agency (MIGA) designed to provide foreign investors with insurance coverage for non-commercial risks faced by their investments in developing countries as well as to provide a consultative forum among member governments to encourage adoption of policy environments that encourage a hospitable business climate in general and the flow of foreign investments in particular. The United States just signed about two weeks ago the MIGA convention which completes the minimum membership requirement of five developed and fifteen developing countries. MIGA is thus expected to be operational by the end of 1986 or in early 1987.

In terms of operating policies and instruments, the World Bank has also introduced several innovations during the last ten years both to promote better government policies, strategies and institutional capabilities as well as to encourage private sector investments and the flow of foreign capital to developing countries. Before 1977, the World Bank had limited its financial assistance in the petroleum industry to downstream investments such as pipelines, refineries and LNG or LPG projects. Starting in 1977, the World Bank began a modest effort of directly supporting petroleum exploration and development and evolved a range of petroleum policy objectives and lending instruments. At the beginning of this decade, the World Bank also enhanced its co-financing techniques which included introduction of the "B-loan" arrangements with commercial banks to increase their lending to developing countries. Finally, the World Bank also introduced its structural adjustment lending operations designed to assist developing countries in restructuring key sectors of their economy in response to the major changes in the global economy—particularly in terms of energy and commodity prices as well as the patterns of trade. A key element of these structural adjustment loans is the implementation by the government of policies and strategies to improve the climate for private investments as well as to encourage greater operating efficiency of public sector enterprises. Such policies and strategies incorporate elements essential for restructuring, sustained economic growth as well as for harnessing the enormous productive potential of the private sector.

THE WORLD BANK OBJECTIVES IN THE PETROLEUM SECTOR

Let me turn now to the objectives of the World Bank in the petroleum sector. The World Bank generally pursues certain sector specific objectives in lending within the various sectors of the economy. This is particularly true in the case of the petroleum sector because of some special features which make this industry unique. The petroleum industry is characterized by a very high level of risk in the exploration and appraisal stages, as well as by large capital requirements in all stages, from exploration and appraisal, through development, transportation, refining and up to marketing. It also involves a high level of technology, and more importantly, there is a large number of international companies with the capital, technical, managerial and operational resources and know-how which are willing and able to invest anywhere in the world where the petroleum geology offers the potential for adequate returns and the contractual terms are sufficiently attractive. Finally, the energy field, in which the petroleum sector is very important, is a critical part of any country's economy—it is indeed the engine of economic development.

It is the intention of the Bank as well as its government shareholders that the Bank's involvement in the petroleum sector would be to complement, rather than to compete with, private investors. In general, Bank lending for petroleum has several financial and non-financial objectives. The financial objectives are to ensure the viability of the project and the implementing entity, as well so to mobilize both risk (equity) and loan capital for project financing. The non-financial objectives, which are generally equally if not more important, include:

- improvements in sector policies such as pricing and legislation to encourage efficiency in energy use, development of local energy resources and investment by the private sector;

- technical assistance at the sector level to help design and implement better sector policies and strategies, as well as technical assistance at the project level to ensure sound project conceptualization, implementation and operation;

- technology transfer to ensure efficient and optimal development of domestic energy resources; and

- institution building to strengthen the long-term managerial and technical capabilities for sustained growth and improvements in the operation of the petroleum sector.

The non-financial objectives associated with the Bank's lending for petroleum projects are essential to the economic adjustment process of the developing countries and are the primary rationale for the Bank's involvement in this sector.

APPROACHES TO ENCOURAGE PRIVATE SECTOR INVESTMENTS IN PETROLEUM

The various approaches and instruments used by the World Bank to encourage private sector investments in petroleum can be grouped into three main classifications: eliminating or reducing the barriers to entry; facilitating or accelerating specific investment decisions; and assisting the government in its ownership or functional divestiture of public sector enterprises. Let me briefly discuss each of these.

Eliminating or Reducing Barriers to Entry

The two oil price shocks in 1976 and 1979 made it imperative that developing countries quickly adjust their energy consumption and production patterns to the new era of high energy costs, but unfortunately the transition was initially very slow. The international oil companies were prepared to increase their oil exploration efforts but most of these investments ended in the already established oil exporting regions or countries, such as the North Sea, the Middle East, North Africa and Nigeria. The oil importing developing countries did not attract a significant share of the additional petroleum investments in the late 1970s. Until this period, most developing countries, particularly the smaller ones, did not have the modern legislative or contractual framework, nor the overall development policies and strategies, needed to effectively attract private risk capital for petroleum exploration. They also did not have the institutional capability to design such a framework or strategies or to monitor the exploration and development activities once the private sector had begun its operations. There was also a second group of countries, but only a few, that had severely restricted, or in some cases prohibited, the entry of the private sector in their petroleum industry. With respect to the first group of countries, the serious legal, policy and institutional deficiencies raised the perceived political risk and discouraged investment initiatives by the private sector. The deficiencies also made the government cautious and unable to make timely decisions. Thus, they had effectively become barriers to the entry of the private sector.

One of the most widely used and successful lending instruments of the Bank in the petroleum sector, called the exploration promotion project was specifically designed to overcome these deficiencies and in addition, to obtain and package geological data in order to actively market the country's exploration acreage to the international oil industry. Since 1980, the Bank has financed exploration promotion projects in some 33 countries and has provided informal advice to various other countries regarding their own promotion efforts or refinements to their contractual frameworks. About half of these promotion projects are still under implementation but those completed to date have already led to about 50 new exploration contracts. However, the impact of these exploration promotion projects goes far beyond these 50 contracts. The legislative, contractual and policy framework, as well as the institutional capabilities within the Government, that these projects have helped develop, will provide the basis for a favourable business climate over the longer term and a sustained presence of the private sector. These are truly long-term developmental impacts. Exploration promotion projects account for the largest number, about 45%, of Bank petroleum projects that represent the smallest financial commitments, usually in the range of US$5–25 million per project. The expected start-up of MIGA in the near future should also provide a means for foreign investors to insure part or all of their investments in developing countries and thereby encourage more private foreign investments, including hopefully, in the petroleum industry.

In a few countries, petroleum exploration and production until the end of the 1970's was more or less limited to the public sector enterprises. The Bank, in lending for petroleum in any country, always encourages a more "open-door" policy, not only in the downstream operations and support services, but also in exploration and production. Of the 50 or so countries where the Bank has lent for petroleum projects, only two countries (both in Eastern Europe) have not opened their country to exploration and production by the private sector and even one of these has begun to allow specialized foreign service companies to enter. In several countries, the Bank has encouraged a more liberal policy and an improved contractual framework where the entry of the private sector had either been geographically restricted or had not materialized as expected.

Facilitating or Accelerating Specific Investment Decisions

In many cases where the private sector is already involved in exploration, the subsequent appraisal or development phases are delayed because of financial, institutional or marketing issues not explicitly covered in the original exploration agreement. For example, the Government may wish to exercise its option to participate but does not have the financial or managerial resources to be an effective partner. In other situations, there may be a need for some related infrastructure investment which the private investors are not prepared to participate in because it will raise their financial exposure and political risk beyond acceptable limits. And in yet another scenario, the development of marginal oil fields or the pricing and utilization of natural gas may become contentious subjects which prevent development of discoveries or discourage continuation and expansion of private sector efforts. In these cases, the World Bank can be of assistance and has in fact been involved in resolving such issues by providing financing, policy advice and technical assistance to both the government and the project itself. The Bank can also provide loans to local financial institutions for onlending to domestic private companies involved in the various facets of the petroleum industry in need of foreign exchange resources. One of the earliest petroleum projects supported by the Bank was the LNG export project in Algeria in 1964 which had an 80% private sector ownership and 20% government shareholding. Since 1977, the Bank has provided financing for the Government's share of six joint-venture projects covering exploration, appraisal or development in four countries, has helped finance three infrastructure projects intended to serve development investments sponsored by the private sector, and has provided in one case foreign exchange facilities through a local bank for petroleum investments of private sector companies. Bank lending specifically designed to facilitate or accelerate private sector investments so far accounts for the second largest share of petroleum loans, in terms of both the number of projects and dollar amount of lending.

Finally, the Bank is also prepared to provide a "letter of cooperation" to indicate its willingness to participate in the financing of the government's share of any joint development project with a private company should exploration lead to a commercial discovery which meets the Bank's economic feasibility guidelines. The Bank is also prepared to provide a "guaranteed loan" arrangement whereby the Bank finances a portion of the exploration program of the local subsidiary of an international oil company and the responsibility for repayment rests with the parent oil company in the event of commercial or technical failure and with the host government in the event its interference renders continued operations impossible for more than a predetermined period of time. Three "letters of cooperation" and two "guaranteed loan" arrangements have reached advanced stages of negotiations. Although the actual number of cases in which the Bank has become directly involved in a project with the specific purpose of stabilizing a government/investor relationship is small to date, interest in such arrangements has continued.

At this point, let me say a few words about IFC and its involvement in the petroleum industry. IFC always had the mandate to participate, with equity and loans, in petroleum development and downstream activities in developing countries. However, about two years ago, it decided to also invest with risk equity in petroleum exploration ventures that are predominantly or exclusively private sector. It is a modest program by oil industry norms—about $100 million of risk capital for exploration over five years—but it represents a serious effort and commitment to help nurture a domestic exploration financing capability as well as attract into the developing countries the smaller and medium-sized foreign oil companies who may not be able, on their own, to shoulder the full exploration risks.

Assisting Ownership or Functional Divestiture. Ownership divestiture, in which the government totally or partially sells its ownership shares of a public sector enterprise, and its twin, functional divestiture, in which a public sector enterprise sells off some of its activities or operations to the private sector, are very dramatic events. They capture the public eye and have a large political impact. They also involve a major political decision by the government and the public sector enterprise. Such decisions could be motivated by financial or efficiency considerations or both. Several countries and national oil companies are reported to be examining these options. To be successful however, such divestitures require a legal and policy framework supportive of private sector involvement, the availability of financial resources within the private sector (particularly domestic private companies), and the potential for profitable operations. In most cases, the domestic capital market is not large enough to provide financing for a substantial government divestiture. In some cases, the public sector enterprise is an unprofitable operation or its assets are in bad physical shape and therefore can not attract buyers or investors.

Whatever the specific situation, the Bank is prepared to assist the government or the public sector to undertake a divestiture or any other project intended to eventually lead to some type of divestiture. There are only a few actual cases in the petroleum sector that fall into this category so far. One example involves a Bank loan to help finance the first stage of rehabilitation of a public sector enterprise in order to restore its physical assets as well as its financial viability to acceptable levels. The private sector had earlier declined to participate in the equity of this enterprise. The intention is that during the second stage rehabilitation, once the financial viability of the enterprise has been established, private sector partners will be sought. The Bank is also currently discussing with a few countries the desirability of restructuring their petroleum industry and adopting pricing and fiscal policies that would lead to additional private investments. This restructuring would also involve some functional divestiture of their national company for efficiency and financial reasons.

While the Bank has not been directly involved in many divestitures, its lending for petroleum has sought to bring together the public and the private sector either as partners or contractual parties. Ever since the Bank started lending for petroleum projects in 1977, it had always encouarged a more "open-door" petroleum policy for its borrowers including the formation of joint ventures between public and private enterprises. Starting in 1984, the Bank went one step further. In lending for oil exploration by a national oil company, the Bank now explicitly seeks or encourages a process for eventually attracting private sector participation in the exploration project or in the subsequent appraisal or development phase in the event of a commercial discovery. While this process is not strictly a divestiture, it is common practice in the international oil industry to farm-in other participants in an exploration or appraisal venture. Such an approach in the case of developing countries provides an excellent opportunity for technology transfer as well as for attracting risk capital. It may also be a particularly attractive option at this time when many international oil companies are cutting their exploration and development budgets and may be less inclined to take on large commitments, but may be persuaded to take a share in a venture sponsored by a national oil company. In another approach, the Bank has encouraged the national oil companies to contract for specialized support-services such as seismic survey, drilling, electric logging, cementing and production testing from the private sector, rather than expand their own capabilities, as a means of reducing capital requirements, focusing scarce managerial talents, and maintaining operational flexibility.

RECENT TRENDS IN GOVERNMENT POLICIES REGARDING THE RELATIVE ROLES OF THE PUBLIC AND THE PRIVATE SECTOR

Now that I have described the World Bank's approaches to promote petroleum investment by the private sector, allow me to share with you some of my own perceptions about the trends in developing country policies with respect to the relative roles of the public and private sector in the petroleum industry. Firstly, I see an increasing degree of "open-door" policy and an improving trend in the legal and policy framework that would be favourable to private sector investments. Even countries that have geographically restricted the private sector involvement in the past have now begun to ease such restrictions. Joint ventures between public sector and foreign private companies are also being encouraged. Developing countries are also fine tuning their contractual frameworks to encourage development of marginal oil fields as well as gas discoveries. Secondly, more governments are encouraging the growth of the private sector in the support and downstream operations, particularly through joint ventures between private local and foreign companies, in order to spread the development impact of the petroleum investments. In this context, there could be scope for significant functional divestitures by public sector enterprises of activities related to downstream and support services. Thirdly, there will probably be only a few cases of partial ownership divestitures. Such ownership divestitures, however, will likely be motivated more by financial and operational considerations at the enterprise level than by a major change in government policy regarding the role of the public sector.

The most important element that will encourage a larger private sector role will continue to be the government's legal and policy framework—particularly its "open-door" policy with respect to private sector involvement in all facets of the industry. Once such a framework is established and the private sector participates to a significant degree, it will provide competition to the public sector enterprises. This, in turn, means the public sector will also eventually become efficient, or it too will be privatized.

In summary, it appears to me that the private sector will become increasingly involved in more facets of the petroleum industry in the developing countries during the coming decade. The public sector will also continue to be involved but in a more focused and strategic way. There will also be more private/public sector joint ventures. This augurs well for the progress of the petroleum industry in the developing countries. It is also a scenario which the

Bank is helping to achieve, and the Bank will continue to provide assistance in support of these objectives.

Thank you very much.

Innovative Financing of Petroleum Projects: Options During the Cyclical Downturn

by Edward L. Morse

In a glutted world market, sources of finance, both concessional and commercial, for oil-related projects are less accessible than before. At the same time, internally generated funds have been reduced as corporate investment in petroleum operations has declined. As a result, multilateral organizations, such as the Asian Development Bank and the World Bank, will become more important than in recent years in the funding and cofinancing of projects. Within this framework, the author examines how innovative financing techniques, combined with changes in fiscal and contractual terms, can assist in the formulation of exploration agreements that are necessary if developing countries are to achieve energy project goals.

All of the activities normally associated with the petroleum industry have dramatically declined in volume as oil prices have fallen and as corporate profits and governmental receipts have been reduced. Exacerbating the situation, especially for developing countries eager to continue to promote the development of their hydrocarbon resources, has been the reluctance, if not the refusal, of private sector lenders to finance petroleum and natural gas development projects due both to price uncertainty and the enormous debt burdens carried by most developing countries. Energy lending, once a prime growth sector for international financial institutions, has virtually dried up.

There are good reasons to believe that the current downturn in the petroleum business cycle has not yet reached its trough and will not until the current overhang in surplus production capacity is substantially reduced, by a combination of declining supply availability and increased demand. But, it is also likely that in the absence of special programs, the international petroleum industry will over contract, through unnecessary reductions in exploration drilling and the financing of development projects. The result will be a tightening market and a new round of price escalations in the 1990s that will probably be steeper and faster than necessary. Accompanying such a price increase there will also again be overinvestment in exploration and development, a bunching of new supplies brought to market, and the setting of the stage of another cyclical downturn.

Therein lies the significance of finding new ways to retard the cyclical slowdown in capital expenditures as far as individual countries, specific companies and the entire international petroleum sector are concerned. It is in the interest

of all parties that participate in this sector—exploration and production companies, governments, drilling and service companies and financial
institutions—to find mechanisms to reduce the extremes in cyclical activity to
which the petroleum sector has now succumbed.

This essay examines a variety of approaches that can be adopted to stabilize
the level of business activity during the current cyclical downturn. Some of
these are already being adopted by governments and the industry as a result of
market pressures. This is particularly the case with respect to the relaxation of
certain terms and conditions in exploration agreements. Other approaches still
require nurturing by the industry. A number of these are examined in the body
of this paper. Bringing them to fruition will require innovation and change in
business practices in the petroleum industry.

Experience in other cyclical downturns gives rise to some hope. In the past,
the petroleum industry has proved to be enormously capable of adaptation and
innovation in responding to changes in market and political conditions. There
are good reasons to believe that the industry and the financial community to
which it relates will once again confront difficult challenges and provide interesting and novel solutions to the problems associated with the apparent relative
lack of capital and obstacles to its being used efficiently as they endeavor to position themselves for the new cyclical upturn.

PETROLEUM EXPLORATION AND PRODUCTION AGREEMENTS

The petroleum industry has always been responsive to changes in the international environment for exploration and production. Several key factors, beyond the availability of capital, have traditionally played a central role in determining where and when exploration takes place. Among these, geological
prospectivity and contractual terms and conditions are pre-eminent. It is perhaps surprising to those not familiar with the petroleum industry that, political
stability per se in a host country, while important, ranks far lower in significance as a factor in capital expenditure decisions.

The two key factors—geological and contractual risks—are fundamentally
intertwined. This condition can be understood with references to Exhibit 1. By
way of background, it is now understood that the cyclicality of the petroleum
industry extends well beyond long term fluctuations in the price of petroleum,
as a reflection of secular changes in the relationships between supply and demand patterns. Exhibit 2 depicts the real price of oil in the United States over
the period 1901-1985. Four pricing cycles are apparent in this period and, if
the graph had been extended back over another twenty years, a fifth would also
have been apparent in this period and, if the graph had been extended back over
another twenty years, a fifth would also have been apparent. Without arguing at
this point the relationship between prices prevailing in the United States and international prices—a subject which involves numerous distinction and
explanations—I have taken it as given that U.S. prices are a valid proxy for in-

ternational pricing conditions. During each of these pricing cycles, the petroleum industry has responded through changes in the terms and conditions of contracts.

It can be argued that a cycle exists, paralleling the pricing cycle, which characterizes the terms and conditions of exploration and production agreements. There are two major elements to such agreements—the definition of property rights and the definition of fiscal terms. These are determined in negotiations between those that want to explore for and produce oil (oil companies and financial institutions) and those who have acreage available (usually governments, but in some contexts private parties, including other oil companies and financial institutions).

In broad terms, an exploration agreement is a license to explore for and/or to produce hydrocarbons. The price of the license, or exploration and production right, also responds to market forces. In an expanding market, the demand for exploration rights tends to increase relative to available supply, and the terms and conditions of exploration licenses—or the price of exploration rights— also tends to increase. The reverse is the case in a soft market, where the avail-

EXHIBIT 1

The Supply and Demand for Exploration Rights

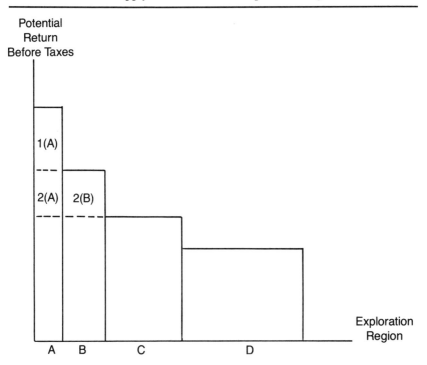

Source: R. Gordon, Phillips Petroleum Company, 1981

ability of exploration rights tends to be higher than the demand for them, resulting in the lowering of the price or cost of exploration licenses.

The latter situation depicts the current state of affairs in the international petroleum sector. During this contractionary period, government companies and international oil companies are experiencing a reduction in cash flow and earnings. They will enter into new agreements only if they are able to define risks in a far more favorable way than was the case in the late 1970s and early 1980s. Similarly, sellers of exploration rights—governments—are discovering that the only way they can induce companies to explore for oil or to develop commercial discoveries is by reducing the costs to companies.

In practical terms, one should ask what corporate responses typify circumstancs such as those found today? In general, companies will seek to limit their capital expenditures to the degree possible, taking into account their desire to position themselves for the next cyclical upturn. This is especially the case for companies which are highly leveraged, financially, due to debt assumed in taking over other companies or in warding off takeovers during the past few years. They will try to increase the options available to them in the future, especially in terms of acreage acquisition and the deferring of work requirements. They will favor relatively low cost production at the expense of high cost, frontier exploration. They will seek production in discoveries that can be brought on stream rapidly. They will seek partners to help reduce their exposure to risk and to participate in costly capital programs. And, they will favor contract

EXHIBIT 2

Real Price of U.S. Oil, 1901-85 (In 1972 Dollars)

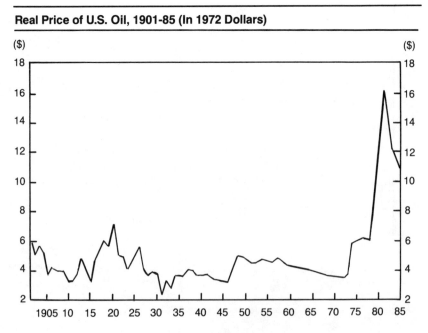

terms and conditions which provide them real equity rights (as opposed to fixed rates or return) and fiscal regimes that offer them the promise to reap the rewards of eventually increasing oil prices.

As noted earlier, there are two principal parameters determining where exploration takes place: geological promise and fiscal attraction. The petroleum industry is aware that the dominant long term trend has been the movement of exploration activities into areas of progressively higher expected costs and risks, and away from the more rapidly depleting, lower cost areas, given the finite nature of petroleum resources. This is obviously not the case over the short term, especially during a cyclical downturn as at present, since exploration expenditures reflect current and immediate expectations and are limited to least costly production. But it is the case over the longer term.

It is useful in this regard to turn to Exhibit 1, which depicts exploration areas of the world in broad groups related to costs of discovery and production and, therefore, potential return to oil companies before taxes. Each bar on the bar chart on the exhibit represents an area available for exploration and production. The width of each bar indicates the relative availability of acreage and the height the total potential cost of production, including government "take" or "rents" from oil exploitation.

In the interdependent and competitive petroleum sector, the amount of potential government take in any one region depends on the extent to which the industry seeks to explore in regions offering lower potential returns. For example, if demand for new reserves is so high that it cannot be met by available low cost supplies (area "A"), that excess demand will drive up the price paid for that area (i.e. government take). The limit of increases in government take is the point where return to industry in that area after taxes meets or surpasses the level of return in area "B." This process continues as one moves out to the right of the bar chart.

In short, as the industry moves to explore in higher cost areas, it creates a taxable surplus for the premium regions. This contrains government take in any region through the differences in returns across areas as they become more marginal. Also, as demand for exploration rights increases during active, expansionary periods, the industry is pushed into frontier regions and government take tends to rise, with take being the highest in the least cost areas.

This theoretical gloss on how competition works in the market for exploration licenses provides the background for a discussion on mechanisms that governments can adopt with respect to exploration agreements, to help mobilize capital for new exploration and, potentially, for early production.

Flexible Fiscal Regimes

Governments seeking to attact petroleum investment in the current period need to meet the competition for expenditures on petroleum exploration and production. It is clear that industry is on the better side of the negotiation table at present and is interested in investing in areas of low geological risk and high return. There has also in this regard been a pronounced preference among most international exploration and production companies to avoid service contracts offering fixed rates of return and, instead, to focus on contracts which provide terms that approach equity ownership.

In addition, for reasons outlined earlier, companies are interested in low cost geological plays and low tax rate areas, which create better opportunities for lower cost known petroleum provinces as opposed to oil importing countries with no petroleum production, at the other extreme.

There are a number of steps governments can take to try to attract exploration capital by meeting competition from abroad in the fiscal area. Since all parties to an agreement seek to achieve contractual stability, flexible fiscal arrangements have become useful vehicles to attract investment. Flexibility can exist along a number of dimensions. For example, governments can attempt to create a number of "trigger points" in the fiscal systems designed to increase or decrease taxes as those points are met. Fiscal regimes can be designed to favor early cost recovery. They can embody features to assure a minimum rate of return. And they can be structured so as to enable a government to increase or decrease its share pari passu with specified changes in oil prices, as well as in profits.

The purpose of flexibility in the design of a fiscal system is to assure that through counter cyclical public policy a government is able to meet competition for exploration expenditures by firms willing to risk capital in this activity. It could thereby assist in the maintenance of a flow of investment funds during a cyclical contraction.

Special Exploration Contracts

There has been a longstanding debate concerning whether exploration and development contracts should be separated into two distinct processes. The recent contraction in petroleum activity has fostered the argument that these two processes ought to be treated as distinctly different from one another. There are several reasons for this. First, since companies are seeking ways to increase their options at low cost, contractual terms that enhance company options while reducing their obligations are seen as favorable. Governments that accommodate corporate needs thus can potentially attract more foreign interest than otherwise. Second, and coming at this from a different direction, an argument has been made that risk capital can be made available for exploration under novel terms that offer both new options and financial reward. We will explore these below.

Seismic Options. One element of an exploration agreement, separated from any development obligation, is the provision to companies of a pure seismic option, involving limited expenditures and providing a foreign company time to decide whether to proceed with a work program.

Flexible Work Programs. Another potential change in contracts pertains to work obligations. While it is true that governments continue to have an interest in timely exploration leading to timely development, as a practical matter, when companies have limited resources available for exploration and seek to postpone decisions for development until price and other uncertainties are resolved, it is in the interest of governments to provide greater flexibility in terms of work requirements. This is true with respect to the extension of relinquishment requirements as well as with respect to drilling obligations and financial expenditures.

Exploration Payback. Another potential contractual innovation, not yet embodied in any contract of which I am aware, would provide an immediate financial reward for an exploration company. Under this type of arrangement, an exploration company would undertake a work program. If at the end of the program a commercial discovery had been made, the government would guarantee the exploration company a fixed and high rate of return on its investment, on the order of 100%. This could satisfy the desires of a company to create early and profitable cash flow. It could also bring a potentially new set of entities into international petroleum exploration activity. It is conceivable as well to amplify such an agreement with a number of options, including the exploration company being given an option to forego payment in exchange for proceeding on a development program, similarly guaranteeing a minimum rate of return.

Exchanging Equity for Services

An entirely different class of opportunities exists for attracting capital into exploration, by tapping into sources which were not available during "normal" periods. Petroleum service and equipment companies, including geophysical companies and drilling contractors might well be induced to provide their services at no initial direct cost. Such companies, which are deeply affected by the cyclical contraction in the petroleum sector, are also seeking new opportunities so as to keep their work forces occupied and to position themselves for the next cyclical upturn. Not all services and equipment companies are now in a position to take such a gamble, but some are.

Provided that opportunities exist for adequately evaluating services renderd, such companies could be enticed into new areas for exploration if they were provided a carried equity interest in a joint venture arrangement—either with the national oil company or with foreign companies. If they were interested in such arrangements, governments would find themselves potentially giving up more of the rents from petroleum production to such companies than was the case in the 1970s. But the *quid pro* would be a potentially more active exploration program in the near term.

Conclusions

This section has outlined a number of approaches that governments can take to maintain the momentum of an exploration program, through changes in their traditional way of doing business. The approaches outlined above all relate to the terms and conditions of contracts. They speak only indirectly to marshalling new sources of capital, or traditional sources in innovative ways. These are the subject of the next section of this essay.

FINANCING PETROLEUM OPERATIONS

In the last section a number of contractual issues were raised in the context of promoting foreign investment capital in the petroleum sector during the current cyclical contraction. The approaches a government takes toward foreign investors, its petroleum laws, and the types of contracts it seeks to secure are directly tied to its ability to finance petroleum projects. A government seeks foreign company participation in the development of its energy resources in order to utilize the foreign investor's technical skills in discovering oil, its managerial skills in organizing the development and production of petroleum resources efficiently, and its capital in order to finance exploration and development.

Financing is required in two stages: first in the exploration for oil; and, second in the development of commercial discoveries. Although oil exploration is frequently expensive in frontier regions, it is much less costly than project development.

A government confronts a choice among three options with regard to financing, assuming it will not, on its own, use self-generated funds for exploration and production:

First, it can decide not to participate directly in petroleum activities, but rather be content to tax the oil industry on its commercial production. This option is rare today, although it will certainly be selected by some countries in the new era of relatively low oil prices and tight government budgets.

Second, a government can separate the exploration and development phases in its contracts, as is frequently done in risk-service contracts prevalent in Latin America. Under this type of arrangement, companies will assume all of the risks, including the capital risks, involved in exploration. However, when a commercial discovery is made, the government can opt to participate, by contributing its share of equity in financing the discovery's development. Given the drastic cuts in companies' exploration budgets due to the drop in oil prices, it will nonetheless be increasingly difficult for developing countries to attract capital for risky exploration ventures.

Third, a government can choose full scale participation in all phases of an exploration and production contract, including its financial participation in pre-exploration studies and in exploration drilling. Under this type of arrangement, a government's participation is an indication that it is willing to risk capital on an equal basis with the private sector from its own country (if available) and from abroad.

Issues of financing immediately pose questions about the sources of funds and about the obligations that the co-venturers in an exploration and production agreement incur. In general, there are only a few ways to secure capital. These may be summarized as follows:

First, a government, or its National Oil Company (NOC), can simply allocate funds through the normal government budgeting process including from its general borrowings, or from funds generated by earlier production and sales. Self-financing of exploration has been the traditional manner in which major oil companies have carried out the first phase of E and P activities (i.e. exploration), as well as of substantial portions of their development work. Self-financing is a viable option for some national oil companies, especially those which are more mature and which have substantial existing production. It is all but excluded as an option for poor countries and those with little or no oil production.

Second, a government or its NOC may undertake to borrow general funds from outside sources to carry out its overall activities, and allocate those funds within the authority granted by its lenders. Such funds might be secured from public sector sources, including the multilateral lending institutions like the World Bank; or they might come from syndicated lending from large international banks. These types of funds have also become relatively scarce as a result of the deep financial crisis confronted by the developing countries, and the unwillingness of private sector lenders to provide this type of loan. Some general funding is available on an increasingly contingent basis from the multilateral institutions.

Third, financing can be secured for specific projects through specialized project financing. This type of financing is generally secured by the assets involved in a project, which means that it is not generally available for the purpose of funding exploration, but it can be made available in some circumstances for the development of commercial discoveries. Project financing usually works either in the form of a special syndication of private banks or through bonds that are widely placed in the international market. Public sector project financing from the multilateral lending institutions is also available.

The main problem associated with the securing of such loans from the private sector is that private lenders are generally unwilling to finance projects on a non-recourse or limited recourse basis (i.e. they generally insist on the government guaranteeing that the debt will be repaid if the project fails) in addition, most private lenders have reached their credit limits for any type of lending in most developing countries and are therefore unable or unwilling to undertake new projects; and energy lending has lost its luster with commercial banks because many of the most problematic and non-performing loans are in the oil and gas sector to oil producing countries.

In short, there is a significant set of problems confronting developing countries with respect to the financing of energy projects. These problems include the level of developing country debt, the inability of these countries to undertake new obligations, and the unwillingness of private banking institutions to lend to the energy sector. Regardless, outside financing can be secured through innovative methods and prudent investment strategies. When a government or its NOC seeks outside funding for energy projects, it should be more adroit on how best to secure funds, be more aware of the types of financial institutions to tap, and be more cognizant of the terms involved.

The increased difficulties in securing financing must also be understood in a wider context. On the one hand, with the dramatic decline in oil prices in the mid-1980s, the once-immediate needs of some developing countries to develop indigenous petroleum reserves have been postponed. For other developing countries, like India, Brazil, Nigeria, Egypt, Indonesia, Mexico and China, the tremendous population growth that is anticipated in the next decade makes the need for stepped up exploration all the more imperative due to the spiralling energy demand which will accompany this growth. In many cases, however, both the costs of not developing reserves or of developing them has been dramatically reduced.

For oil importers, foreign exchange requirements to finance oil imports have been dramatically lowered, as have the costs of financing in terms of interest rates. At the same time, the requirements for financing energy development have been sharply circumscribed. The World Bank had once stated that over the course of the 1980s, developing countries would require close to $2 trillion in investment in energy. This estimate has been substantially reduced. Not only was this original figure always well beyond attainment, but more significantly now is the time to make funds available for exploration purposes, with the costs of exploration and of development much lower than at any point since the early 1970s.

Given the fundamental changes in the international petroleum markets in the mid-1980s, it is clearly important for developing countries not to be complacent. Unless adequate investments are made in the next few years, governments run significant risks for the future. The main risk, of course, is of another cyclical tightening in the oil market in the early to mid-1990s. Underinvestment in the short term will lead to a significantly tighter market in the longer term, with higher oil prices, higher inflation, higher import bills for oil importing countries, and lower export coalmines, and thus revenues for the exporters.

Multilateral Lending Institutions

As private sector sources of financing have diminished in absolute levels, the relative role played by multilateral and bilateral public sector (i.e. governmental) financing has increased proportionately. Such financing can be in the form of direct grants or indirect grants (i.e. very low interest rates and long maturities); or it can involve terms similar to what would be available on a commercial basis, when private financing would otherwise be unavailable.

Financing can also involve complex combinations of bilateral and multilateral official lending, along with private sector funding and oil company participation. But it always has a "soft" quality.

There are two principal functions of public sector financing. The first is to overcome obstacles to commercial development by, for example, assuming risks that the private sector is unwilling to take or providing information on geological conditions that is not yet available. This can be achieved either by direct risk reduction through the elimination of obstacles or indirect risk reduction in the form of "insurance." The second role of public sector financing is to act as a catalyst so as to trigger private sector investments.

This latter role is also borne of necessity, since the resources of multilateral and national development agencies are far too limited to ever provide more than a fraction of the funds required. Public sector financing, however, does represent as much as 25% of the energy financing for the Third World and most of it is directed at power generation and infrastructure (e.g. pipelines, roads, port facilities). The catalyst role is one which best utilizes these limited public resources, as each dollar of concessionary lending will be multiplied by additional dollars of funds from commercial sources. The recent emphasis on private sector co-financing, which unites public and private sector financing sources, is the clearest example of the public/private multiplier at work.

The role of catalyst ensures that commercial funds are not displaced and that uneconomic projects are not financed. Thus, public sector moneys are often provided at an early stage in a project, when private parties are reluctant to become involved. Similarly, when the focus of lending is infrastructure-building, it is undertaken because private sector involvement is inevitably reduced until the overall or ancillary projects become sufficiently attractive for investment by commercial entities.

Over the past quarter century, there has been a lack of oil exploration in most developing countries, other than those with already proven production. Part of the problem has been linked to political factors, which create unsuitable or hostile investment environments. In such cases, the catalyst role is severely constrained, if not entirely constricted. However, it is now recognized that loans from the public sector for pre-development and exploration can reduce perceived risks and inspire confidence. In these respects, the intimate country knowledge and project evaluation skills of institutions such as the World Bank can do a great deal to attract attention and development funds to projects, which would otherwise be overlooked. Country risk appears to be the one obstacle which public sector funds can most effectively alleviate. This is especially the case in the current depressed petroleum sector.

While this is not an appropriate vehicle for examining the energy lending programs of the World Bank and its affiliates or of the regional development banks, their programs are introduced primarily because of their significance to developing countries and because they can provide potential building blocks for some of the financial mechanisms discussed below. It is clear that the solution to the long-term structural problems of maintaining and enhancing investment in oil exploration and production will require innovation on the part of governments, financial institutions and international petroleum companies. Some of these are in the process of development. Others will need to await the design of new financial structures to reduce and spread risks.

In the remainder of this chapter a number of potentially innovative mechanisms will be reviewed. An array of examples is also provided showing how inventiveness tailored to specific problems can potentially result in the marshalling of additional financial resources for petroleum exploitation. In particular, some of the experiments currently under way in the multilateral lending institutions to provide additional resources through the co-financing of projects are examined. Attention is then turned to ways to tailor new private and public sector arrangements for limited recourse project financing. Finally mechanisms through which oil can be used as a financial tool through counter-trade, pre-export financing and hedging are examined.

Co-Financing

Co-Financing is a well-established mechanism, which recently has been applied in innovative ways to facilitate the flow of private sector funds to developing countries. There are a number of innovations that can still be created for co-financing techniques and that are applicable in either a multilateral or regional context, including the Asian area. Co-financing is normally an arrangement where two or more financial institutions or corporate lenders, seeking different repayment terms, are formally associated with each other for the purpose of financing a designated project.

Private sector co-financing normally involves the association of two types of lenders—one set, usually commercial banks, having an interest in rapid paybacks and another set, usually pension funds, seeking long-term maturities. Mortgage markets in the United States have involved this form of co-financing. In the case of international lending for projects in developing countries, co-financing usually involves two official institutions, or a combination of private and public sector institutions.

Examples of international co-financing involving two public sector institutions include two multilateral concessionary lending institutions (e.g. IDA and the OPEC Development Fund), aid agencies from two different countries (e.g. the United States and France), or one multilateral and one national donor. This latter type of co-financing grew substantially during the 1970s as a result of OECD country efforts to coordinate and streamline official assistance and also as a result of the substantial growth in assistance from OPEC. However, to date, relatively few energy projects have been targeted.

The form of co-financing that has received the most attention recently involves a combination of private and public sector (multilateral) financial institutions. This type of co-financing has been used on an experimental basis in an attempt to expand the flow of private sector resources to developing countries. It lessens the commercial banks' risks through use of the multilateral banks' funds to subsidize interest rates and carry the risk of the tail-end payments. It also involves using their expertise to help in evaluating and supervising projects and, crucially, though not always infallibly, using their influence with the creditor governments to obtain repayment. Although the World Bank (IBRD) has been in the forefront of these efforts, other multilateral development banks have also been involved, including the International Finance Corporation (IFC), the Inter-American Development Bank (IADB) and the Asian Development Bank (ADB). Energy projects have been preeminent among these types of arrangements.

The original co-financing program typically had the World Bank and the private sector institutions providing separate loans for a single project. These loans were loosely linked by cross-reference provisions (including cross-default clauses) and an overall letter of agreement. Since the relationships between the two classes of lenders was not tight, the World Bank had the right—but was not obligated—to follow the private sector side in suspending disbursements or accelerating repayment.

These co-financing schemes were regarded as having created "additionality" in the sense of making available funds that would otherwise not have been committed for specific projects. This is because the participation of the multilateral development banks provided additional comfort to the private sector through staff work done in project appraisal, loan preparation and the monitoring of the implementation schedule. However, several major obstacles impeded the expansion of the program. These obstacles can be summarized as follows:

- *Legal Obstacles.* The loose relationship between the World Bank and private lenders and, in particular, the World Bank's freedom not to invoke cross-default provisions, was worrisome to the private sector. Even the tighter structure of IADB co-financing was a concern, since banks did not wish to relinquish their own freedom to invoke a default provision to the judgment of a multilateral agency.

- *Developing Countries' Resistance.* Many LDCs preferred project loans to be made wholly by the multilateral lending institutions. Some of this attitude was ideological—many governments did not wish to be tied to the private sector. Some of it was tactical—some governments did not wish co-financing to succeed if it would mean that industrial countries would reduce their contributions to the multilateral institutions. And some of it was based on terms and conditions. As opposed to wholly public sector loans of the period, co-financing loans carried floating rates, shorter maturities and grace periods, and more onerous conditions, especially on choice of law and the settlement of disputes.

- *Multilateral Institution Resistance.* The multilateral lending institutions, themselves, impeded the expansion of co-financing. Some of this stemmed from bureaucratic inertia, cumbersome procedures, and inflexibility in dealing with concerns of the private sector banks.

- *Private Sector Impediments.* Constraints on the private sector side are partially attitudinal, partially related to regulatory limitations and partially reflective of the fact that numerous banks have reached their limitations on lending to particular countries, especially in the period of high levels of indebtedness by developing countries.

In response to these constraints, the World Bank developed a new set of co-financing mechanisms in an experimental program instituted in 1983. This program is being further modified and improved. These so-called B-loans, described below, have been important, as illustrated in Exhibit 3. These loans, totalling $1.4 billion, should be placed in the context of other lending. In the same period, because of the emphasis on reschedulings and the limitations placed on new borrowings by LDCs, total new commercial lending was on the order of only $5 billion. Co-financing was traditionally 1% of new voluntary syndications to developing countries, but reached 12% in FY84 and grew further in FY85.

The new World Bank, B-loan facility has three major variants, which are designed to make co-financing more attractive to all parties. They have made capital available in a period when such capital was increasingly scarce, at terms that represent improvements over what otherwise could have been achieved. In particular, these terms can include extended payments and fixed rates.

The new B-loans, unlike the traditional loans, have the World Bank as a direct participant in the later maturities of the loans. Thus the new loans overcame some of the obstacles, which were posed earlier, to the expansion of co-financing. Not only did banks receive comfort from the direct link between the two classes of loans, but also tangible benefits could be brought to borrowers

EXHIBIT 3
Private Co-Financing Operations of the World Bank: Competition of Market
Placements, FY 1976-85
(U.S. $ Millions)

Year	Traditional Loans		B-loans	
	Number	Amount	Number	Amount
1976	1	55	—	—
1977	1	50	—	—
1978	8	304	—	—
1979	9	225	—	—
1980	12	597	—	—
1981	5	175	—	—
1982	6	332	—	—
1983	3	125	—	—
1984	0	0	6	564
1985	0	0	5	922

Source: World Bank, *Annual Report 1985*, p. 55.

and lenders—the availability of the Bank's analysis to the latter and the facilitation of long-term credits to the former.

The three B-loan options include the following: (1) direct Bank participation in the late maturities of the loan (with an option by the Bank to sell off all or part), thus providing the lengthening of maturities by up to four years beyond what would be available in the commercial market alone; (2) the provision of a Bank guarantee on late maturities; and (3) the provision of a level payments option, with the Bank taking a contingent liability on the final amount of potentially deferred amortization, due to floating interest rates and the variable amount of principal actually repaid.

Co-financing is in its infancy. It could well become one of the primary financing vehicles for energy projects in the developing world. The World Bank program—and others which emulate it—can be improved upon, with enhanced benefits to borrowers.

One potential improvement relates to an option available in the World Bank pilot program. It involves the prearranged sale of participants in Bank loans on commercial terms. This option is important in that it could enable borrowers to tap into markets or financial sources, which have been more difficult to obtain thus far. These would include institutional investors, such as pension funds, and second-tier banks. It could also be a helpful mechanism in restoring lending to countries as they emerge from the debt crisis.

A second potential innovation is one adopted from the secondary mortgage markets of the U.S. and which could reduce overall rates to the borrower. This innovation involves the creation of a special dedicated assets fund of about 15 percent of total financing. These assets can be invested in liquid holdings earning a market rate. Withdrawals would be made from this interest earning account to provide commercial banks with a market rate of return while, in effect, subsidizing the borrower's rate and providing a grade period in the early years. For example, a special account of $15 million in a $100 million financing, would generate about $1.65 million of interest income at 11% during the first year. This amount, plus some capital could be drawn down to service the overall debt. Such a procedure could be an added inducement to private lenders to enter co-financing arrangements; and, it could attract new borrowers by helping to provide attractive rates. Sound financial engineering allows this to be accomplished without requiring the Bank to provide additional funds or exposing its assets to project risk.

A third innovation is, mechanically, a variant of the latter one. It would involve the establishment of a revolving loan fund for oil development projects. Such a fund, using co-financing techniques, could be used not only for the financing of new projects, but also for the refinancing of earlier loans. It could be established on a regional basis (e.g. by the ASEAN countries) or through existing facilities of the regional and other multilateral lending institutions.

A properly structured revolving loan fund could substantially enhance the leverage to be gained from public sector financing. A public sector institution, administering the revolving loan fund, could structure its participation in the form of a "convertible zero coupon bond." The public sector institution could retain a variety of options concerning the form of its participation. One choice could involve the establishment of a trust account to be used to leverage private sector funds when concessional financing is deemed desirable. The use of a trust account offers the possibility of serving as a catalyst to increase private sector investment in a project. The option to employ a trust account could also be used in conjunction with direct equity financing by the public sector institution, or not at all.

A fourth type of innovation in co-financing would be to establish the elements of limited recourse financing of energy development projects in the developing world. The World Bank has begun to consider ways to do this in its energy lending program.

Limited recourse financing techniques were developed in the United States on the basis of production loans and production payment loans, where the security for the loan was based on the revenues generated by the particular project for which the loan was made. Under limited recourse financing the lender does not have direct recourse to other assets of the borrower beyond the project being financed. In other words, the lender assumes, or shares, some of the risk of the project along with the borrower.

Limited recourse financing to date has been restricted on an international basis largely to development projects undertaken by the large international oil companies, especially in the North Sea. Lenders have thus far been reluctant to extend limited recourse financings to government-owned enterprises because of the numerous risks involved, including foreign exchange convertibility, market, price and general political risk.

It should become a major task—and opportunity—for multilateral lending institutions to become engaged in the design of project financing on a limited recourse basis of oil and gas projects in the developing world. This could well be accomplished if mechanisms could be developed to segment projects into appropriate stages and if the public sector or multilateral institutions provided means to reduce the riskiness of projects for lenders. The nascent Multilateral Investment Guaranty Agency (MIGA) of the World Bank, for example, could reduce overall country or political risk, once it is fully implemented. Beyond this form of insurance, the multilateral lender could also provide contingent loans for governments to back up the government's obligations (or more simply to offer guarantees) in such areas as completion obligations or foreign exchange obligations.

As was argued earlier, co-financing techniques offer enormous promise for oil and natural gas development projects, even for those designed to meet domestic needs rather than providing export surpluses. The crisis now being confronted by governments in the financing of energy projects should create an exceptional environment for testing the inventiveness of governments, their financial advisors, and the multilateral lending institutions in developing new approaches in this area.

Countertrade Finance

Another general category of innovative financing for energy projects is countertrade finance. Countertrade, or barter in its most basic form, is as old as trade itself. The debt crisis has revived the practice in a myriad of innovative uses and mechanisms. "Countertrade" in the energy context normally implies exchanges of oil at some discount, for industrial goods, agricultural commodities, military equipment, or construction projects. In this context, we will examine countertrade as a mechanism of trade finance for the procurement of energy equipment and services as well as of a development project's financing.

Countertrade can be defined as any international transaction in which imports of goods or services are linked to exports from the importing country. A decade ago, it was estimated that some fifteen countries were actively involved as initiators of such trade. These were largely Eastern Bloc countries, which sought to reduce the volatility of their export earnings, reduce their outlays of hard currency, and gain access to Western technologies and markets. World economic instability and mushrooming debt have fueled countertrade as cash short countries have sought out markets for their goods to pay for their imports. It is estimated that more than 100 countries—mostly LDCs—are now engaged in countertrade. These countries see countertrade as a way to expand and diversity exports, while making imports self-financing at a time when they are facing hard currency shortages and lost access to trade credits.

Despite theoretical arguments that countertrade is inefficient for countries and for the world trade and payments system, it has clear advantages to some countries in the practical world. In a world of restrictions and inefficiencies, countertrade can conserve scarce hard currency, facilitate development with limited reliance on credits, and increase access to new markets.

For many oil exporting countries, countertrade served as a way to disguise discounts from the official price of their oil in efforts to increase their market share, especially between 1983 and 1985 when official selling prices were still being maintained. Today it is used to enhance market share beyond a country's given OPEC production allotment. In addition to using countertrade as a trade finance tool, Iran, Iraq, Nigeria, Libya and Qatar have all used oil countertrade to pay for construction projects. Libya is also known for using oil to settle arrears on its debt.

The use of oil in direct barter transactions has been appropriately criticized. It has been alleged that too often countertrade involves deep discounts not warranted by the marketplace, is a temptation to corruption, or results in transactions significantly les remunerative than utilizing the cash generated from oil sales to purchase products freely on the open market.

A carefully constructed countertrade strategy can, however, assist a government in achieving trade financing and project financing objectives in both oil exporting and oil importing countries. In order to facilitate the use of oil as a financial instrument in such transactions, several criteria must be met. For example, the government must have a clear understanding of the projects it wishes to finance, the vendors from which it is purchasing equipment and services, the schedule of payments it wishes to make, and the mechanisms by which it can doubly leverage its trade by building an export credit facilities offered by foreign governments in the vendors' home countries. It must also have available in the economy spare production capacity of readily marketable commodities to be used in the countertrade project.

The first type of countertrade arrangement we will review relates to the financing of procurement of oil related equipment and services. These are financial/trade transactions designed to help a national oil company maintain a level of imports of parts and services so as to continue an active drilling program without placing undue burdens on foreign exchange reserves.

For example, a National Oil Company would devote a specially budgeted amount of local currency for the purpose of buying goods on the local market for sale abroad. For these purposes it could either create its own trading company, as Peterobras of Brazil has (Interbras), or engage the services of a trading company, on contract. These goods would then be exported, generating foreign exchange. The foreign exchange would be escrowed, or maintained in a special account. This special account, in turn, would be used to pay for oil equipment and services from outside vendors (see Exhibit 4).

There is a variant on this approach, which is workable under certain circumstances, and which abstracts one step beyond pure barter transactions involving goods exported for goods imported. In this variant, an NOC will issue a promissory note for payment to its equipment suppliers. These notes will have no alternative redemption features. On the one hand, like the promissory notes once issued by Petrobras to its suppliers, these notes could be redeemed for full payment at the end of two years (principal plus interest)—or they could be sold to a party wishing to hold them. Depending on the credit rating of the issuing NOC, such notes could also be insured for repayment. On the other hand, such notes could be redeemed for local currency through the central bank and made available for the purchase of local services or for goods to export. In this type of procedure, the countertrade burden would be placed on the shoulders of the supplier rather than the NOC.

There are a number of prerequisites for making this type of program workable. These include the creditworthiness of the NOC, the agreement of the central bank, and the availability on the local market of goods for export. A major factor is the willingness of the parties involved in the countertrade to price goods competitively without dumping them on the international market. The overall thrust of the example, however, is to postulate that there is much to be done through the innovative and imaginative use of countertrade finance to help an NOC in securing its procurement objectives.

A second area in which countertrade finance can be used innovatively is in the co-financing of specific projects, such as refineries (grassroots, expansions or modernizations), pipelines, and oil field development. Countertrade can be used in such projects and when a financing gap emerges. Let us assume, for example, the case of a small grassroots refinery with capital costs on the order of $50 million.

Let us assume, further, that 60%, or $30 million of the project is being financed by a multilateral lending institution and 25%, or $12.5 million by the export credits of the country, whose company has been the winning bidder on the refinery. The remainder—15% or $7.5 million—is to be financed by an NOC, which has not generated the cash equivalent in foreign exchange and either cannot or prefers not to borrow the difference. In this circumstance it is feasible to require the contractor to generate the remaining amount through countertrade. In this situation, the NOC will allocate local currency, deemed equivalent to the financing gap ($7.5 million) to the contractor to buy goods in the local market for export. It would be up to the contractor to market the goods selected as best it can, or to sell the goods below market and absorb the "losses."

EXHIBIT 4
Countertrade: Finance

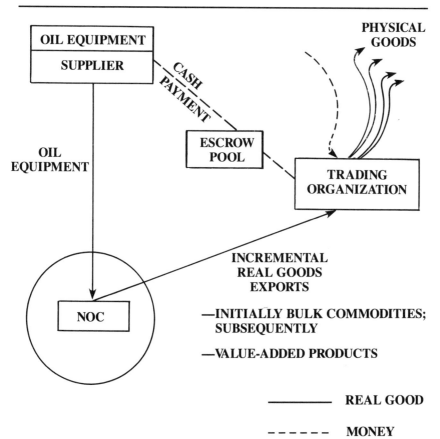

A common variation on this type of countertrade co-financing is where the supplier agrees to be paid back "in-kind" from the facility's future production. Often referred to as a buy-back arrangement, the contractor in the above example would be allocated petroleum products from the refinery equal to the financing gap plus interest. One actual proposal calls for the financing of a gas fired power station in Peru through payment in iron ore from the mining company which would receive its payment in electricity. Again, the point is that countertrade can have a useful role in the financing of a capital project. This is even more true under current circumstances, wherein suppliers are competing actively with one another for business and their home governments are eager for them to generate business, since it has a positive impact on employment levels in the home country.

Pre-Export Finance

Akin to a number of forms of project financing is the development of advanced payment facilities. These are mechanisms, which can be made available for general revenue purposes for oil exporters, provided that the level of exports is in excess of any existing financial obligations. This type of facility has been created on a large scale on a government-to-government basis as well as on a government-to-company basis. The largest such facility was created in 1982 between Mexico and the U.S. whereby the U.S. provided $1 billion to Mexico as advanced payment for future delivery of oil to the U.S. Strategic Petroleum Reserve. Some oil exporting countries use a simple variation of this type of facility by obtaining a bankers acceptance credit for a cargo of crude, rolling it over for subsequent cargoes. This method, however, can provide only a small amount of financing and does nothing to stabilize marketing arrangements for these countries.

The importance of stable marketing arrangements has grown dramatically since 1981 as the petroleum sector entered a period of uncertainty which now appears likely to last for another five to ten years. This uncertainty relates primarily to the surprising and radical decline in the demand for crude oil in the industrial world together with an increase in supplies from non-OPEC sources and the consequent downward pressure on prices. This has led to a decline in crude oil term contracts and a broad move to spot market sales and pricing based on netback formulas or baskets of spot crude prices.

Crude oil exporters need to assure themselves that they can:

- sell all of the crude oil available for export;

- have an assured income stream for planning purposes;

- have the flexibility to use their oil resources for obtaining credit, when needed, at rates more favorable than conventional borrowing.

An appropriately designed advance payments facility can help meet these objectives. By structuring a facility to include a trust account, the borrowing can be over-collateralized, thus enabling the borrower to obtain a low interest rate and also providing a buffer against fluctuations in the selling price of the oil.

For illustrative purposes, consider a hypothetical case where an NOC desires to borrow $50 million to finance a development project. Working together with an external agent, the NOC enters into a contract to deliver oil cargoes worth a total of $75 million over eighteen months. This contract would be committed as security for the $50 million loan. Since at current oil prices and interest rates the contract has a present value of $70 million, the loan would be over-collateralized by forty percent. This provides considerable security to the lender, enabling a favorable lending rate.

A trust account is then established and is funded from the proceeds of the monthly oil sales. Principal and interest payments on the loan are then made out of this account. The trust account balance rises steadily over the eighteen month period (bearing a sharp drop in oil prices) and the surplus is invested in high yielding debt instruments, with the excess balance being paid back to the NOC. If oil prices fall during the eighteen months, the trust account acts as a buffer, with the surplus falling, while the debt servicing continues unimpeded. Likewise, a rise in oil prices inflates the trust account balance, and the surplus funds are passed through to the NOC. Below are three examples demonstrating this:

1) Oil prices unchanged:
   - Loan proceeds to NOC — $50.0 million
   - Trust account end balance — $22.8 million
   - Present value of oil — $70.0 million
2) Oil prices fall by half:
   - Loan proceeds to NOC — $50.0 million
   - Trust account end balance — $ 3.3 million
   - Present value of oil — $52.6 million
3) Oil prices rise by half:
   - Loan proceeds to NOC — $50.0 million
   - Trust account end balance — $42.2 million
   - Present value of oil — $87.6 million

While the trust account provides a substantial buffer against price declines, the advanced payments facility can be used together with a hedging strategy to reduce the downside risks. This facility can be used in a number of ways, providing flexibility. It can be used to back a straight syndicated borrowing, or, if desired, as security for a stand-by line of credit.

In summary, using innovative financing techniques, advanced payments facilities can be tailored to provide a government or NOC money at highly favorable terms for financing development or other purposes. The strategy can be further tailored by using hedging techniques so as to minimize potential losses related to fluctuations in the price of petroleum. And, the buyer will also be better off by receiving a term contract for petroleum at a market rate.

Petro-Bonds

Finally, another innovative approach to medium-term financing for oil producing countries would involve the development of a petroleum backed security. By combining sovereign borrowing with the best aspects of commercial, collateralized credits, the oil producing state can obtain financing on favorable terms.

There are many potential ways to develop a petroleum backed security. One mechanism would work as follows:

- The oil producer enters into a contract to deliver a fixed value of crude oil at a specified maturity in the future (5 years or more could be tried).

- A financial source lends money against the contract and gains title to oil.

- At maturity, the oil is shipped and proceeds from the sale are used to pay off the principal and interest.

This arrangement looks very much like the advanced payments mechanism outlined above. It results in a hybrid credit with potentially better terms than an unsecured sovereign loan or a loan collateralized by assets within the oil producing country. The terms should approach those that a "AAA" international oil company (IOC) might obtain on a fully secured credit. The perceived risks to the lending bank are reduced to the following:

- Risk of non-delivery of the oil under the contract.

- Risk of non-payment of the bank loan after the oil is delivered.

These risks can be substantially reduced, if not eliminated, by the following actions:

- Arranging for a "AAA" IOC to enter into the contract as a guaranteed purchaser of the crude oil, in order to ensure an orderly disposition of the oil and a reliable source of funds.

- Providing for a pricing formula that assures the IOC a fair and competitive price for the oil in the year of maturity (i.e. a transparent price, such as a netback formula or crude basket formula, which can be verified by an independent third party) and, given this pricing arrangement, provides that a sufficient quantity of oil is delivered to cover the loan obligations.

- Allowing the IOC a small discount on its purchases, thus providing the company an incentive to enter into the contract. The contract should also have no negative balance sheet impact on the IOC.

- Providing a bank or transfer agent to act as escrow agent to transfer, upon delivery of the oil, the proceeds from the IOC directly to the lender. In addition, the trustee will locate a buyer for the oil, should the IOC fail to fulfill its commitment.

- Including in the contract a provision that the bank or trustee, as holder of the title to the oil, has a legal "first claim" after maturity to any crude shipped by the oil producer, up the amount due so as to satisfy the loan. This would include an agreement of choice of law, guaranteeing an appropriate jurisdiction of the bank or IOC's choice, and the right, if necessary, to claim cargoes of oil outside of the oil producing country in order to meet legal claims under the loan agreement.

These provisions would virtually eliminate the risk of non-payment or non-delivery of the oil, unless the oil exporter has depleted its resources to the point that it has ceased to be an oil exporter. This reduced risk should enable the oil producer to obtain far more favorable terms. This hybrid credit carries advantages over traditional forms of finance, such as banker's acceptances, which have short maturities, or longer term loans, which carry a higher risk premium associated with concerns over possible foreign exchange difficulties or inability to make claims on collateral within the borders of the borrowing country in question.

A number of potential interesting variants could also be worked out. In one variant, the lender could be an individual IOC or a group of IOCs. The price of the bond could be discounted for the net present value of oil, priced in today's terms, but delivered in five years or longer. The bond would be tied to barrels of crude rather than the value of crude in question, although a government would almost certainly need to assure delivery of a minimum value of crude. With the potential for price increases, the bond holders (initially IOCs) could share the windfall with the issuing government, perhaps with a cap. The virtue of this arrangement from the perspective of a lender is that it is almost equivalent to buying oil in place. Another potential element, alluded to earlier, could involve making the petro-bond instrument transferable and sold in capital markets in many denominations.

CONCLUSIONS

The mid-1980s have marked a sharp break with trends in the international petroleum sector that had been set off in the early 1970s. In particular, the abrupt cyclical downturn in business activity in this sector has created a crisis in the financing of conventional oil and gas projects for developing countries seeking to continue the momentum to reduce imports or oil or to increase exports.

The reduced cash flows of the international and national oil companies have substantially reduced their ability to engage in exploration or to finance the number of energy development projects open to them. If one accepts the view that the international oil industry is substantially under-investing today to meet the demands of the 1990s, then it is crucial to find ways to encourage both early exploration and development.

This paper has taken the view that mechanisms are available to developing countries, both through changes in the terms of exploration agreements and through innovative financing techniques to assure that some of their project specific energy goals are met. Not all of the mechanisms outlined in this paper will work. They certainly will not be appropriate for all countries under all foreseeable circumstances. But variants of many of them do open up the possibility to governments to proceed with projects which would otherwise remain dormant until the next upturn takes place in the petroleum business cycle.

Joint Development of Petroleum Resources in Overlapping Claim Areas*

*by Mark J. Valencia***

Overlapping claims and unresolved boundaries resulting in disputes between sovereign governments can impede petroleum exploration and development. Since resolution of disputes typically takes years to achieve, governments must devise new ways of conducting exploration activities in disputed territories to ensure secure sources of future supply. The Asian-Pacific region offers important examples of joint development arrangements. The author examines features common to joint development arrangements in the region and explores the obstacles to their implementation.

INTRODUCTION

With the extension of jurisdiction over resources and certain activities to 200 nautical miles ("nm") or more, many seabed areas have become subject to overlapping claims. Petroleum resources are likely in some overlap areas. Presently, oil prices are down and supplies are in overabundance with exploration and drilling having been cut back. However, many economists believe that demand will again eventually outstrip supply. Then the new cycle of exploration and drilling will trend further offshore into deeper and sometimes disputed waters.

The UN Law of the Sea Convention provides that pending agreement on boundary delimitation of the exclusive economic zone and continental shelf, the States concerned shall make every effort to enter into provisional arrangements and in the meantime not jeopardize or hamper the reaching of the final delimitation.[1] International joint development—the setting aside of a boundary dispute and jointly exploring and developing any resources in an agreed area—is one such provisional arrangement.[2] This paper reviews precedents for

---

*This paper draws on and updates previously published works by the author: Mark J. Valencia, 1986. Taming Troubled Waters: Joint Development of Oil and Mineral Resources in Overlapping Claim Areas. *San Diego Law Review,* v. 23, p. 3; Mark J. Valencia and Masahiro Miyoshi, 1985. Southeast Asian Seas: Joint Development of Hydrocarbons in Overlapping Claim Areas? *Ocean Development and International Law Journal,* v. 16, pp. 211–254; Mark J. Valencia, 1985. *Southeast Asian Seas: Oil Under Troubled Waters,* Kuala Lumpur, Oxford University Press, 155 p.
**Research Associate, Resource Systems Institute, The East-West Center, Honolulu, Hawaii.

joint development, defines the essential elements of a joint development agreement, reviews problems in implementation, and sketches the basic parameters of possible joint development schemes for five areas of overlapping claims in Southeast Asia.

Potential hydrocarbon-bearing areas in Southeast Asia with unresolved boundaries and thus candidate areas for joint development include the eastern Gulf of Thailand (Vietnam, Thailand, and Kampuchea), the Timor Sea (Australia and Indonesia), the southwestern Gulf of Thailand (Malaysia, Thailand, and Vietnam), the area north, west, and east of Natuna (Vietnam, Indonesia, Malaysia, and China?), offshore Brunei (Brunei, Malaysia, China?, Vietnam?), the Gulf of Tonkin (China and Vietnam), and the Dangerous Ground (Malaysia, Vietnam, the Philippines, and China)[3] (Figure 1). Such areas in East Asia include those between South Korea and Japan, South Korea and China, China and Japan, and China and Taiwan (Figure 2).

JOINT DEVELOPMENT IN AREAS OF OVERLAPPING CLAIMS

Joint development agreements between Thailand and Malaysia[4] (Figure 3), South Korea and Japan[5] (Figure 4), Saudi Arabia and Kuwait[6] (Figure 5) and Iceland and Norway[7] (Figure 6) are sufficiently well-documented to delineate elements in common and their variation. Supplemental information can be drawn from a similar agreement between Sudan and Saudi Arabia[8] (Figure 7) and that recommended for Tunisia and Libya.[9]

The extreme north-western end of the Malay Basin is claimed wholly or in part by Thailand, Malaysia, and Vietnam. Although both Malaysia and Thailand agree on the boundary extending approximately 50 km (31 mi) from land, from that point their respective boundary claims diverge north and south. The area of overlap is roughly a triangle situated north-east-south-west, athwart the north-western shore core of the Malay Basin with its apex pointing towards land. The overlap area includes a gas discovery by Texas Pacific and is believed to contain some 14 trillion cubic feet of gas or as much as the estimated gas reserves for the rest of the Gulf of Thailand. A line of equidistance between Thailand and Malaysia would extend even further south than the Thai claim and include the gas discovery in Pilong 1. Assuming that the new Vietnamese government has not relinquished the 1971 continental shelf claim of South Vietnam, the Vietnamese claim encompasses the north-western tip of the area claimed by both Malaysia and Thailand. Thailand had let concessions in the north-eastern part of the disputed area to Texas Pacific and in the south-eastern part to Triton 1.

On 21 February 1979, the prime ministers of Thailand and Malaysia, General Kriangsak Chomanan and Datuk Hussein Onn, signed a memorandum of understanding establishing the Malaysia-Thailand Joint Authority. Both governments agreed that it was in their best interests to exploit the resources of the

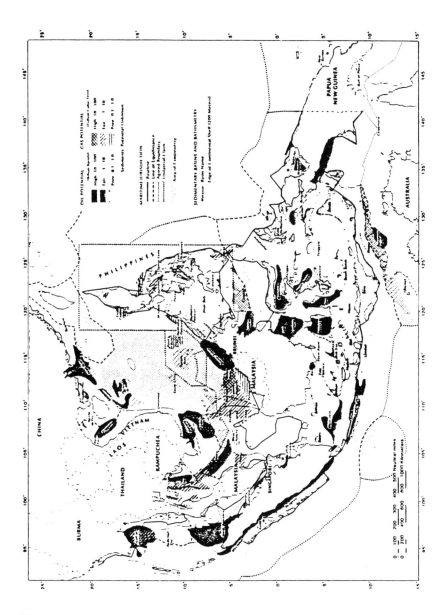

Figure 1. The South China Sea: Extended Maritime Jurisdiction and Petroleum Potential. Source: Mark J. Valencia. Oil and Gas *in* Joseph R. Morgan and Mark J. Valencia, eds., *Atlas for Marine Policy in Southeast Asian Seas.* University of California Press, Berkeley.

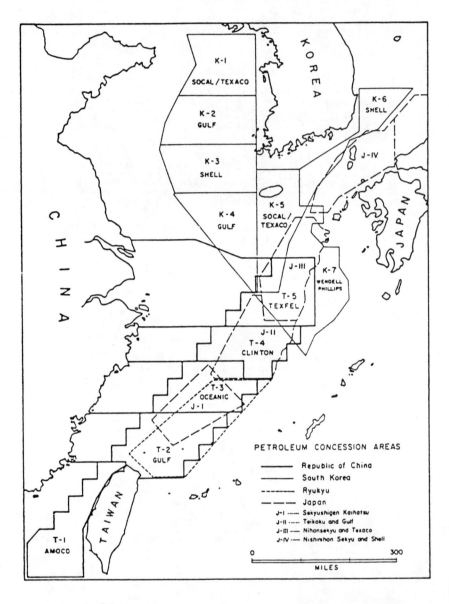

Figure 2. Unilateral claims and concessions in the Yellow Sea and the East
China Sea (based on U.S. State Dept. Office of the Geographer map
No. 2617-71). Source: C. H. Park, *Harvard International Law Journal* 14, 219 (1973). Reprinted with permission © 1973 Harvard
Law Journal Association.

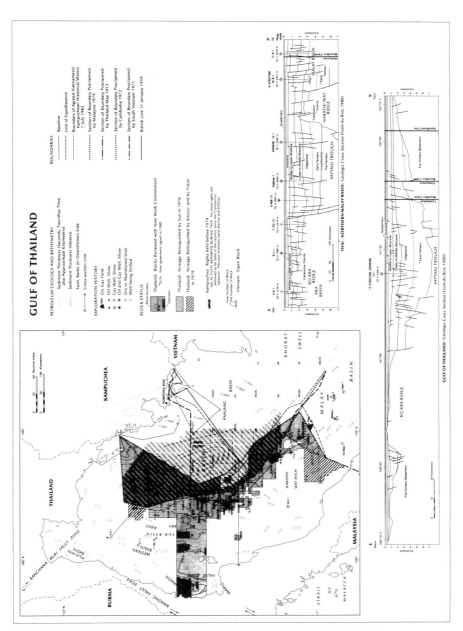

Figure 3. Gulf of Thailand: maritime claims and petroleum geology. Source: Valencia *supra* source Fig. 1.

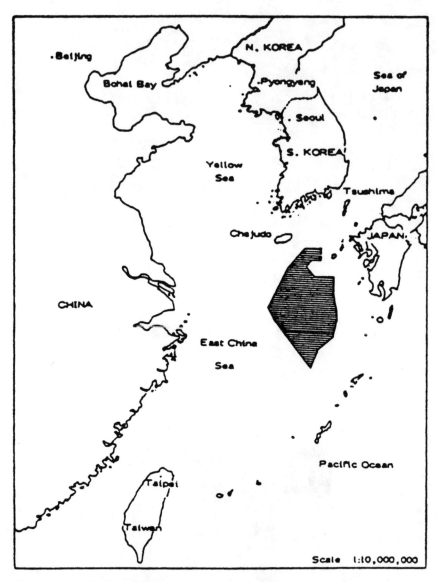

Figure 4A. The joint development zone.

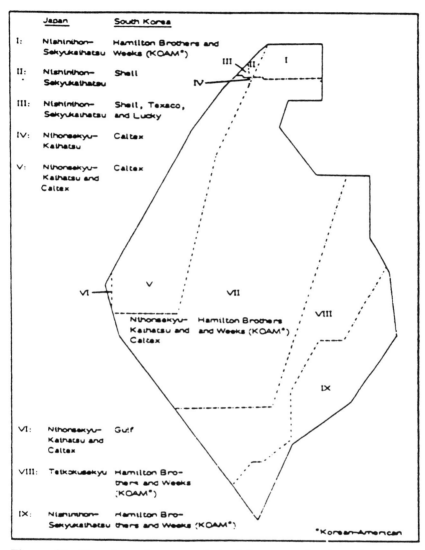

Figure 4B. The nine subzones and the joint concessionaires. Source: M. Takeyama. Japan's Foreign Negotiations Over Offshore Petroleum Development: An Analysis of Decision- Making in the Japan-Korea Continental Shelf Joint Development Program *in* R. Friedheim et al. *Japan and the New Ocean Regime;* 1984, Westview Press. Reprinted by permission of Westview Press, Boulder, CO, copyright © 1984.

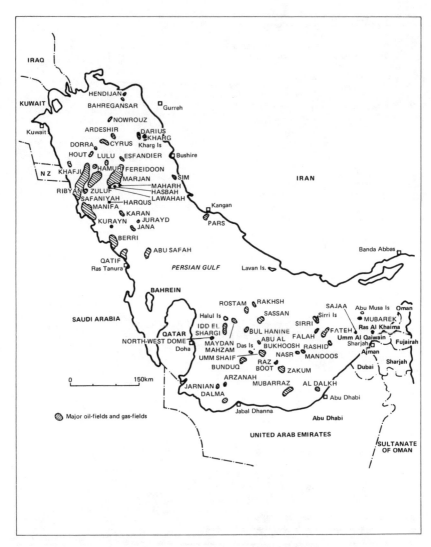

Figure 5. Joint offshore oil developments in the Persian Gulf. Source: H. Whitehead, *An A–Z of Offshore Oil and Gas.* Gulf Publishing Co., Texas (1976). Kogan Page Ltd. publisher outside the U.S.A.

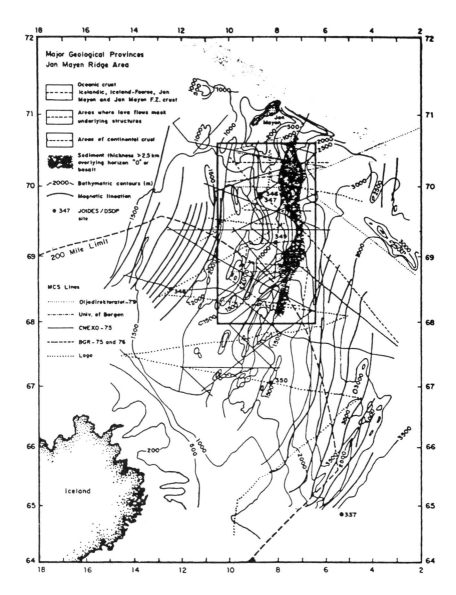

Figure 6. Area subject to joint development. Source: Reprinted with permission from W. Østreng, Reaching agreement on international exploitation of ocean mineral resources *in* M.J. Valencia, ed., *Geology and Hydrocarbon Potential of the South China Sea and Possibilities of Joint Development,* Pergamon Books Ltd., p. 561.

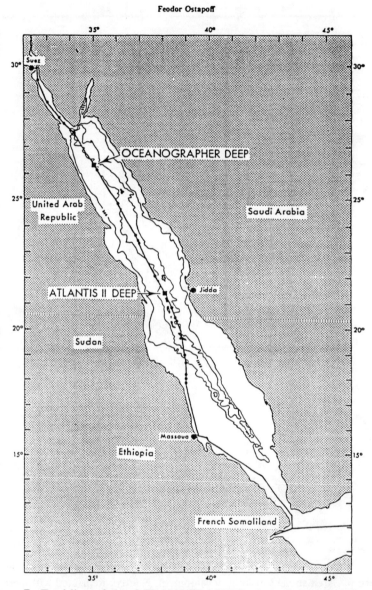

Figure 7. Trackline of the OCEANOGRAPHER through Red Sea showing geographic locations of Atlantis II Deep and Oceanographer Deep: 500m and 1,000m contour lines after Drake and Girdler (1964). Source: Reprinted with permission from E. Degens and D. Ross, eds., *Hot Brines and Recent Heavy Metal Deposits in the Red Sea: A Geochemical and Geophysical Account,* 1969, New York Springer-Verlag. Permission also granted by Blackwell Scientific Publications, Ltd.

seabed in the area of overlapping claims as soon as possible. Thus they agreed to jointly explore and exploit the seabed and subsoil non-living resources in a defined Joint Development Area (JDA) for a period of 50 years and to share equally the costs incurred and the benefits derived. During this time the countries will continue to negotiate the boundary. The memorandum of understanding was ratified by an exchange of the instruments of ratification on 24 October 1979, and the Joint Authority to manage the area came into being.

The case of Japan and South Korea has both similarities and differences with the Thailand-Malaysia case. Stimulated by a 1969 ECAFE report that the continental shelf between Taiwan and Japan may be one of the most prolific oil reservoirs in the world, Japan, South Korea and Taiwan made overlapping claims to the continental shelf situated between them. These disputes were further complicated by a dispute between Japan and Taiwan over the Senkaku or Diaoyutai islands. In 1970, Japan, South Korea and Taiwan agreed to put aside the surface boundary issues for future negotiation and to jointly develop any oil in the overlap area. However, Chinese protests resulted in the abandonment of this arrangement. Japan and South Korea then entered into a joint agreement in January 1974. The agreement was ratified by South Korea in December 1974 but not by Japan until 1978.

The joint development zone between Kuwait and Saudi Arabia is situated in the northeastern corner of the Saudi Arabian peninsula along the eastern head of the Gulf. The zone was created in lieu of a boundary as a buffer between rival nomadic tribes. The zone lay dormant until the petroleum exploration boom. On June 28, 1948, the American Independent Oil Company obtained a concession from Kuwait covering its undivided half of the zone. On February 20, 1949, Pacific Western Oil Corporation, later Getty Oil Company, acquired a corresponding concession from Saudi Arabia for its undivided half of the zone. Kuwait's "special relationship" with Great Britain ended in 1961 and on 7 July 1965, the two fully independent States agreed to formally partition the zone and drew an international boundary to divide it equally. However, the agreement maintained the unified joint development of petroleum reserves in the zone as well as the existing rights of the concessionaries.

In February 1979, the Norwegian government declared its right to establish an exclusive economic zone (EEZ) around the island Jan Mayen. Iceland countered by maintaining that Jan Mayen was a rock and that under international law was not entitled to a continental shelf or exclusive economic zone. Two problems evolved from negotiations—control of fishing in the area and continental shelf rights. On May 28, 1980 the parties reached an agreement in which Iceland recognized Norway's right to an EEZ around Jan Mayen while Norway limited the zone to the median line with Iceland. However the agreement applied mainly to fish, explaining Norway's next day declaration of a 200 nm zone for fisheries only. Article 9 of the agreement stipulated that a Conciliation Commission be established to make recommendations with regard to a dividing line for the continental shelf. The Conciliation Commission drafted a geological report on the area involved, resolved various questions of international law and most important, recommended a joint development of hydrocarbons in the area. On 22 October 1980 Iceland and Norway accepted the Conciliation Commission's recommendations. The joint area is permanent but flexible depending on petroliferous structures extending beyond the initially defined area; it is divided into distinct national jurisdictional areas; its function as a resource regime for exploration and exploitation of petroleum; and it requires active cooperation to be operative.

COMMON ELEMENTS[10]

Frequently appearing elements in precedents for joint development define the extent of the area, the contract type, financial arrangements, the process of selection of concessionaires and/or operators, the length of the agreement, and the nature and functions of the joint management body. Joint development does not have to be *in lieu* of a boundary; indeed boundaries were agreed in the land portion of the Saudi Arabia-Kuwait arrangement[11], and for the continental shelf and exclusive economic zones between Norway and Iceland[12], and between Sudan and Saudi Arabia.[13] However, agreement on the extent of the area in question is fundamental to a joint development arrangement. In the Thai-Malaysia[14] and South Korea-Japan[15] cases, boundary delimitation was shelved and the area of overlap of the respective claims become the agreed joint development area. In the Saudi Arabia-Kuwait case the land portion of the joint development area was originally a neutral zone established as a buffer to prevent classes of nomadic tribes.[16] In 1965 a boundary was agreed and the zone was partitioned; however the Partitioned Zone, i.e., the area covered by the neutral zone before partition, became the joint development area. The submerged area adjoining the Partitioned Zone has not been partitioned and the two countries have agreed to joint exploration outside territorial seas of 6 miles.

In the Iceland-Norway case, the recommended joint development area is based on the extent of the prospective sediments and is 70 percent on the Norwegian side of an agreed EEZ boundary.[17] An interesting variation is the recommendation that if a field extends outside the joint development area into Icelandic shelf, then Iceland should have sole rights to that partition in its territory, but if a field extends into Norwegian shelf, the whole field should come under the joint development scheme. In the Saudi Arabia-Sudan arrangement in the Red Sea, the joint development area is that between the 1000 m isobaths extending from each coast and includes the main Red Sea brine deposits.[18] In the minority opinion recommendation for Tunisia-Libya, the joint development area would be that formed by lines deviating 10–15 on either side of an adjusted equidistance line.[19]

Jurisdiction is clearly defined in the Japan-Korea,[20] Thailand-Malaysia,[21] Iceland-Norway[22] and Kuwait-Saudi Arabia[23] agreements; it is not so clearly defined in the Saudi Arabia-Sudan[24] arrangement. In the Thailand-Malaysia arrangement, the governments jointly retained sovereign rights to the area and regulation of customs, fishing, navigation, hydrographic and oceanographic surveys, marine pollution and security. Criminal jurisdiction was divided by a line equidistant between the two claim lines.[25]

If the two countries have different contractual systems, e.g., concessions versus production-sharing, they must agree on one or the other. Also difficult are questions of respective management rights, taxation, and the allocation of financing. If the area is sufficiently prospective, financing could be arranged by private companies, but that must be agreed as must the choice of company. Thailand and Malaysia agreed to use a production-sharing contract system even though Thailand was using a concession system.[26] The agreed tax formula amounted to half the total rates in both countries. Under the South Korean-Japan arrangement, each country names a concessionaire and taxes are collected by each party from its own concessionaire.[27] The Saudi Arabia-Kuwait scheme uses concessions, and OPEC tax rates, royalties, and prices, and production and maintenance costs.[28] A joint venture contract was the recommended approach for the Norway-Iceland arrangement.[29] The Conciliation Commission also recommended that each party participate with a 25% share in joint ventures with oil companies in the other's portion of the joint development area. However it also recommended that if no commercial companies became involved and the countries each financed exploration themselves in their own portions of the joint development area, Norway should carry Iceland's interest in Norway's portion. Similarly, Saudi Arabia will bear all the expenses of operation of the joint commission.[30]

In both the South Korea-Japan and Saudi Arabia-Kuwait land agreements,[31] both parties nominate a concessionaire for the entire subzone or area and these concessionaires reach an operating agreement between them, or in the South Korea-Japan agreement, by drawing lots, if necessary.[32] Saudi Arabia and Kuwait agreed on one operator for the offshore portion of the joint development area. No specific reference to a contractual system was made in the Saudi Arabia-Sudan agreement.

The duration of the agreement must be decided as well as the reasons and procedures for terminating the agreement. A short-term agreement (say 10 years) may provide impetus to hasten exploration and development but may also make investors shy away from a situation which will obviously change. A long-term agreement (say 50 years) provides a more stable investment climate but a longer commitment. The Thailand-Malaysia agreement is for 50 years or until the parties agree on delimitation.[33] The South Korea-Japan arrangement is also for 50 years; however it can be terminated by mutual consent if the parties recognize that the natural resources are no longer exploitable.[34] The Saudi Arabia-Kuwait agreement is of indefinite duration and can be terminated by either party. However a 60 year concession in the area was given to one company.[35]

There also needs to be agreement on the degree of autonomy and authority to be vested in the joint development body, if one is established. Should it be strong—a full legal person with powers to license, stipulate terms and exemptions and enter into contractual agreements with foreign companies—or should it be weak—simply a liaison or consultative body between national oil companies? The Thailand-Malaysia and Sudan-Saudi Arabia arrangements produced joint authorities with strong powers in contrast to the consultative status of the joint commissions produced by the Japan-Korea and Kuwait-Saudi Arabia arrangements.

In the Thailand-Malaysia case, a Joint Authority was established for the purpose of exploring and exploiting the non-living natural resources of the seabed and subsoil in the overlapping area.[36] The Joint Authority assumed all rights, responsibilities, and powers on behalf of both parties in this regard, and for the development, control and administration of the area. The assumption of such rights and responsibilities by the Joint Authority was not supposed to affect or curtail the validity of concessions or licenses hitherto issued or agreements of arrangements made by either party. The Joint Authority has a constitution; it has licensing powers; it can retain profit and will be taxed. It consists of two joint-chairmen, one from each country and an equal number of members from each country; there are one legal and two technical subcommittees.

The Saudi Arabia-Sudan agreement stipulated that a joint commission would be established to survey and delimit the common zone, carry out the requisite studies concerning the exploration and exploitation of the natural resources there, encourage specialized bodies to undertake exploration activities in the zone, and look into applications for licenses and concessions concerning exploration and exploitation in the common zone, and specifically, render a decision on the previous agreement between Sudan and Preussag for exploration rights.[37]

South Korea and Japan established the Japan-Republic of Korea Joint Commission with a mandate to review operation of the agreement and *recommend* action to the parties.[38] The Commission has a permanent secretariat and a subcommittee of experts. However the operating agreement between the concessionaires must be approved by the parties and the laws of each party apply to its concessionaire if its concessionaire is the operator. One interesting variation is that the Japanese Ministry of Agriculture, Forestry and Fishery must be consulted in approving the operating agreement and can restrict exploration and exploitation in designated fishing zones.

Saudi Arabia and Kuwait established a Joint Operating Committee to supervise the concessionaires' field operators.[39] The Committee studies projects and new licenses, contracts and concessions relating to exploitation of shared natural resources and recommends action to the respective Ministers of Natural Resources. It can sign contracts. A permanent consultative committee was recommended in the Tunisia-Libya case.[40]

Standard ingredients which may become important later include unitization provisions for deposits which straddle the boundaries of the joint development area, and procedures and principles for conflict resolution such as direct negotiation, provisions for, or governing, a conciliation commission or bringing the matter to the International Court of Justice. Transfer of technology may be important, particularly if there is a great gap between the technical levels of the two entities, or if political difficulties exist between one of the partners and the home country of interested companies, e.g., Vietnam and the United States.

PROBLEMS IN IMPLEMENTATION

How well has joint development worked? The only arrangement which has proceeded from political agreement through the establishment of the necessary legal and institutional organizations to successful exploration and development of resources is the Saudi Arabia-Kuwait arrangement. The Saudi Arabia-Sudan agreement has functioned successfully through a three month pre-pilot mining test but a commercial project has not yet been implemented due to uncertainty as to its commercial viability.[41]

The success of the Saudi Arabia-Kuwait agreement can be attributed to (1) an "unwritten agreement" to keep oil out of political differences, (2) the practical desire of both parties to develop the oil fields quickly, and (3) the small portion of total oil production by these states from the joint development area.[42] The Saudi Arabia-Sudan agreement also was reached relatively easily and has worked relatively smoothly because of the good relations and practical attitude of the two countries. In implementation of both of these agreements, perhaps pan-Arabism and familiarity with the Islamic concept of *mushaa*—equal shares in joint and undivided property[43]—were additional factors in their success. In both arrangements, the agreement of both countries on one company which played a constructive and cooperative role in the exploration and development of the resources was also a definite contribution to their success. And the discovery of actual resources in the joint development area certainly cemented the effort.

Implementation of other joint development agreements has not yet been successful for a variety of reasons. The Iceland-Norway agreement is too recent to ascertain major problems in its implementation. From the beginning, the South Korean-Japan joint development scheme has been a highly sensitive political issue straining the relations between the coastal states. Although the agreement has been in force since June 1978 and much drilling has occurred, no petroleum has yet been found. Although discussions on joint development began in 1970, and the agreement was signed in 1974, it was not ratified until 1978 for two reasons. Japan was concerned about its relations with China, which also claimed the area, and Japan felt that under the median line principle, it was entitled to the entire area in dispute.[44] Discussions on joint development between Indonesia and Vietnam and Indonesia and Australia have been plagued by difficult political relations.

The litany of problems in implementation of the Thai-Malaysian scheme is illustrative. Initially, Thailand accommodated Texas Pacific by allowing it to keep its concession in the joint development area and Malaysia agreed to this. Then Thailand's disagreement with Texas Pacific over the pricing of gas in its

"B" structure heated up. Consequently Thailand apparently wanted to revoke Texas Pacific's concession in the joint development area in order to pressure the company in the pricing disagreement. Texas Pacific on the other hand did not recognize the Joint Development Authority.

The fact that a line of equidistance between Thailand and Malaysia would extend the boundary further south than the initial (1973) Thai claim and include the gas discovery in Pilong 1, produced a disagreement between the Thai government and its concessionaire Triton Oil Company. When Malaysia agreed that Pilong would be included in the joint development area, Triton claimed that its concession boundary moved with the international boundary and extended southward to the equidistance line. Thailand initially agreed to allow Triton to include Pilong in its concession area but internal Thai interagency disagreement on this point followed. Indeed, in May 1985 government sources in Malaysia announced that implementation of the joint development agreement was being delayed because of Thai government problems with contractors in the area.[45]

Another problem was that Malaysia preferred to have one concessionaire, not three—Petronas, Triton, and Texas Pacific, as proposed by Thailand. To break the logjam, Malaysian Prime Minister Mahathir promised to Thai Prime Minister Prem Tinsulanonda that the Petroleum Authority of Thailand (PTT) enter a joint venture with Peteronas and international oil firms approved by both governments. According to this scheme, the foreign firms would then settle among themselves their respective equity in the joint venture and choose a representative to negotiate with the Joint Development Authority. However the Thai government may have been wary of this proposal because PTT is not as experienced in petroleum exploration as Petronas.[46] Also, Triton Oil Company was reported to have formally rejected joint operation by the three as economically unfeasible.

However, after nearly five years of negotiations beginning in April 1980, Malaysia and Thailand, under the spirit of ASEAN cooperation, finally decided to jointly develop the disputed area in the Gulf of Thailand. A committee to be jointly headed by Thailand's Director General of Treaties and Legal Affairs of the Foreign Ministry, Suchinda Yongsunthorn, and Malaysia's Deputy Secretary of the Foreign Ministry, Mon Jasmaluddin, will be responsible for developing the area. The committee is expected to invite foreign contractors to bid for tenders announced in May 1985. The terms of these bids will be different from the terms presently offered by Malaysia and Thailand for contractors involved in the development of offshore oil and gas in those countries.

Presently Malaysia offers production-sharing contractors 20 percent of oil and 25 percent of gas as cost recovery, while the remaining 70 percent of the gross oil production and 65 percent of the gas sold is shared between Petronas and the contractors to pay 12.5 percent and 50 percent to the government as royalty and income taxes, respectively. However, neither set of terms would apply for the joint development area. Instead, contractors would be allotted 25 percent of gross production as cost recovery with 70 percent of the remainder shared equally between the two countries, and the rest to the contractor, subject to a 40 percent income tax. The contractor will also be given a period of 15 years to develop the area. The 40 percent income tax revenue derived from the contractors would be shared equally between Malaysia and Thailand, and no other tax would be imposed on the contractors.

Also, both countries agreed that Carigali, Petronas' exploration subsidiary, should not be allowed to participate in the tender. This could pave the way for Promet Bhd, a favorite of the Malaysians and Thais, to be one of the successful contractors. Promet already holds a concession block in Thailand and is expected to play a major role in Malaysia's offshore oil and gas exploration activities this year. The decision of the two countries to resolve their differences might also see a return of Triton Energy Corporation, one of the concessionaires that pulled out pending a resolution of the demarcation lines separating the two countries.[47]

APPLICATIONS

Joint development is at best an interim solution and may not be appropriate for each or any of the suggested candidate areas. The schemes developed below emphasize this option and are useful only if the countries concerned choose to consider joint development.

There are two areas in Southeast Asia that are currently being considered for joint development by the countries concerned—the "Timor gap" between Indonesia and Australia,[48] and the Natuna Sea between Indonesia and Vietnam.[49]

The "Timor Gap" (Figure 8)

In 1971 and 1972 Australia and Indonesia concluded treaties that established seabed boundaries extending from Papua New Guinea in the east to the waters between Ashmore Island and Pulau Roti in the west. A gap of about 200 nm was left in the boundary south of eastern Timor which was then a colony of Portugal. When Indonesia formally incorporated eastern Timor in July 1976, the closing of the gap became the subject of negotiations beginning in February 1979.

Geology is the main factor in the dispute although the talks ebb and flow with the state of Indonesian/Australian relations. For the boundary south of Timor, Australia argues that there are two continental margins between Timor and Australia—a more than 200 nm wide Australian margin to the south and a 40 to 70 nm wide Indonesian margin to the north, separated by the Timor Trough. Further, Australia claims that either the trough's axis or—more generously—a line half-way down the Australian margin, should be the boundary. Indonesia claims that there is a single continental margin between the two countries with the Timor Trough just a depression in this continuous feature, and that the boundary should be the line equidistant between the two countries' territories. The disputed area measures some 12,000 nm².

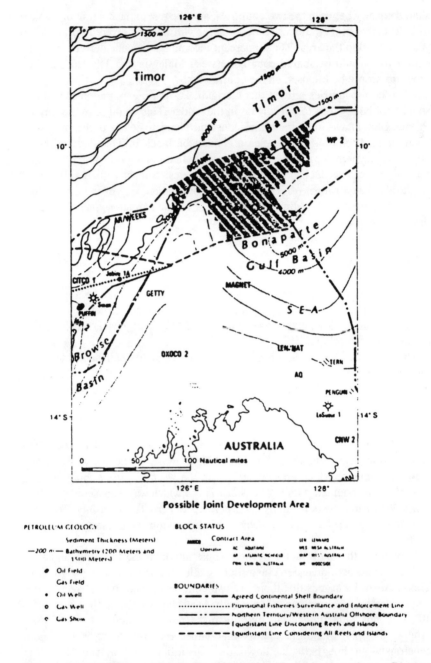

Figure 8. The Timor "Gap": Possible Joint Development Area. Source: Reprinted with permission form Mark J. Valencia, *Southeast Asian Seas: Oil Under Troubled Waters.* Oxford University Press, Kuala Lumpur, 1985, p. 123.

The "Timor Gap" presents an interesting problem because it includes two prospective basins, Timor and Bonaparte Gulf. Little is known of the petroleum potential of the Timor basin although it is generally considered poor. However, in December 1983, there was supposedly the most significant find in Australia since the Bass Strait—Jabiru 1A in the Timor Sea (Vulcan subbasin of the Browse basin). Test flows reached 7,500 BOPD and preliminary recoverable reserve estimates were at least 200 million barrels. However the results of appraisal wells were disappointing and this plus Australia's resources rent tax or the politics associated with it may postpone production. Kelp, another structure of interest overlaps the northeastern portion of the "gap." Its oil reserves were estimated to range from 500 million to 5 billion barrels of oil and 50 TCF of gas.

An equidistant line would cut the core of the Bonaparte Gulf basin's closure in a two-thirds/one-third proportion in favor of Australia, with Kelp falling to Indonesia. A continuation of the agreed continental shelf boundaries to close the "Timor gap" would place the entire Bonaparte Gulf basin and Kelp in Australian jurisdiction. The basin is also divided almost in half by the northwest-southeast boundary between Australia's Northern Territory and the State of Western Australia. Several holders of Australian contracts had acreage beyond the equidistant line: Trioentrol (awarded in 1980), Woodside Petroleum 2 (WP2) and Aquitaine in the Northern Territory portion and WP2 and MES/WAP in the Western Australia portion. The WP2 and the Aquitaine acreages extended to the hypothetical connection across the "gap," which is halfway down the Australian continental "margin," thus lapping over into the Timor basin. The government subsequently reduced the areas of the permits for Aquitaine and Mesa to fit within the undisputed Australian area.[50] Pertamina is considering offering Timor Block A for bidding but it is expected that alterations in location and size will be made to exclude the disputed area.[51]

The Timor basin would be completely within Indonesian "shelf" if the equidistant line were to become the agreed boundary. If the middle of the Australian margin is used as a guide to complete the "gap," a small portion of the core of the Timor basin would accrue to Australia, which has already leased it for exploration. Former Portugese Timor had leased the area extending to the hypothetical "gap" connection and thus the bulk of the basin to Oceanic.

Australia has proposed to Indonesia that they form a joint authority to administer the disputed area or at least those areas with the highest oil and gas potential. Indeed, after eight rounds of talks some agreements on joint development have been reached but further progress is likely to be tied to improvement of Indonesian-Australian relations.[52] In a joint development agreement, Australia and Indonesia could agree that the boundaries of the area to be jointly developed are the line connecting the two agreed boundaries, the equidistant line and two longitudes connecting these lines. Given this agreement, the line connecting the agreed continental shelf boundaries could be set as the continental shelf boundary in the area and Australian criminal jurisdiction and defense could prevail in the joint development area.

The joint authority established by the Federal Governments of Indonesia and Australia or their assignees could be strong, but it must accommodate the interests of the Australian states of Western Australia and the Northern Territory possibly through a division of powers similar to that between the Regional Fishery Management Councils and the Federal Government in the United States under the Fishery Conservation and Management Act of 1976. Pari Petroleum has operated in both Australia and Indonesia and as operator might satisfy all parties concerned. The contract could be on the Indonesian production-sharing model which is more favorable to oil companies than current Australian tax regulations. All risk would be borne by oil companies. To cement and stabilize relations between the two and allay suspicions, the agreement could be long-term. Conflict resolution could be by conciliation, although recourse to arbitration should not be ruled out.

The Natuna Sea (Figure 9)

In the Natuna Sea, the disputed area includes in the west, the northeastern West Natuna basin, in the north, the Khorat basin, in the center, the extension of the Natuna arch, and in the east much of the "South China Sea Block A, Eastern Part." The portion of the northeastern West Natuna basin includes a small part of a three second core (two-way reflection time; one second approximately equivalent to one kilometer of sediment) and another three second thick sediment pod aligned northeast-southwest; both have been drilled once with dry holes. However, the disputed area is surrounded by proven oil fields in Indonesian, Malaysian and Vietnamese waters. Conoco discovered oil in Block B. However, reserves are only 20 million barrels and the discovery is not likely to be declared commercial.[53] Marathon was given approval to proceed with development of its KH field in the Kakap block and commercial production at 22,000 Barrels of Oil Per Day (BOPD) is expected by 1986.[54] In late 1981, Conoco and Pertamina announced the discovery of "highly significant" natural gas.[55] In April 1982, Sumatera Gulf Oil reported a significant discovery of high-gravity clean oil in Block A.[56]

The central portion of the disputed area is an extension of the nose of the Natuna arch where sediment thicknesses are about one second, and thus, unprospective. However, thicknesses increase to two seconds across the arch in the northern part of the disputed area, offering some possibilities. The Vietnamese boundary claim line runs latitudinally across the middle of this basement high.

The "South China Sea Block A, Eastern Part" is a transition zone between the Saigon Basin and the Outer Basinal Area. Sediments generally thicken eastwards without large closure. AGIP made a significant gas discovery approximately 250 kilometers north-northeast of Natuna Island near the northern limit of the thick pod of Plio-Pleistocene sediments referred to as the "Outer Basinal Area." Six dry holes were drilled in Indonesian concessions in the disputed area before the reunification of Vietnam. These dry holes contrast with the Dua and other discoveries just north of the Indonesian claim line. Fur-

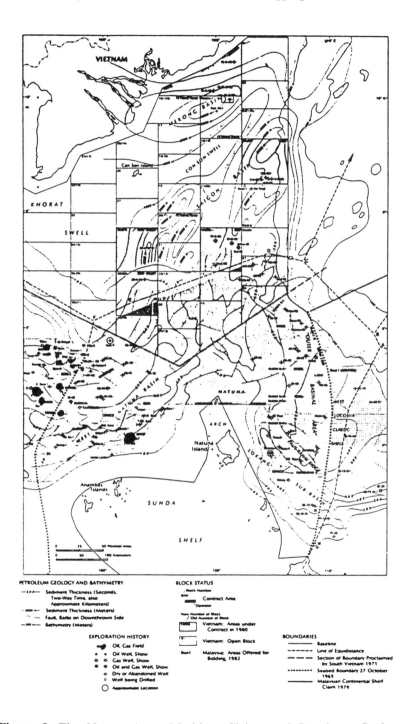

Figure 9. The Natuna Area: Maritime Claims and Petroleum Geology.
Source: Valencia, *supra* source Fig. 8, p. 67.

ther north on the shelf, VietSovpetro, the joint venture between Vietnam and the Soviet Union has discovered commercially exploitable quantities of oil, is preparing to extract it, and plans to build an oil refinery to process it.[57]

Thus the disputed area is divided east-west in terms of hydrocarbon potential into two geologically distinct, relatively unknown but prospective basinal extensions separated by an unprospective basement high. The eastern area appears gas prone whereas the west appears somewhat oil prone. In the early negotiating sessions it was allegedly proposed that Indonesia have jurisdiction over areas in which Pertamina has contracted to American Oil companies since 1970 who are currently exploring for, or developing known reserves (West Natuna basin) and that Vietnam obtain the northeastern portion (the South China Sea Block A, Eastern Part) of the overlap. Clearly the two sides were getting closer to a solution and the area in dispute was diminishing, although the northeastern portion remained a problem.[58] Discussions on joint development are ongoing but progress is doubtful because it is tied indirectly to progress on the issue of Vietnam's occupation of Kampuchea.[59]

The exact area still in dispute is unknown. The following scenario assumes that the area in dispute is that situated between the continental shelf boundary claim made by South Vietnam in 1971 and a line equidistant between the northernmost Natuna Islands and the southernmost Vietnamese islands. It is not necessary to delimit a boundary, but if one is deemed desirable, the boundary could be the line equidistant between the two claims. An east-west line would be logical given the north-south geographic relationship of the two countries and would fairly divide the oil-prone west, gas-prone east and unprospective central portions, in contrast to a north-south line along the crest of the unprospective Natuna Arch. Rather than be a full jurisdictional boundary, this east-west line could divide national authority for security and criminal purposes.

Given the tenuous relations between the two countries, any joint commission should have consultative status only and recommend action to the respective governments. The area has already been the site of successful exploration by private companies—Gulf, Marathon and Amoseas—all U.S. companies. Thus there is no need for the states to bear exploration expenses. However Indonesia might consider carrying Vietnam's interest for the operation of the joint development commission. Although experienced Indonesia should perhaps take the lead in managing development of the area, training of Vietnamese counterparts should be a first priority.

Given the antipathy between Vietnam and the United States, the contract holders should be non-American, perhaps French, German, Italian, or Canadian, all of which have operated in Vietnam recently. The contract could be on the sophisticated Indonesian production-sharing model with all risk borne by the oil companies. The agreement must be sufficiently long-term to bolster the confidence of the companies and the countries in the stability of the agreement but it must also be sufficiently flexible to accommodate changing conditions without breaking under tension.

The remaining candidate areas are less amenable to joint development because of the complexity of the overlapping claims or the poor relations between the claimants.

The Eastern Gulf of Thailand (Figure 10)

The area of overlap between Vietnam and Kampuchea can be divided into three areas based on claimants, the jurisdictional regime, and the geology—the joint historical waters over the Panjang Basin (Area 1), the area of continental shelf overlap extending from the outer boundary of the joint historical waters to the Thai claim line and overlying an unnamed basin (Area 2), and the area of continental shelf also claimed by Thailand and overlying the margin of the Pattani trough (Area 3). (Area 4 is claimed only by Kampuchea and Thailand and is not considered a good candidate for joint development at present.)

In Area 3, Thailand should be invited to participate in any joint development. If it does not participate, a trust fund equaling one-third of the proceeds minus one-third of the costs should be established on its behalf by the developers. Management rights and criminal jurisdiction could be allocated on the basis of the equidistant line—Vietnam and Kampuchea to the east, Thailand to the west. The authority could be a liaison body between the Petroleum Authority of Thailand (PTT) and Petro Vietnam/Kampuchean Government. Non-U.S. foreign companies such as French or German firms should be invited to participate. As Thailand is moving toward the production-sharing contract, this contract system could be used. The oil would be owned by the countries but the contractual terms should be liberal to entice Western companies to invest in exploration and exploitation in this unstable area. Unitization clauses could provide for Thai ownership of pools extending west of the Vietnamese/Kampuchean claim line and Vietnamese/Kampuchean ownership for pools extending east of the Thai claim line. The arrangement could provide for reexamination and renegotiation in ten years as more information on the potential and its distribution becomes available. Dispute settlement could be by conciliation between the parties.

In Area 2, the petroleum geology is poorly known. For this reason the entire area could be subject to a joint development agreement by the two claimants—Vietnam and Kampuchea. An equidistant line between the two claims could be the basis for allocation of criminal jurisdiction. Vietnam, being better off economically, and having more and better management resources and experience in its national oil company, could take responsibility for the management of the operation and pay the management costs, including the exploration costs for the entire area. If commercial hydrocarbons are discovered, Kampuchea could have the option to pay half of the costs of exploration and then to participate in the exploitation and derive equal benefits after costs. Alternatively, exploration and exploitation might be undertaken by the Soviet Union on behalf of both Vietnam and Kampuchea for some share of any hydrocarbons produced. The joint authority could be strong—a legal entity similar to the Thai-Malaysian

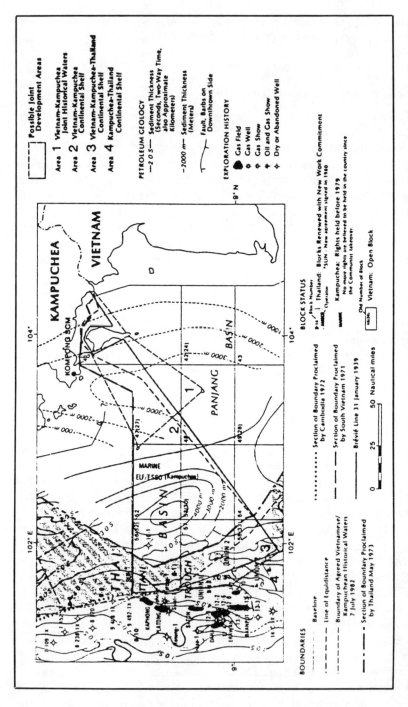

Figure 10. The Eastern Golf of Thailand: Possible Joint Development Areas. Source: Valencia, *supra* source Fig. 8, p. 120.

Joint Authority.[60] Unitization could be in Kampuchea's favor, i.e., any pool extending into undisputed Kampuchean territory could be entirely Kampuchean whereas that extending into undisputed Vietnamese territory or into Thai-claimed territory could be split equally between Vietnamese and Kampuchea. Any conflict should be resolved between the two countries through direct negotiations. Given the alliance between the two countries, the duration could be long-term, e.g., 50 years.

The differences between Areas 2 and 3 are that in the latter the two countries have agreed on the boundaries of a joint area, and there is a need to accommodate Kampuchean concerns for the vital Kampchean port of Kompong Som. In Area 3, the existing treaty allocates control and patrol to both countries. However, the existing equidistant line could divide criminal jurisdiction. This would allow Kampuchea to police and defend its vital port of Kompong Som. The equidistant line could also be a convenient geographic division of management rights; each could manage its half but with Vietnam financing the risk. Alternatively, Vietnam could manage the whole area although Kampuchea could have a management veto. The contract system could be production-sharing; however, the Soviet Union or Vietnam could bear the risk. The joint authority could be strong and the duration of the agreement long-term. Unitization and the process of conflict resolution could be similar to the arrangement for Area 2.

The Spratly Area (Figure 11)

Very little is known of the geology of this region. The irregular shoals, submarine plateaus, and small intermediate-depth basins have been interpreted as representing a foundered mass of continental crust. The crust beneath the shoal areas to the northwest of the basin, including Macclesfield Bank and the Paracel Islands, may also be continental. It is hypothesized that the Reed Bank-Calamian microcontinental blocks, possibly extending from Luconia shoals in the south to southwest Mindoro Island in the north, were rifted from the continental margin of China in Middle Eocene time and moved southward. The Chinese mainland as well as the microcontinental blocks themselves would have been the source of sediments to the block and their margins. Considering that the Reed Bank may once have been adjacent to the Chinese continental shelf and that oil has been found there, the Dangerous Ground could also have potential.

The thickest sedimentary section in the Reed Bank area is under the Southern Bank and in the southeastern part of the Reed Bank proper, and in the inter-deeps between these two banks. Tertiary thicknesses of 4,000 meters or more are known geophysically and from drilling. The oldest known beds under the Reed Bank are of Lower Crustaceous age, and consist of coal-bearing sandstones, with conglomerates, siltstones, and shales deposited under marginal marine conditions. The thickness of Cretaceous and possibly Jurassic sediments may reach 5,000 to 6,500 meters in the southeastern portion of Reed

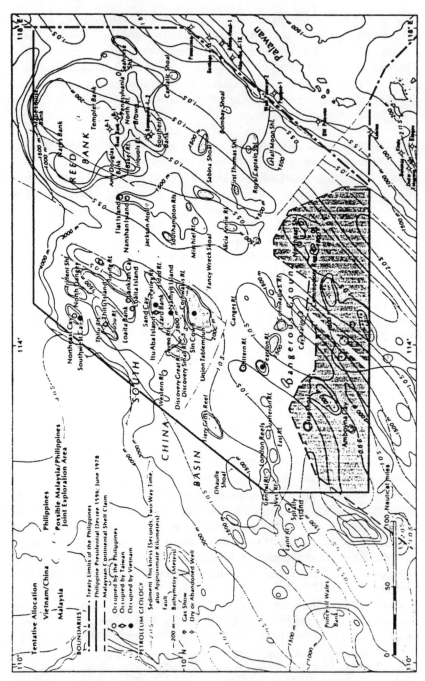

Figure 11. Spratly area: maritime claims and petroleum geology. Source: Valencia, *supra* source Fig. 8, p. 126.

Bank. The stratigraphy suggests a dominantly continental shelf environment, interrupted by episodes of shallow water clastic deposition, and occasional deep water conditions. Such data provide incentive to examine the bathymetric highs within the intermediate shelf zone for their hydrocarbon potential in both the pre-Tertiary and Tertiary sedimentary section.[61]

Of the disputed areas, the Spratly area seems the most hopeless for a cooperative response. However, restraint is dictated by consideration of the number of claimants, the variety of their rationales, the probability that no one country can hope to obtain the whole area, and most important, the political visibility of the area and the influence of the superpowers. Delaying tactics have been purposefully and rationally employed. Direct confrontation has been avoided, and although the disputes remain open-ended and may be resurrected at any time, non-settlement avoids dealing with deeper underlying issues such as the China/Taiwan question. Thus avoiding settlement of the disputes appears to be in the interest of all the parties. A tacit agreement on ownership may be arrived at and the disputes will then have been settled de facto. The major unpredictable factor is the possible resumption and spillover of Chinese-Vietnamese hostilities.

North of the Malaysia/Philippine overlap, the area could be divided based on island occupation, proximity, reasonableness, and bathymetry. Under one scheme, the Philippines could get the northeast portion extending from Marie Louise Bank in the north to Half Moon Shoal in the south and to Southhampton Reefs in the west. This area includes the Reed Bank and sediment thicknesses up to 1 kilometer. Vietnam and China could jointly get the western cluster extending from Trident Shoal in the north to Cay Marino in the south and westward to Ladd Reef. This area includes most of the occupied islands and sediment pods up to 1 kilometer in thickness. This area could perhaps be further divided between Vietnam and China along a latitude north of Fiery Cross Reef.

The southern part of the area where Philippine and Malaysian claims overlap could be allocated in several ways. Vietnam might get the western part including Amboyna Cay which it occupies, and Stag Shoal. The entire area which includes sediment pods of at least one kilometer thickness could be allocated to Malaysia.

Almost nothing is known of the potential of the area. While the Chinese isopachs must be viewed with considerable skepticism, they do indicate that the area includes some elongated sediment pods several kilometers thick and reefs such as An Bang, Barque Canada, Mariveles, and Commodore which are so situated as to be used as drilling platforms.

If allocation among the claimants is not feasible, then joint exploration of the southern portion could be undertaken by Malaysia and the Philippines. Under their joint auspices, perhaps through a liaison committee, reconnaissance surveys could be undertaken by universities which have been active in the area— Lamont-Doherty Geological Observatory or the Federal Republic of Germany's Geological Survey. Such joint action could strengthen both Malaysian and Philippine claims to the area and possibly stimulate settlement.

The Philippines has not acted unilaterally in the southern part although Malaysia has occupied Terembu Layang Layang. A possible problem or opportunity is that this claim by Malaysia is intended to be used as a bargaining chip to persuade the Philippines to fully relinquish its claim to the Malaysian state of Sabah. The Philippines needs oil desperately; Malaysia has ample potential elsewhere. Neither country's claim can be said to be particularly well grounded in international law. The United States would prefer to see these two friendly countries strengthen their claim to the area.

Only four islands or reefs are involved. However, the major difficulty for such a scheme is that Vietnamese troops occupy An Bang (Amboyna). Perhaps Vietnam can be persuaded to trade control of that island for concessions and consolidation of its holdings in the western part of the area outside of Philippine and Malaysian claims.

The Gulf of Tonkin (Figure 12)

Although the Gulf of Tonkin is not considered a priority candidate for joint development due to the poor relations between the claimants, political relations do change—often rapidly—and thus it is interesting to speculate on a hypothetical agreement which might be instituted in future. The extent of a candidate area for joint development has already been agreed to by the claimants— the Neutral Zone. The Neutral Zone encloses the north-central quarter of the Yinggehai Basin as well as parts of the southern North Bay basins. However there is disagreement over the eastern boundary. Vietnam claims that the eastern boundary of the agreed Neutral Zone coincided with the 1083'13" East meridian stipulated in the 1887 Sino-French Convention which Vietnam claims divides the land and seabed in the Gulf. China maintains that the Convention only divided the islands in the Gulf and not the seabed, and that the eastern boundary of the agreed Neutral Zone is 108 East.[62] Although China has already leased to Amoco and Total three miles of seabed that Vietnam claims is within the Neutral Zone, this sliver could be included in the joint development scheme as a show of good faith on China's part to get the process started. In turn, Vietnam could agree that the equidistant line to be used for criminal jurisdiction is that discounting the island Bach Long Vi. No boundary should be drawn because it would prejudice the drawing the boundary segments north and south of the Neutral Zone.

The joint authority could initially be simply a liaison body. The first step could be reconnaissance exploration which could be undertaken by universities operating under the auspices of the International Energy Development Authority of the U.N. Committee for the Co-ordination of Joint Prospecting (CCOP). If reconnaissance exploration gives favorable indications then each could choose an operator. The area could be subdivided into blocks of agreed size and number, and lots could be drawn for exploration or exploitation rights in each area. The contract system could be the production-sharing model and the operators should be non-Soviet or U.S. entities, preferably French or Italian, since

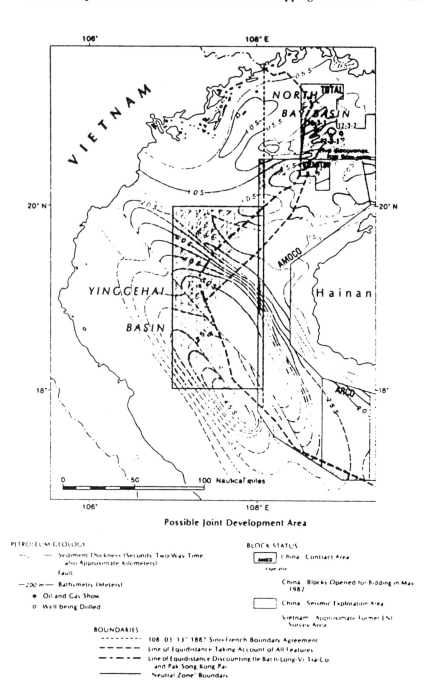

Possible Joint Development Area

PETROLEUM GEOLOGY
---, — Sediment Thickness (Seconds Two-Way Time, also Approximate Kilometers)
    Fault
—200 m — Bathymetry (Meters)
◆ Oil and Gas Show
○ Well being Drilled

BOUNDARIES
--------- 108° 03' 13" 188° Sino-French Boundary Agreement
— — — — Line of Equidistance Taking Account of All Features
— · — · — Line of Equidistance Discounting Ile Bach-Long-Vi Tra-Co. and Pak Song Kong Pai
———————— Neutral Zone" Boundary

BLOCK STATUS
[AMOCO] China Contract Area
    Operator
    China Blocks Opened for Bidding in May 1982
[   ] China Seismic Exploration Area
    Vietnam Approximate Former ENI Survey Area

Figure 12. Gulf of Tonkin: Possible Joint Development Area. Source: Valencia, *supra* source Fig. 8, p. 125.

such companies have operated recently in both China and Vietnam. The duration could be long-term to cement relations and give confidence to potential operators. The countries could continue to negotiate the boundary during this period.

In East Asia, Japan and South Korea have proceeded with joint development. At the other extreme, China does not recognize South Korea, so settlement of their boundary overlap is extremely difficult. However, China has proposed joint develoment to both Taiwan and Japan for its respective areas of overlap with each. In China's 1981 nine-point proposal to Taiwan for unification talks was accompanied by a proposal for the joint development of offshore petroleum resources. And in November 1980 in unannounced preliminary seabed negotiations, China advocated the creation of joint development zones that would give China a share of the richer resources on the Japanese side of the continental shelf. China continues to propose joint development to Japan. However, both Taiwan and Japan are presently opposed to the idea—Taiwan refuses to even discuss the matter and Japan refuses to accept China's precondition for discussions, viz., that its sovereignty over the Senkaku Islands is uncertain. Nevertheless, the parties could resolve the issue by (1) creating a 12 nm enclave around the Tiao-yu-t'ai Islands and leave that area for future settlement; (2) agree on joint jurisdiction and development to the southernmost portion of the overlap area; and (3) apply a modified equidistance principle to the remaining area of overlap, ignoring the Okinawa Trough.[63]

CONCLUSIONS

International joint development is the common exercise of sovereign rights by two or more States for the purpose of exploration and exploitation of the non-living resources of an area under national jurisdiction. An international joint development zone may be established on a continental shelf or in an exclusive economic zone that has been delimited or it may be established pending delimitation. As a minimum, the joint development agreement should specify the area covered by the agreement, the jurisdiction(s) to be applied within the zone, organization(s) which will manage the area, and the law(s) under which the mining license(s) will be issued. The determination of the applicable contractual law can be left to the private companies operating within the zone, or to the States concerned. Resources in the zone may be explored and exploited in various ways such as unitization, production sharing, or scientific cooperation. Good political relations, practical mindedness, discovery of actual deposits and cooperative private companies favor successful implementation of joint development arrangements.

Joint development is clearly not the optimal nor permanent solution to unresolved boundaries. However, in some situations it may be the only alternative to no action and thus no hydrocarbon development, or to confrontation and conflict. In an energy-poor world with many areas of offshore hydrocarbon potential claimed by more than one desperate country, joint development is an idea whose time is coming. Indeed, it will look increasingly attractive as the need for oil intensifies and precedents mount.*

* See Appendix A for further discussion and summary.

Footnotes

[1] United Nations Convention on the Law of the Sea, *done* at Montego Bay, Dec. 10, 1982, UN Doc. A/CONF.62/122 (1982), reprinted in 21 ILM 1261 (1982), art. 83(3). "Pending agreement   , the States concerned, in a spirit of understanding and cooperation, shall make every effort to enter into provisional arrangements of a practical nature and, during this transitional period, not to jeopardize or hamper the reaching of the final agreement."

[2] Lagoni, *Interim Measures Pending Maritime Delimitation Agreements,* 78 AM. J. INT'L. L. 345 (1984).

[3] Mark J. Valencia, "Oil and Gas Potential, Overlapping Claims and Political Relations," in George Kent and Mark J. Valencia, eds., MARINE POLICY IN SOUTHEAST ASIA (Berkeley: University of California Press, 1985), pp. 155–187.

[4] Valencia, SOUTHEAST ASIAN SEAS: OIL UNDER TROUBLED WATERS 62 (Oxford Univ. Press 1985); Ariffin, *The Malaysian Philosophy of Joint Development* in GEOLOGY AND HYDROCARBON POTENTIAL OF THE SOUTH CHINA SEA AND POSSIBILITIES OF JOINT DEVELOPMENT 533 (Valencia ed. 1985); Polahan, *Thailand-Malaysia Memorandum of Understanding* in THE SOUTH CHINA SEA: HYDROCARBON POTENTIAL AND POSSIBILITIES OF JOINT DEVELOPMENT 1355 (Valencia ed. 1981); *PETROLEUM NEWS,* February, 1985, p. 18.

[5] Miyoshi, *The Japan-South Korea Agreement of Joint Development of the Continental Shelf* in: GEOLOGY AND HYDROCARBON POTENTIAL OF THE SOUTH CHINA SEA AND POSSIBLILITIES OF JOINT DEVELOPMENT 545 (Valencia ed. 1985); Park, *Joint Development of Mineral Resources in Disputed Waters: The Case of Japan and South Korea in the East China Sea* in THE SOUTH CHINA SEA: HYDROCARBON POTENTIAL AND POSSIBILITIES OF JOINT DEVELOPMENT 1335 (Valencia ed. 1981); Takeyama, *Japan's Foreign Negotiations Over Offshore Petroleum Development An Analysis of Decision-Making in the Japan-Korea Continental Shelf Joint Development Program* in JAPAN AND THE NEW OCEAN REGIME 276 (Freidheim et al. 1984); Miyoshi, *Licensing in Japan-South Korea Joint Development Arrangement,* paper presented at Third East-West Center Workshop on South China Sea Hydrocarbon Potential and Possibilities of Joint Development, Bangkok, Thailand, February 1985.

[6] Onorato, *A Case Study in Joint Development: The Saudi Arabia-Kuwait Partitioned Neutral Zone* in GEOLOGY AND HYDROCARBON POTENTIAL OF THE SOUTH CHINA SEA AND POSSIBILITIES OF JOINT DEVELOPMENT 539 (Valencia ed. 1985); Fesharaki, *Joint Development of Offshore Petroleum Resources: The Persian Gulf Experience* in THE SOUTH CHINA SEA: HYDROCARBON POTENTIAL AND POSSIBILITIES OF JOINT DEVELOPMENT 1325 (Valencia ed. 1981).

[7] Richardson, Anderson & Evensen, *Report and Recommendations to the Governments of Iceland and Norway of the Conciliation Commission on the Continental Shelf Area between Iceland and Jan Mayen,* 20 ILM 797 (1981); Østreng, *Reaching Agreement*

on International Exploitation of Ocean Mineral Resources with Special Reference to the Joint Development Area between Jan Mayen and Iceland in GEOLOGY AND HYDROCARBON POTENTIAL OF THE SOUTH CHINA SEA AND POSSIBILI-TIES OF JOINT DEVELOPMENT 555 (Valencia ed. 1985); Østreng, *Delimitation Arrangements in Arctic Seas: Cases of Precedence or Securing of Strategic/Economic Interests?,* 132 MARINE POLICY 10 (1986).

[8] El-Hakim, THE MIDDLE EASTERN STATES AND THE LAW OF THE SEA 180-188 (Syracuse Univ. Press 1979); Blissenbach & Nawab, *Metalliferous Sediments of the Seabed* in OCEAN YEARBOOK 3 77 (Borgese & Ginsburg eds. 1982); Emery, Hunt & Hays, *Summary of Hot Brines and Heavy Metal Deposits in the Red Sea* in HOT BRINES AND RECENT HEAVY METAL DEPOSITS IN THE RED SEA 557 (Degens & Ross eds. 1969).

[9] Evensen, *Dissenting Opinion, Case Concerning the Continental Shelf (Tunisia/Libyan Arab Jamahiriya),* International Court of Justice, Reports of Judgements, Advisory Opinions and Orders, Judgment of 24 February, 1982, at 321.

[10] This section is based on a paper *Elements for Negotiations: An Introduction* presented by the author of the Third East-West Center Workshop on the Hydrocarbon Potential of the South China Sea and Possibilities of Joint Development, Bangkok, Thailand, February 1985.

[11] Miyoshi, *Some Comments on Legal Aspects of Precedents for Joint Development* in THE SOUTH CHINA SEA: HYDROCARBON POTENTIAL AND POSSIBILI-TIES OF JOINT DEVELOPMENT 1359 (Valencia ed. 1981).

[12] Id. at 1359; Østreng, "Delimitation arrangements ” *supra* n. 8, at 141.

[13] El-Hakim, *supra* note 8, at 185.

[14] Ariffin, *supra* note 4.

[15] Miyoshi, *supra* note 11, at 1359.

[16] Onorato, *supra* note 7, at 540.

[17] Østreng, *supra* note 7, at 560.

[18] El-Hakim, *supra* note 8, at 185.

[19] Evensen, *supra* note 9, at 321.

[20] *Agreement Between Japan and the Republic of Korea Concerning Joint Development of the Southern Part of the Continental Shelf Adjacent to the Two Countries* in Park, *supra* note 5, arts. XIX, XXI at 1347.

[21] Polahan, *supra* note 4.

[22] Østreng, *supra* note 7, at 560.

[23] *Agreement Between the State of Kuwait and the Kingdom of Saudi Arabia Relating to the Partition of the Neutral Zone* in Fesharaki, *supra* note 6, arts. III, VII at 1331.

[24] Miyoshi, *supra* note 11, at 1359.

[25] Polahan, *supra* note 4.

[26] Ariffin, *supra* note 4, at 535.

[27] *Agreement* in Park, *supra* note 20, art. IV at 1343, art. XVII at 1347.

[28] Fesharaki, *supra* note 6, at 1329.

[29] Richardson et al., *supra* note 7, at 841.

[30] Blissenbach and Nawab, *supra* note 8, at 98.

[31] Onorato, *supra* note 6, at 54.

[32] *Agreement* in Park, *supra* note 20, art. VI at 1344.

[33] Polahan, *supra* note 4.

[34] *Agreement* in Park, *supra* note 20, art. XXXI para. 4 at 1352.

35 Either party shall be relieved of its obligations under the agreement if the other cedes or alienates all or part of [its] equal rights to any other State or if the other refuses to abide by [a] judgment made against it, *Agreement* in Fesharaki, *supra* note 23, art. V at 1331, art. XXII at 1334.

36 Polahan, *supra* note 4.

37 El-Hakim, *supra* note 8, at 186.

38 Miyoshi, *supra* note 5.

39 Onorato, *supra* note 6, at 541.

40 Evensen, *supra* note 9, at 321.

41 Blissenbach & Nawab, *supra* note 8, at 94; Blissenbach, *Technical and Economic Aspects of Ocean Mining,* paper presented at *Pacific Marine Mineral Resources Training Course,* East-West Center, Honolulu, Hawaii, June 1985, at 7, 11.

42 Miyoshi, *Some Comments on Legal Aspects of Precedents for Joint Development,* in THE SOUTH CHINA SEA: HYDROCARBON POTENTIAL AND POSSIBILITIES OF JOINT DEVELOPMENT (Valencia ed. 1981); Fesharaki, *supra* note 6, at 1329, 1330.

43 Onorato, *supra* note 6, at 540.

44 Park, *supra* note 5, at 1341; Park, South Korea and the Law of the Sea, *Korean International Law,* Institute for Asian Studies, University of California, Berkeley, 1981.

45 ENERGY ASIA (10 May 1985).

46 PETROLEUM NEWS (11 July 1985, at 11).

47 PETROLEUM NEWS (February 1985, at 18).

48 Valencia & Miyoshi, *Southeast Asian Seas: Joint Development of Hydrocarbons in Overlapping Claim Areas,* OCEAN DEV. INT. L.J., v. 16, pp. 211–254; FAR EAST. ECON. REV. 1 (22 August 1985).

49 ENERGY ASIA (30 August 1985).

50 ENERGY ASIA (June 1985).

51 ENERGY ASIA (19 April 1986).

52 Richardson, *Drawing the Seabed Line,* FAR. EAST. ECON. REV. 79 (3 October 1978); *Talks with Indonesia on Fishing, Seabed to Japan,* The Weekend Australian, Dec. 27-28, 1980 at 9, col. 3; Richardson, *Tying up Timor's Loose Ends,* FAR EAST. ECON. REV. 44 (5 January 1979); ENERGY ASIA (13 June 1986); PETROLEUM NEWS (December 1984, at 15).

53 The Ikan Pari 1-A flowed 6,085 Barrels of Oil Per Day (BOPD) from two zones and 2,953 BOPD from a confirmation well, ENERGY ASIA 5 (14 October 1983); PETROLEUM NEWS (August 1983).

54 PETROLEUM NEWS (July 1983).

55 The Tembang-1 well flowing at 325 Million Cubic Feet Per Day (MMCFD), ENERGY ASIA (January 1982).

56 The Anoa-1 well flowing at 4,300 BOPD and 1.7 MMCFD, ENERGY ASIA (16 April 1982; 30 April 1982).

57 The AL-1X well reported gas-in-place of 130 to 140 Trillion Cubic Feet (TCF) of which 80 percent is said to consist of inerts, leaving 28 TCF; ENERGY ASIA (30 August 1986); Chanda, *Diplomatic Isolation Hinders Investment from Abroad,* FAR EAST. ECON. REV. 28 (10 April 1986).

58 FAR EAST. ECON. REV. 9 (15 May 1981).

59 PETROLEUM NEWS (October 1985); (December 1984, at 15).

60 Ariffin, *supra* note 4.

[61] J.A. Katili. "Geology of Southeast Asia with Particular Reference to the South China Sea," in Valencia, ed., 1981, *supra* note 4 at 1077-1093; Karl Hinz and Hans Schleuter, "Results of SONNE Cruise SO-23 and SO-27," in Valencia, 1985, *supra* note 4.

[62] C. La Grange. "South China Sea Disputes: China, Vietnam, Taiwan and the Philippines," East-West Environment and Policy Institute Working Paper (May 1980).

[63] Selig S. Harrison. The Taiwan issue and seabed petroleum development in the East China Sea. Paper prepared for a conference on "Major Current Issues in East Asia," St. John's University, Jamaica, New York, October 25, 1985; PETROLEUM NEWS 16 (July 1985); Kim, The Northeast Asian Continental Shelf Controversy: A Case Study in Conflict Resolution among South Korea, Japan, China (PRC) and Taiwan (ROC), unpublished Ph.D. Dissertation, Florida State University, 1980, at 248.

Appendix A
Joint Development of Petroleum Resources in Overlapping Claim Areas: Summary of Discussion*

Cooperation is an emerging rule of international law and should be taken into account in negotiations on boundaries. It is also increasingly a State practice. In particular, a State interested in a common international petroleum deposit, or an area in which potential reserves exist, may not unilaterally exploit them over the timely objection of another State. To do so would be a violation of international law. Thus States with overlapping claims are compelled to enter into good-faith negotiations to arrive at agreement on a boundary or an agreement to jointly exploit the area of overlap. An indirect precedent may be found in the Trial Smelter case in which an international tribunal found that there was economic injury by one State to another. The unilateral exploitation of a resource in an area that has valid, viable overlapping claims would also be an economic injury by one State to another, would be actionable, and depending on the power of international tribunals, would be enjoinable. But enforcement would be more difficult and doubtful.

Joint development might be considered an extension of unitization, i.e., the principle that a deposit which straddles a boundary line should be developed as a unit for maximum recovery. This principle was instituted by States because competitive drilling into, and production from, the same deposit by several owners significantly reduced maximum possible recovery by too rapid depletion of the natural pressure drive in the reservoir. In unitization, a formula for the sharing of produced oil is developed based on, e.g., estimated recoverable reserves in place, or acre-foot of overlay by the respective contract areas. How-

---

* The following summary was written by the author of the preceding paper based primarily on contributions by C.Y. Li, William Onorato, Datuk Harun Arrifin, and Ernst Wilheim.

ever, there are significant differences between unitization and joint development. Joint development is for an *area* of overlapping claims often with unknown potential, whereas unitization is for a particular known reservoir or field that is divided by an agreed boundary. Thus, joint development presupposes a government-to-government relationship and the creation of a bilateral body, i.e., a joint authority. Joint development is plausible because, typically, neither party knows how much oil may be found on its side of the putative boundary. Rather, it is simply a 50:50 agreement in advance of exploration and exploitation.

The Asian region has good prospects for resolving its boundary disputes or developing agreements for joint development because most Asian nations are anxious to attract private capital, expertise and technology and are more practical, flexible and accommodating in such matters than some nations in many other areas of the world. Cooperation or joint development in the ASEAN region will not be too difficult because of the ASEAN spirit. In Northeast Asia, China has shown a reasonable attitude by not drilling in areas claimed by other nations such as Vietnam, Japan and South Korea, and when the time is right, China will probably negotiate with these other claimants. However, joint development of overlapping claim areas with Vietnam in the eastern Gulf of Thailand and the Gulf of Tonkin are impossible at present. On the other hand, for some areas like the Spratly Islands, resolution of the conflicting claims is impossible and thus joint development may be the only solution.

With oil prices so low, it would initially seem that there is little incentive to pursue a complicated plan like joint development. However, for Indonesia and Australia, the price of oil has had no apparent effect on negotiations for joint development. Also, it may be better for countries to begin discussions before oil is discovered, because once oil is discovered, complications will increase. Thus, lack of knowledge of any hydrocarbon potential may actually enhance prospects for agreement on joint development. With low oil prices, the countries involved now have time to think about the joint development option carefully and to develop a solid lasting arrangement. In general, the more unimportant a matter appears to be, or the more uneconomic an area appears to be, the easier it will be to reach an agreement; otherwise bureaucrats become afraid of the responsibility and politicians become more involved in politicizing the issue and making it more difficult to resolve.

The incentive for joint development from the oil companies' perspective is that without some agreement among the contending claimants, the political risk factor becomes insurmountable for the prime risk takers—the private international oil companies. For States it represents the possibility of having something rather than nothing. But it is not enough for private capital risk takers for the claimants to agree to agree. The operational scheme has to be fairly clear, well defined, and systematized, and its duration has to be sufficient to allow for the logical development and decline phases of a discovery. First and foremost, the oil company must believe there is sufficient potential to provide a return on investment. From the oil companies' perspective there is no problem in exchanging information in joint operations; there are many precedents in many parts of the world. However, because of PSCs in many places, oil companies are not allowed to exchange information without the consent of the national oil company.

There is presently a rationalization of the oil industry in progress with some companies being taken over by others. Companies have saddled themselves with greater debt and exploration budgets have decreased, as have profit margins. Companies say (1) that they need terms that are more attractive because money is unavailable for high risk projects; and (2) that they are inclined to spend less and to look for better prospects, particularly where there is political stability, and where the boundary lines are clearly drawn. If a joint development area is being offered, the companies say they need to be assured that the regime will be perpetuated, and that the governments will be cooperative and the incentives reasonable. Thus, with the decline in oil prices, countries may actually be more inclined to settle their boundary disputes, including joint development, to provide the stable environment necessary to attract private investment.

In the present situation of low oil prices, the World Bank has been taking the lead in helping countries all over the world to create data bases and technical, fiscal and legal regimes to attract private capital investment. Normally, at the request of a country, the World Bank helps the country collect and enhance available data, and put together a series of presentations by the oil industry on the potential and prospects for hydrocarbons in that country. The Bank also helps the countries put together legal and fiscal regimes which are realistic and attractive.

For Malaysia, the problem of unresolved boundaries has hampered exploration and development of hydrocarbon resources. Malaysia inherited its land boundary problems from the British colonial administration at independence. No offshore boundaries had been established. After independence in 1957, other countries and companies began to raise the issue of offshore boundaries but Malaysia was not well prepared to deal with these issues then. Malaysia claimed its continental shelf on 28 July 1966, and granted a concession to Esso Production Malaysia, Inc. on 16 April 1968 which was later assumed by PETRONAS, the Malaysian national oil company. Thailand passed its petroleum mining act in 1971 and granted concessions to Texas Pacific Thailand on 8 March 1972, and to Triton Oil Company of Thailand on 12 October 1972. In 1972 Malaysia began meeting with Thailand to negotiate their mutual offshore boundary. On 15 May 1972 Thailand and Malaysia agreed on a boundary extending offshore about 50 km from their land border on the Gulf of Thailand. However, the two countries could not reach agreement on the remainder of the shelf boundary.

In 1979 Malaysia and Thailand reached a Memorandum of Understanding in which they acknowledged the existence of overlapping claims and agreed to create a joint authority with the responsibility to explore and exploit all natural resources in the seabed for the next fifty years. According to the agreement, costs and benefits would be shared equally and all previous arrangements or licenses issued by either of the parties would not be curtailed.

The next objective for Thailand and Malaysia was to work out the terms of reference of the joint authority—its constitution—and the powers that were to be delegated to it—the legislation for the formation of the joint authority. Also needed was resolution of the boundary in the area. It was agreed that these matters were to be treated as a package. The initial discussions also produced agreement to treat the area as one contract area and to adopt the production sharing contract model for the area.

The next step was to draft the legislation to apply to the area. The legislation could have been entirely based on either Malaysian or Thai law, or it could have been entirely new law. The solution desired by the respective governments was to harmonize the laws of the two countries. However, a number of legal and non-legal problems ensued. First, the Thai negotiator did not have good communication with his minister, causing a year's delay. Then the negotiator had an accident. Finally, Thailand had several changes in government which caused further delays. Another problem was that to negotiate terms with companies which had concessions in the area, the negotiators first had to be fully aware of the technical knowledge of the area, and the necessary technical and economic assessment took some time.

The joint technical committee's deliberations went smoothly; the legal committee's deliberations were more difficult and contentious. For example, the Malaysian petroleum development act did not contain any reference to production-sharing contracts (PSC); these provisions were only in the individual contract agreements. The Thai negotiators said that the law must contain the specific PSC terms, so the Malaysians had to extract all the relevant PSC references from the contracts and put them into law. Another problem was the decision on geographic allocation of civil jurisdiction. It was agreed that a line equally dividing the joint area would divide criminal jurisdiction, but the Memorandum of Understanding was silent on civil jurisdiction. This matter took some time to resolve but eventually it was agreed that the line dividing criminal jurisdiction would also divide civil jurisdiction except for laws dealing with finance, taxation and customs. The matter of customs was straightforward: the equipment under a PSC will be owned by the government or in this case, the joint authority. But taxation laws of the two countries—particularly relating to income tax and royalties—had to be rationalized.

The Thai claim line itself was a problem. Up to 1971, the original shelf claim by Thailand extended from the coast right up to the easternmost edge of the Texas Pacific concession. But the negotiations in 1972 led to an agreement on the line from the coast to the southwestern point of that triangle and later on, the line was extended from that point to the easternmost edge of the Texas Pacific concession. Malaysia eventually adopted the easternmost line for the eastern boundary of the joint development area, and Thailand agreed.

A further problem was that Triton and Texas Pacific had concessions from the Thai government, and since the PSC was to be the operative model for the area, these companies might object. Thailand agreed that the terms of the concession agreements made by them were applicable only in its half of the area. To resolve this problem, different concepts were explored based on the area to be involved. However, to propose subdivisions of the area for the concessionaires, the negotiators needed to know the geographic distribution of the potential. It turned out that 85 percent of the resources in the area were on the Malaysian side. Thus it again became clear that in order to be profitable, the area had to be treated as one. Malaysia was willing to share with all concerned, as an incentive to Thailand and the companies, to get them to agree to implementation of the agreement and the PSC. But the companies were not very cooperative. Texas Pacific has not replied to the incentive offered by Malaysia, probably because they have problems with the Thai government over pricing of gas in another area. Triton claims that under its interpretation, when Thailand's boundary moved south, so did its concession area.

Overall it took the British and Norwegians some ten years to conclude and implement their joint agreement; perhaps implementation of this agreement will also take as long. If it is successful, it will be a bonus for the two countries, but not a necessity. The difference between Thailand and Malaysia and Korea and Japan is that the latter are not so concerned with the sovereignty of their shared areas whereas Thailand and Malaysia put this concern above exploitation.

In the case of the boundary issue between Australia and Indonesia, the seabound boundary was negotiated in the early 1970s based on the then prevailing doctrine of the continental shelf. Thus, the key feature determining the boundary was the bathymetric axis of the Timor Trough which is only 30 to 60 miles from the coast of Timor. The actual boundary is a little way up on the Australian side of that axis.

At the time the boundary was negotiated, East Timor was a colony of Portugal and thus the boundary was not extended off its shore. Australia was discussing this section of the boundary with Portugal in 1975 when the Portugese regime in East Timor disintegrated. East Timor was then incorporated into Indonesia, but it took several years for Australia to recognize Indonesian sovereignty over the area. Meanwhile, the Law of the Sea Convention had been concluded and some of the ground rules for seabed delimitation had changed. Actually, the Convention provides little direct guidance on seabed delimitation. But it does provide the right of each coastal state to exercise seabed rights out to 200 miles, regardless of depth. Indonesia maintains that distance has taken priority over geomorphology and that because the distance between the opposing claimants' coasts is less than 400 miles, it is the equidistant or median line that is the prevailing principle for boundaries. The median line would put the boundary considerably to the south of its present location. However, Australia has never accepted the median line as a basis for negotiations and maintains that the structure of the shelf remains the primary consideration for seabed boundary delimitation. The Kelp structure is in the unresolved area and simple closure of the existing line would give it entirely to Australia whereas a median line would give it wholly to Indonesia.

These opposing views have created a deadlock and neither State is prepared to compromise its basic legal principle. However, both States are anxious to find a way out of the impasse. The way out seems to both parties to be a joint development zone under which the disputed area would be developed jointly, pending resolution of the boundary.

First, however, the parties must define the extent of the joint development area. The eastern and western boundaries are unlikely to create much difficulty, but agreement on the northern and southern boundaries may be more sensitive because any such lines may have implications for future delimitation. These matters were discussed at the eighth round of talks in Jakarta in June 1986.

But the most formidable task is the merging or other application of the legal and administrative systems of the two countries so that joint development can be viable. An operator derives title from both States jointly; it follows that the legal and administrative systems of neither country are paramount. This creates great difficulty when the legal and social systems of the two States are very different. There is a wide range of matters to be considered: granting of titles, contractual agreements with operators, supervision of operators, the collection and sharing of revenue, the application of public regulatory laws such as customs, immigration and quarantine, and the application of a system of private law, general and civic law, and criminal law.

Envisaged is the establishment of a joint authority comprised of officials of the two governments which would grant title by operators and be responsible for contractual arrangements, including their supervision. There may also be a ministerial council above the body of officials. The authority would perform, on behalf of the two governments, the administrative and supervisory functions normally undertaken by a national mines administration. Titles would be secured because the operator's title would be derived jointly from the two governments.

Revenues would be shared equally between the two governments. However, Australia and Indonesia have quite different revenue collection systems. Australia has a concession system with royalties and excess income taxes; Indonesia has a PSC. The PSC might lend itself more readily to a revenue sharing arrangement between the two governments than the Australian concession system would.

The licensing and revenue collection systems are among the easier of the issues to resolve in a joint development scheme. More difficult is the application of the system of civil law, e.g., labor and criminal law, because of the great difference in the legal and social systems of the two countries. For example, if an Indonesian worker fell on a rig and injured his back he might be sent back to his village to be cared for by his extended family. If he were an Australian worker, he could retire in comfort on the compensation award he would get.

And what if a national of one country murdered a national of another country? Each State would have a case for trying the murder.

One possible solution is to leave these matters to the joint authority to resolve; perhaps to determine in negotiations with particular operators, perhaps by contract. However, as in the Malaysia-Thailand arrangement, this simply defers the problem. For Australia, it is necessary, when presenting an arrangement to parliament for approval, for the government to demonstrate that these problems have been resolved and that the people's interests have been adequately protected.

Although the Malaysia-Thailand arrangement divided criminal jurisdiction geographically in the joint development area by a single line, this solution would not work for Australia and Indonesia because of the possible implications of any such line for future delimitation. In the South Korea-Japan joint development arrangement, the area is divided into blocks which are allocated alternatively to license holders of each country, and the law of the nationality of the relevant license holder applies. This system does not appeal to Australia because if it is known that one particular area is especially prospective, the joint development area could become functionally one block and thus this system would not offer a solution.

Another approach is based on the concept of personal jurisdiction. In this situation, Indonesia would have jurisdiction over Indonesians and Australia over Australians. However, this approach does not provide guidance on the application of laws or jurisdiction over nationals of third States, it does not deal with criminal conduct between an Australian and an Indonesian, and the idea of people working alongside one another but being governed by different laws would be opposed by Australian trade unions.

Thus Australia favors the application of a single legal system to the joint development zone. Since most of the movements to and from the zone are expected to be through the Australian city of Darwin, Australian law is an obvious choice. Perhaps a variation of the single system approach in which Australian law is combined with residual personal jurisdiction by agreement would be acceptable to Indonesia. In this solution, Indonesia, by agreement, could exercise jurisdiction over an Indonesian national. Certainly, the application of the system of civil and criminal law to structures in a joint development zone is one of the most difficult issues to be resolved in implementing such a zone.

New legal ground is being broken here. Although it will not be a new legal system, the solution must combine the ordinary existing civil and criminal laws of each nation in a suitable mix. It may be useful to look for guidance in these matters beyond the petroleum field to examples of other joint resource development such as the joint development of hydropower between Paraguay and Brazil or Paraguay and Argentina. In the former agreement, Brazil prefinanced Paraguay's share and gets repaid with priority out of production. Or take a recent Caribbean example, in which a part of a country with offshore oil potential in its part separated from the other part, leaving the latter with no offshore potential. The condition for the independence of the former was that it gives the country from which it separated 15 percent of its future petroleum revenues. This was a kind of intergovernmental farm-out, plus relinquishment, plus separation plus a cessation agreement. The situation is even more complicated because a third country claims these two islands. There is a joint commission supervising the petroleum arrangement and it is trying to formulate a fiscal regime for the newly independent country. The definition of the revenues to be shared is extremely complicated. If we assume a PSC whereby costs are recovered before production sharing is triggered, and from which comes the 15 percent share for one country, it is quite important to define costs. For example, if one country were to levy high income taxes on employees, the higher salaries will be recoverable costs; the same applies for custom duties for certain taxes called fees. Indeed, there are many quasi-levies by which the government can increase or reduce costs. Thus, it is very important in a sharing arrangement not to let one country obtain additional revenues by influencing costs.

A new legal system might be necessary for mining and environmental standards, although they could be based on international standards. Some guidance in this matter can be derived from unitization agreements. For example, take a situation where there are platforms on both sides of a boundary with interconnecting pipelines, and the pipelines flow to a terminal in country B. Now say there is an explosion on the rig in country B and the resulting fire is transmitted to, and damages the facilities of country A. The question of liability is unresolved. The parties must argue the liability question and the payment of insurance, and the problem can escalate because the two countries have different legal systems. The same problem can arise in the administration of joint development.

However, if the participation formula is agreed, operators may be willing to operate in an uncertain civil and criminal legal environment and to argue their cases later if necessary. Private parties may be able to agree where States cannot. Another solution is simply to insert a dispute resolution clause in the joint development agreement. Existing law can never cover all contingencies. Needed, however, is a draft analysis and guidelines for these issues—model agreements and contracts for joint development—like the OECD drafts of double taxation agreements or the United Nations model taxation agreement used by many developing countries when negotiating with developed countries.

The Development and Trade of Petroleum Resources in the Pacific Rim: The Roles Played by Governments*

*by Corazon Morales Siddayao***

Dynamic economic growth is expected in the Asia-Pacific region in the coming decade—growth characterized by high levels of export activity and demand for energy resources. A relatively favorable investment climate and existing refining and marketing facilities provide the basis for increased intra-regional trading opportunities. The author analyzes the policies adopted by Asian-Pacific governments to influence these trade and investment flows and assesses the implications of current and emerging governmental action for the petroleum industry of the region.

It is generally observed in investment circles that the Asia-Pacific region is a growth area and, except for pockets of instability, a generally stable area for investments. Because the region is a growth area—implying an increasing demand for modern fuels, especially petroleum—some of these investments will be in the oil and gas sector. Furthermore, structural changes in the petroleum industry which principally originated with the sharp oil price increases in the 1970s, plus the accompanying technical improvements and institutional changes, have made the region attractive to risk investors. The petroleum resource potential of the region has generated increased intra-regional and extra-regional trade and investment opportunities. The significant importance assigned by national governments to energy as consumption and production inputs has, in the process, increased its involvement in petroleum production and trade. Although the traditional view of the nature of public enterprises has been that of utilities providing the public with electricity, gas service, water, transport, etc. (see, for example, Turvey, 1968), this is no longer the case. National oil companies and other government bodies with oversight responsibility over the petroleum industry abound.

* A shorter version of this paper has appeared in Peter N. Nemetz, ed., *The Pacific Rim: Investment, Development, and Trade,* Vancouver, B.C.: University of British Columbia Press, 1967. It was released in its current version as Working Paper WP-85-2 of the Resource Systems Institute, The East-West Center, Honolulu, Hawaii.
** I wish to acknowledge with thanks the contributions of Barbara McKellar to Tables 4.3 and 4.4.

The increasing involvement of the public sector in traditionally privately-run economic activities raises many issues concerning allocative efficiency. This trend allows analyses of such developments in the context of applied microeconomics (especially in the areas of industrial organization and public economics), international trade, and capital theory. It is not the author's intention to dwell on the theoretical aspects of these theories. Rather, using the basic notions of this body of knowledge, this paper will, initially, look briefly at the petroleum potential in the region and the determinants of its trade related investment flow (the discussion will cover the flow of petroleum in both its primary and processed form). It will then inquire into the related implications of existing or emerging government involvement in both upstream and downstream operations[2] directly and indirectly.

FRAMEWORK FOR ANALYSIS AND SCOPE

Basic premises

1. Energy is regarded as a critical input in the socioeconomic progress of a society. Petroleum is at this time the technologically most economical—and, therefore, the most desirable—energy resource, with oil preferred to gas. Because petroleum accumulations are not located in all countries in amounts or at costs that will meet each country's demands, an international market for this commodity exists. There are thus net oil exporters and net oil importers.

2. The development, processing, and transportation of petroleum requires significant amounts of capital investment. The volume of capital or investment flows (defined as flows of physical, human, and monetary assets) is determined by the yield from such investments, measured in terms of the investor's desired positive net present value or internal rate of return (IRR). The IRR, which may also be viewed as the cost of capital or the measure of an investor's opportunity cost, is at least equal to but may be higher than the real interest rate. The IRR will, however, differ among stages in the industry as well as among economic units involved, projects, and environments, because of variations in the parameters chosen, e.g., the degrees of risks involved.

3. Each economic agent is assumed to want to maximize the benefits and minimize the costs from the decisions it makes in the oil and gas sector; that is, each decision maker "optimizes." The measures for optimality are not assumed to be identical for each decision maker, nor are the goals or the time frames against which each agent measures such optimality. Hence, private investors will seek, where possible, to maximize profits by generating the maximum revenues attainable and minimizing direct costs to themselves within their own sets of time frames. The receiving country's government will act similarly with respect to revenues and costs to the state, according to the priorities it sets and according to its own time frame.

4. Attitudes towards risk differ, but it is assumed that investors are basically

risk-averse. Given the availability of various investment opportunities, foreign investors will rank areas according to expected income streams and the stability of those streams. Thus, the revenues from the operation and the cost of the venture are principal determinants of project choice, given equal technical risks. The stability of the institutional framework within which a project will be operated influences final choice; the stability factor includes what is often referred to as "political risk" (as opposed to technical—associated with hydrocarbon search—and economic or commercial risks).

5. The institutional framework is defined as including (a) the contractual framework delineating the relationship between economic agents, (b) government policies affecting the net gains from sanctioned behavioral relations among economic agents, and (c) other institutional factors that may inhibit or enhance perceptions of the attractiveness of such relationships. This framework affects both commodity and financial flows in the petroleum sector in the region. Hence, the role of government in influencing such flows will be given principal attention.

6. Government is only one among several institutions of social control. Government is the agent, the mechanism, by which the ends of the people associated in a state are pursued. The state is only one of many human associations in a society. Governments may change, but the people living in a definite territory, with some kind of government, make up a continuing association. The state is legally supreme, but this does not mean—unless the form of government is a dictatorship—that it is all-powerful and that it controls *every* activity. And if it attempts to do so, individual economic units with the freedom to make economic choices will reflect their choices in the elasticities of demand and supply.

7. The institutional framework is assumed to provide for the transfer of technology to nationals of the home country through various provisions governing employment and training skills, etc.

Additional premises

The basic purposes for setting up a state-owned or national oil company (NOC) are assumed to be the following:

1. In a situation where private investments are available for the operation of an oil enterprise engaged in the usual activities the oil industry has been experienced in doing, the establishment of a publicly owned national enterprise can be economically justified under the following set of circumstances (which is not complete): (a) A suspicion of severe market imperfection exists with regard to the operation of privately-owned oil enterprises. (b) The national oil company is used as a yardstick against which the performance of privately-owned companies will be measured. (c) The establishment of a national oil company will not severely hamper the operation of the market, by worsening a distortion in the allocation of the nation's resources, if such already exists. (d) The market imperfection that initially justified the creation of the national oil company is

seen as a possible source of national insecurity in the provision of energy goods considered vital to the operation of the economy.

2. Where a national enterprise is created to serve as a yardstick for measuring private performance, the national enterprise is required to operate and be managed under the usual efficiency conditions required of a privately-owned enterprise. That is, least costs and maximum revenues remain the guiding principles in management decisions. Profits generated would be used (a) to expand capital bases where necessary, as in a private enterprise, and (b) increase government revenues, in the same way that a private enterprise would be expected to pay corporate taxes. "Dividends" would accrue to the national treasury.

The foregoing justifications will not always hold true, but they are provided as the starting points for discussion.

Scope and Approach

This paper will focus on the countries on the western rim of the Pacific Basin. To keep the analyses within manageable bounds, the discussion will be limited to the following countries: Japan, South Korea, the Philippines, Thailand, Malaysia, Brunei, Singapore, Indonesia, Australia, and New Zealand. References will be made to Burma, China, and the Indochinese countries where appropriate. As an important buyer of petroleum and supplier of capital, the United States will also be referred to where appropriate.

The discussion will cover both upstream and downstream segments of government involvement in the industry. Treatment will be uneven, as developments of a more recent nature will be given more space because the implications of such events may not have received as much attention as earlier ones. Data availability will also be a constraint.

This paper will not provide econometrically based analyses to support inferences drawn. Rather, this paper will raise policy-oriented research issues about such government involvement that need to be addressed more carefully and in depth in a systematic way.

THE FLOW OF OIL AND GAS IN THE REGION

There is a market for crude oil and natural gas as well as for the products processed from these two basic sources. In the countries under review, the nature of the market depends on the capability of the buyer to receive crude oil and to refine products for domestic use, as well as the ability of the buyer to receive natural gas in liquefied form. Gas is less easily transportable than oil, but with improvements in technology and cost-price ratios, an international market has also developed—although this has occurred more recently than for oil.

Current Dependency, Resource Bases, and Trading Patterns

Table 3.1 shows patterns or oil and gas consumption in the countries under review for the years 1970, 1978, and 1982. Notwithstanding the sharp changes in oil prices that have occurred over the period under review, the table shows only slight changes in levels of dependency on hydrocarbons as a group, with a shift in favor of natural gas occurring in some countries.

Table 3.2 shows the flow of oil to and from the Western Pacific rim countries. The table shows that Japan and other Southeast Asian countries receive some petroleum from Canada and the United States, and that Japan and the United States are currently the major markets for Southeast Asian output. Overall, however, the Middle East remains the principal source of oil supply for Japan, Australia, and Southeast Asia as a whole.

Southeast Asia is defined in this matrix as consisting of Brunei, Hong Kong, Indonesia, Malaysia, the Philippines, Singapore, South Korea, Taiwan, and Thailand. China is grouped with the U.S.S.R. and Eastern Europe; it can be assumed, however, that most of the flow out of that block into the region comes from China, and that such trade will be in the form of crude oil.

TABLE 3.1
Western Pacific Rim: Patterns of Oil and Gas Consumption 1970, 1978, 1982
(Percent of Total)

	1970		1978		1982	
Country	Oil	Natural Gas	Oil	Natural Gas	Oil	Natural Gas
East/Southeast Asia						
Brunei	25	75	8	92	43	57
Burma	81	1	74	11	58	28
China	7	. . .	18	1	17	3
Indonesia	69	29	84	14	83	16
Japan	70	1	74	5	64	8
Korea, South	52	—	61	—	58	0
Malaysia	95	1	88	10	82	15
Philippines	97	—	94	—	91	. . .
Singapore	100	—	100	—	100	—
Thailand	96	—	95	—	66	8
Australasia						
Australia	47	3	41	10	34	40
New Zealand	58	2	51	17	40	24

Source: Based on United Nations (1976, 1979) and (1984).

. . . = less than or equal to 0.5 percent.

TABLE 3.2
Oil Flow Into and From the Western Pacific Rim, 1983
(Thousand b/d)

From	To	USA	Canada	Southeast Asia	Japan	Australasia
USA		—	80	80	105	15
Canada		540	—	—	5	—
Latin America		2,160	125	5	180	5
Western Europe		550	15	5	—	5
Middle East		575	60	1,615	2,750	120
North Africa		280	25	—	40	—
West Africa		475	15	—	5	—
East and Southern Africa		—	—	5	—	—
South Asia		—	—	25	15	10
Southeast Asia[a]		345	—	—[b]	780	85
USSR, Eastern Europe, China		60	6	240	235	5

Source: British Petroleum Company (1984).

[a] Southeast Asia is defined as: Brunei, Hong Kong, Indonesia, Malaysia, Philippines, Singapore, South Korea, Taiwan, and Thailand.
[b] Trade occurs among Southeast Asian countries, but this matrix does not report intra-regional trade.

The continued large dependence on Middle Eastern supply is not surprising, of course. The principal reason is that the Middle Eastern reserves and production levels are several times larger than those of the whole region; see Tables 3.3 and 3.4. The type of crude produced in the region and the existing product demand patterns also encourage that flow.

The *Petroleum News* shows the following patterns in early 1984:[3]
— Persian Gulf crudes moving to East Asia amount to around 3 million barrels per day (b/d), with Japan accounting for 90 percent, Singapore for 3 percent, and the balance to the others.
— Of approximately 0.5 million b/d of Indonesian crude exports to the region, 95 per cent goes to Japan and a smaller amount to the Philippines.
— Of Brunei's exports of about 0.08 million b/d, about 96 percent goes to Japan, with the rest going to Australia.

The above mentions nothing about Malaysia, which produces low-sulphur crude. In 1979 and 1980, Malaysia exported over 0.2 million b/d. Its major markets were—and should continue to be—Japan and the United States, with shares of over 40 and 25 percent, respectively. Small amounts go to the Philippines, Singapore, Thailand, and New Zealand.[4] (The source cited did not specify if the flows to Singapore include those sent for processing and for re-export to Malaysia.) Taiwan is reported to be considering doubling oil imports from Malaysia, from 1984 levels of 5,000 b/d.[5] Thailand is reported to have signed an agreement to import 5,000 b/d from Indonesia for a one-year period beginning in April 1984, and there is little reason at this point not to expect this to continue.[6]

TABLE 3.3

Western-Pacific Rim: Oil and Gas Reserves and Resources, January 1984

| | Estimated Proved Reserves[a] (Jan 1984) | | Ultimately Recoverable Resources[b] | | | |
| | | | Offshore | | Total | |
Country	Oil (mmb)	Gas (bcf)	Oil	Gas	Oil	Gas
East and Southeast Asia						
Brunei	1,390.0	7,050	D	E	D	D
Burma	30.0	180	D	C C	C	
China	19,100.0	30,300	D	C	C	B
Korea, South	. . .	. . .	D	D	D	D
Japan	58.0	900	D	D	D	C
Indonesia	9,100.0	30,200	C	C	C	B
Malaysia	3,000.0	48,000	C	C	C	C
Philippines	16.3	14	D	C	C	C
Taiwan	6.2	550	D	D	D	D
Thailand[c]	45.0	8,500	D	D	D	C
Australasia						
Australia	1,622.1	17,768	C	B	C	B
New Zealand	169.0	5,545	E	C	E	C
Middle East	370,100.8	775,047	NA	NA	NA	NA

Sources: Reserve data are from the *Oil and Gas Journal* (26 December 1983). Resource data are from Albers et al. (1973). Oil (1 billion bbls.) and gas (trillion cu. ft.) categories as follows: A = 1,000 – 10,000; B = 100 – 1,000; C = 10 – 100; D = 1 – 10; E = 0,1 – 1.

[a] "Reserves" defined as deposits recoverable under existing or forseeable legal, economic, and technical conditions.
[b] "Resources" defined as deposits believed to be present in sedimentary rocks in unexplored or partly unexplored areas.
[c] Thailand's potential resources has been upgraded in light of new information. New onshore discoveries also changes total basin data.
. . . = negligible or zero.
mmb = million barrels.
bcf = billion cubic feet.
NA = not available on a regional basis from comparable estimates.

The imports of the Philippines—a net oil importer—are shown as coming from East Asian producers as well as from the Persian Gulf.[7] China and Indonesia are the country's major Asian sources of crude imports; Saudi Arabia supplies most of the balance.

Japan is the principal importer of liquified petroleum gas (LPG)[8] in the region. This is used mainly in traditional areas for this product (residential, commercial, and industrial). Propane is used in areas beyond the reach of town gas supplies for cooking and water heating. With price controls lifted on kerosene products, consumption of LPG in competitive uses may be expected to increase. In addition, the usual non-energy uses of LPG as feedstock in the chemical sector account for Japan's large demand for this product. LPG shipments to Japan come in bulk refrigerated form from Australia and Indonesia, as well as from the Persian Gulf countries. Australia ships about 90 percent of its LPG to Japan, with the rest going to ASEAN countries. Indonesia's shipments go mainly to Japan and the United States, with about 20 percent going to other Asian markets.[9]

Prospective Shifts

As domestic production of either oil or gas or both increases in several net oil importers, this pattern will change for some countries. For example, Thailand's natural gas production is expected to supply about 70 percent of its primary source for power generation by 1986 and 62 percent by 1991.[10] New Zealand's natural gas production is also expected to displace oil by 1987.[11] Japan's gas reserves have increased considerably from 720 bcf at the beginning of 1983 to 900 bcf at the start of 1984; see Table 3.3. Deliberate policy strategies by national governments to switch away from oil not only to indigenous resources of all types, but to coal imports and nuclear power as well, could eventually reduce intra-regional demand.

Market pressures may, however, slow down this shift. Already China's production is being touted as the source of new production in Asia after 1986.[12] Even at 1984 production levels, China was reportedly marketing its oil in Asia at prices below those of Indonesia (at US$28.45/bbl. in October 1984 against the official US$29.53/bbl. price for Minas crude, Indonesia's major export), a strategy which could open up markets in Japan, Singapore, and Korea. Iran was also reportedly flooding Asia with low-priced oil, as other Persian Gulf prices began falling in mid-1984.[13] With the late October 1984 decrease in North Sea oil prices followed by a drop in Nigerian prices that led to an OPEC pricing meeting in Geneva a few days thereafter, trading among Western Pacific rim countries (including Australia, which approved limited crude oil experts in 1983)[14] may be expected to be negatively affected.

These pressures may not affect the shipment of liquefied natural gas (LNG) where projects have already been committed. LNG contracts run for around 20 years and are associated with a deposit's project development. Malaysia's first shipment of LNG left for Japan in January 1983 to supply Japanese utilities.

TABLE 3.4
Western Pacific Rim: Oil and Gas Production, 1981 and 1983

Country	Oil Production				Natural Gas Production			
	1983		1981		1983		1981	
	Total (mbd)	% Offshore	Total (mbd)	% Offshore	Total (mmcfd)	% Offshore	Total (mmcfd)	% Offshore
East and Southeast Asia								
Brunei	160	76.0	156	75.9	942	95.5	909	96.3
Burma	22	0.0	23	0.0	67	—	56	—
China	2,100	0.0	2,010	negl.	5,500	—	5,184	—
Indonesia	1,420	30.9	1,620	34.9	1,813	36.2	1,620	39.0
Japan	8	0.0	8	12.6	NA	—	150	20.0
Malaysia	383	100.0(?)	258	96.5	723	99.9	234	—
Philippines	14	100.0	5	100.0	—	—	—	—
Taiwan	2	NA	3	NA	140	—	170	—
Thailand	13	52.4	3	0.0	183	96.6	98	100.0
Australasia								
Australia[a]	405	84.2	382	96.4	1,350	45.2	1,060	52.0
New Zealand[a]	15	44.4	10	45.0	243	73.0	177	47.4
Middle East	11,711	30.9	15,694	33.8	5,450	11.8	5,020	20.0

Source: Production data for all but the Middle East and 1981 Australia and New Zealand data are from Association of Petroleum Geologists (1984). Other oil data are from the *Oil and Gas Journal* (25 December 1981 and 26 December 1983). Offshore data are from *Offshore* (20 July 1984). Middle East natural gas data are from *Petroleum Economics* (August 1983, August 1984).

[a] Natural gas annual data originally reported in cubic meters for Australia and New Zealand were converted to mmcfd by multiplying a factor of [(37.3/365)1,000].
mbd = thousand barrels per day.
mmcfd = million cubic feet per day.
(?) As reported but questionable offshore/total relationship.

Similar agreements between Thai and Japanese companies may not be affected, nor will those signed between Japanese companies and Indonesian or Australian suppliers, or that between South Korea's Electric Power Corporation and Indonesia's Peramina.[15]

A major consideration given to energy security in energy policy planning may, however, dampen the true effect of market pressures on the flow of oil into the region from the Persian Gulf. Asian oil importers have not forgotten the 1973 embargo, and how some of them were indirectly affected by an act that was intended to cripple the United States. Hence, the notion of energy security will continue to constitute a significant factor in the oil importers' determination to diversity not only the type of energy used but also the geographical source of imported energy. In this respect, OPEC oil would continue to be taken with caution by most countries. Indonesia may be spared from this bias even though it is an OPEC member, because it is a party to the ASEAN emergency supply agreement (the effectiveness of this agreement has not, of course, been put to the test to date). There is strong evidence that a premium associated with developing alternatives to oil is acceptable to most countries to assure the security of a stream of oil supplies for their economies. The Iran-Iraq war makes short-term contracts at low prices attractive, but long-term contracts continue to be treated with caution. Emergency plans have become standard policy in the region.

Additional shifts have also been occurring in the petroleum product flow in the region. Singapore has long served as the principal refining center for the region, although each country has its own set of refineries. Until Indonesia upgraded its refining capability, the bulk of Indonesian oil that was not exported as crude was refined in Singapore; this contract was cancelled in April 1984.[16] Singapore has also served as a processor for Malaysian crude; excess capacity for some products in Korea and the Philippines was also utilized by other Southeast Asian countries when required. All this is changing, as producing countries achieve their goals to confine processing within their boundaries and complete their refinery construction programs.[17]

CAPITAL FLOWS INTO THE REGION'S PETROLEUM INDUSTRY

Just as oil as a commodity flows into and out of the region, the capital funds required to initiate and develop upstream and downstream petroleum activities in the countries under review have been generated both within the home countries and elsewhere.

Investment Expenditures

Table 4.1(a) shows the amount of capital and exploration expenditures in the Far East for the years 1967, 1977, and 1982.[18] Growth of expenditures are compared for the ten years that include the first sharp oil price increases against the succeeding five years which include the second set of increases and the beginning of their decline to current levels. High and increasing growth rates are shown for both periods for exploratory geological and geophysical expenses at 11.0 and 25.4 percent, development and production investments (crude oil and natural gas) at 23.0 and 31.2 percent, and refinery investments at 14.4 and 17.0 percent.

Table 4.1(b) shows a projection of exploration and development expenditures in individual Asia-Pacific countries to 1990. This shows Australia, Indonesia, and China (offshore) as areas where the bulk of these new investments will occur.

Table 4.1(c) provides details of some commercial financing in the oil and gas sector in some countries in Asia for the years 1982 and 1983. The amounts and the rate bases are also shown. Note that these commercial loans are limited to the development stage of oil and gas projects.[19]

Risk capital flows to areas where the prospects of acceptable returns to investments are reasonable. The expected revenues from the sale of the commodity or service[20] are only one side of the equation; the other side consists of expected costs. These costs will include fiscal elements (taxes, bonuses, output or profit-sharing, royalties, etc.). The net revenue would, however, always be discounted for uncertainty over the future stream of returns. In the petroleum industry, the risks associated with the upstream stage are generally acknowledged to be higher than those for the downstream stage. The size of this difference is influenced, in part, by the institutional framework of the country in

TABLE 4.1(a)

Capital and Exploration Expenditures in the Far East,
1967, 1977, 1982
(Current US$ Million)

	1967	1977	1982	Growth Rate[a] 1967-77	Growth Rate[a] 1977-82
Crude oil and natural gas	130	1,300	6,200	23.0	31.2
Natural gas liquids plants	5	900	800	51.9	−2.4
Pipelines	20	525	525[b]	32.7	0.0
Refineries	350	1,475	3,450	14.4	17.0
Chemical plants	150	300	700	6.9	17.0
Marketing	300	425	875	3.5	14.4
Other	20	125	325	18.3	19.1
Total capital expenditures	975	5,050	12,875	16.4	18.72

Source: Chase Manhattan Bank (1979, 1984).

[a] Computed using the formula $Y_t = Y_0 e^{rt}$.
[b] Investments rose to 625 in 1981.

which the investment is made. Hence, in addition to the technical and economic risks associated with hydrocarbon search, the type of risk often referred to in the foreign investment literature as "political risk" cannot be ignored. The investor's profit function may thus be expressed in the following form:

$$p = \int [R(t) - C(t)e^{-rt} dt]$$

$$R(t) = R(P, Q)$$

$$C(t) = C(T, M, V, K, G)$$

$$r = r(X_1, X_2, X_3)$$

where p = profits, R = revenue, C = costs, t = time, P = selling price, Q = output, T = costs associated with technical difficulty, M = raw material or

TABLE 4.1(b)

Forecast of Capital Expenditures for Petroleum Exploration and
Development in Asia-Pacific Countries (1983-1990)
(US$ million in 1983 current value)

Country	1983	1984	1985	1987	1990	Growth Rate, 1983–90 (%)[a]
East and Southeast Asia						
Brunei	480	390	410	500	960	9.90
Burma	200	220	260	300	500	13.09
China (Offshore)	700	1,100	1,600	3,000	5,500	29.45
Indonesia	3,900	3,900	3,600	4,200	4,300	1.39
Japan	400	420	400	550	530	4.02
Malaysia	1,500	1,400	1,600	1,900	2,500	7.30
Philippines	360	310	390	450	550	6.05
Thailand	560	650	520	500	950	7.55
Australasi						
Australia	2,200	1,800	1,600	2,800	4,100	8.89
New Zealand	240	300	310	350	450	8.98
Others[b]	3,000	3,450	4,300	6,400	7,900	13.83
TOTAL[c]	13,540	13,940	14,990	20,950	28,240	10.50

Source: Based on data in *Resources Asia* (December 1983), Figure 1, p. 4.

[a] Computed using the formula $Y_t = Y_0 e^n$.
[b] Includes India.
[c] Total capital expenditure for petroleum exploration and development in Asia-Pacific countries for 1982 was US$ 16.5 billion.

TABLE 4.1(c)
Western Pacific Rim: Major Petroleum Loans, 1982–83

Country	Borrower	Amount (US$ million)	Total Interest Rate Base	Purpose
Australia	Private	3,481.4	Libor[a]	Cooper Basin development and gas pipeline.
Indonesia	State and private	199.0	Libor and fixed	Term loans, aromatics plant.
Malaysia	State and private	688.0	Libor	LNG project and oil storage terminal.
New Zealand	Private and State	2,720.0	Libor	Methanol plant, synthetic gas-oline plant, refinery expansion.
Korea, South	State	38.0	Libor, USP[a]	Drilling rig.
Thailand	State	257.4	Libor, LTP[a]	Drawdown, gas separation plant.

Source: *Euromoney Syndication Guide* as published in *Far Eastern Economic Review* (1984).

[a] Legend: Libor = London inter-bank offered rate. USP = US prime rate. LTP = Japanese long-term prime rate.

geological costs, V = other variable costs, K = capital costs, G = government costs (e.g. taxes, royalties, etc.), r = the discount rate, X_1 = geological risks associated with petroleum search, X_2 = economic and technical risks associated with ordinary venture capital (such as unexpected changes in the market), X_3 = "political risk."

The Fiscal Regime

The general economic and political framework is the usual starting point for investment risk-ranking of a country. Table 4.2 shows in the countries under review (1) the relationship to total revenues of taxes on income, profits, and capital gains for 1975 and 1980 and (2) comparative macroeconomic information on the relationship to total revenue of corporate taxes and taxes on net income and profit collected in 1981. Since comparable data for the years desired were not available, two sets of data are presented to provide the reader with a feel for the changes over the period of oil price increases. The values in columns 1 and 3 are close, so that the 1981 data may be used as a surrogate for column 3. Indonesia's high percentage rate may be explained by its high dependence on the petroleum industry for revenues, as is usually the case for developing countries with extractive industries. Those of Singapore and Malaysia may only be partially explained by revenues from the petroleum industry. Tax levels could also be explained by the degree of privatization of major economic activities in these countries and the formal incorporation of such activities (see, for example, the Philippines and Thailand, which appear to have similar levels). This latter inference may be borne out by looking at the ratios in column 4 and the corporate tax rate listed in column 1 in Table 4.3. (The efficiency of tax collection systems may be a factor but no systematically collected information is available in this area.)

Table 4.2 shows that the level of government revenues derived from the taxation of labor and capital returns has very little apparent relation to judgements of the stability rankings of a country for investment purposes. In summary, aggregate data indicate very little in terms of the indirect influence of the general tax structure of the countries on the attractiveness of a country tax-wise to the petroleum investors. They do not explain why ratios differ highly even among the developing countries of the region. One can only seek explanations for variations in the country rankings among the specific variables that characterize the institutional framework of each country and influence investment behavior.

Table 4.3 shows that corporate tax rates applicable to petroleum investors in the different countries under review range from a low of 40 percent (the Philippines) to a high of 60 percent maximum (Thailand), where they are applicable. (Burma's national oil company is reported to assume the costs of all taxes imposed on petroleum contractors; the foreign companies that operated in Burma in the 1970s were not successful in their exploration, and this approach is therefore academic at this point.) Most tax rates are in the area of 45-55 percent.

Attempts by the Indonesian government to simplify its tax laws in 1983 have created concern over the effects on the net incomes and cash flows of both foreign employers and employees. These new laws provide, among other things, for elimination of the tax deductibility of employee fringe benefits as expenditures by a company; this means that it would be treated as income for the employee. It also provides for a withholding tax arrangement that is seen as cutting into available operating funds.[21]

There are other aspects of an investor's operation that influence the profitability of a venture. These are physical or monetary shares of the output from a project that must be turned over to the state, either in the form of royalties, output sharing, or profit-sharing. Royalties range from 1 percent (Japan) to 12.55 percent (Korea and Thailand) with variations and qualifications. Output-sharing rates range from 70/30 in favor of the state to Indonesia's latest agreement with Caltex of 88/12 in favor of the state.[22] Cost recovery allowances in production-sharing contracts (PSCs) and their variants affect the net share accruing to investors. The sizes of these allowances differ from 20-30 percent (Malaysia) to 49 percent upwards (China) and 50-70 percent (Philippines). The effective output share—when corporate tax rates, royalties and cost recovery allowances are taken into account—will differ significantly among countries according to the sizes of these variables.[23] Bonuses add further to the cost factor, while any type of control on the manner in which prices are set upstream or downstream affect the sizes of the net revenues. As Table 4.3 shows, a significant amount of intervention exists in the pricing of either crude oil or petroleum products in the countries reviewed. Directives related to the fiscal regime such as those connected with the use of Batam Island instead of Singapore for importing oil exploration and development equipment also affect costs if such directives result in less efficient handling and time loss or higher rates; this could, in turn, affect net revenue to the government if such costs increase the

TABLE 4.2

Western Pacific Rim: Comparative Macro Information on Corporate and
Other Taxes versus Stability Rankings
(Percent of Total Revenues except where not noted)

	Taxes on Income, Profits, and Capital Gains ($%)		Taxes on Net Income and Profit 1981 (%)	Corporate Taxes, 1981 (%)	1982 Stability Rankings by Three Research Firms[a]
	1975	1980			
East and Southeast Asia					
Burma	27.3	2.9	2.7	NA	NA
Indonesia	65.6	78.0	NA	NA	12, 8, NA
Korea, South	22.4	22.3	22.8	10.9	8, 7, 5
Malaysia	38.0	35.6[b]	36.8	29.9	6, 3, 6
Philippines	19.5	24.2	21.7	11.0	9, 10, 9[c]
Singapore	37.3	32.9[d]	31.9	NA	1, 1, 1
Thailand	16.0	19.6	21.4[c]	11.4[c]	11, 12, 7
Australasia					
Australia	64.7	62.2	63.5[d]	12.6[e]	4, 5, 3[f]
New Zealand	65.7	67.3	66.8	6.8	7, NA, NA

Source: Columns 1 and 2 are from the International Monetary Fund (1983).
Columns 3 and 4 are from the World Bank (1983).
Column 5 is from the *Asian Wall Street Journal* (1982).

Note: Data on Japan not available.

[a] Ranking: 1 = highest.
[b] 1979 data.
[c] Prior to economic deterioration of 1984–84.
[d] 1981 data.
[e] 1982 data.
[f] Prior to institution of resource rent tax in 1984.

NA = not available.

TABLE 4.3

Western Pacific Rim: Miscellaneous Revenue Determinants, Upstream and Downstream

Country	Corporate, Income, and Other Relevant Taxes	Royalty, or Output Sharing on Production[a]	Cost Recovery by Contractor	Bonuses to be Paid	Price Regulation
Australia	± 46%, levies on "old" and "new" oil, resource rent tax (RRT) on "green-fields" offshore.	R = Onshore: 10% Offshore: 10%–25% (may be reduced by government). Abolition proposed with use of RRT.	Allowable exploration and development costs.	Not specified.	Prices set by government.
Brunei	50% or rate in effect at time of agreement.	R = 8–12.5%	Normal allowable.	Not specified.	None.
Burma	Myanma Oil Corporation assumes all taxes	PS, sliding scale.	Variable, up to 40%.	Yes.	Prices set by government.
China	50% (on net income).	R = 17.5% per field (includes taxes[b]).	49% minimum.	US $1 million (signature plus variable offer).Not available.	
Indonesia	45% (plus 20% dividend tax).	PS: Variable, latest at 88/12.	Accounting depreciation according to field productivity, double declining method.	Variable.	Graduated.
Japan[c]	56.4%	R = 1%.	Normal accounting procedures.	Not specified.	Not on crude output. Ceiling on products

Country					
Korea, South	50%[d]	R = 12.5%	Assumed to follow normal accounting procedures.	Variable (all stages).	pre-1980 and spot purchases. Ceiling on petroleum products.
Malaysia	45% plus 25% on revenues from exports (imposed in 1980).	R = 10%	20% on oil, 25% on gas (1976); 30% on oil, 35% on gas (1982).	Variable.	Prices set by government.
New Zealand	45%	R = negotiated on individual contracts.	Assumed normal.	Not specified.	Set by government.
Philippines	39.875%[e]	PS: variable.	55–70%	Variable.	Crude at world prices. Product prices controlled.
Thailand	50–60% (maximum).	R = 12.5%.	Assumed normal.	Not specified.	Primary output prices negotiated, product prices controlled.

Source: Siddayao (1980), Barrows (1983), Petroleum Economist/Petro Consultants (1981), U.S. Department of Energy (1981), *Oil and Gas Journal* (3 September 1984), *Petroleum News* (July 1984), and *World Oil* (1 August 1984).

a Legend: R = royalties.   PS = production-sharing.
b In addition to output-sharing undeter terms of PSC or variant.
c Modified terms apply to Joint Development Zone with Korea.
d All other taxes, duties, and other charges are waived.
e Corporate tax = 35%; profit remittance tax = 75% x 7.5% = 4.875%. Total tax = 39.875%.

amount recoverable under the terms of the production sharing contract. Some of these features will be expanded upon in a later section.

The overall investment environment—including the stability of this environment—determines the investor's IRR. To a certain extent, the direction of the flow of commercial loans and direct investment upstream and downstream is an indicator of investors' perceptions of the economic viability of projects in these environments.

Investment Types

Table 4.4. shows the sources of investment funds in the petroleum industry in the countries reviewed. In every country listed, foreign investments are shown; details of the varying levels in the form of the number of investing companies or the amounts of the investments are given elsewhere.[24] The Korean government is reported to encourage Korean companies to seek joint ventures and explore for petroleum in the offshore areas of Korea. Brunei was also reporting to be seeking foreign investors in oil exploration.[25] These foreign investments are not always solely from private companies. State-owned companies (such as the Japan National Oil Company and the Korea Petroleum Development Corporation) are involved in overseas ventures in the region (and elsewhere). The state-run Chinese Petroleum Corporation (CPC) of Taiwan is reported to have entered a joint venture with the PNOC Exploration Corporation in the Philippines in 1984.[26] Japan's Burma Petroleum Development Company is reported to have financed the exploration that led to the discovery of offshore gas fields in the Gulf of Martaban of Burma (although no indications exist at this writing that similar financing will be arranged for the development of those fields.)[27]

Table 4.5 shows the activity level of Japanese exploration companies in different parts of the world. Its drilling level in Asia in the three phases of the upstream stage is more than half its total worldwide. In some cases, drilling participation comes as funds provided for exploration programs, rather than in the form of active participation as operator or technical partner. The returns to such investments or loan repayments are made in the form of oil or natural gas as profit shares.[28] Other forms of innovative financing are reported. For example, a scheme identified as "evergreen revolving hydrocarbon credit" is reported to be already in use in Asia. In this type of financing, a highly discounted value is assigned to proven production reserves and a company can borrow against it on an ongoing basis. The funds received can then be used for exploration.[29]

There is significant direct state involvement in both the upstream and downstream operations in the region in the form of direct investments and subsidies to state-owned companies. These companies may be engaged in exploration for or in developing petroleum resources, or they may be involved in transporting oil or gas from Asian countries to the investor's home countries. Direct state

involvement does not necessarily mean that such funds are from internally generated revenues. China, the Philippines and Thailand, for example, have
received World Bank loans for oil and gas development projects.[30] Some funds
are also borrowed at commercial rates; see Table 4.1(c) again.

Some capital flows are required to address shifts in the market. A good
example is Singapore, which has to upgrade its refinery facilities to cope with

TABLE 4.4.

Western Pacific Rim: Ownership and Contractual Form,
Upstream and Downtream
(Selected Countries)

| Country | Upstream | | Downstream |
	Nationality of Operators	Contractual Form	Types of Ownership
Australia	F, P.	Onshore: varies with each state. Offshore: exploration permits and production licenses.	F, P. 50% Australian equity required.
Burma	F, G.	Concession and PSC.	G.
China	F, G.	PSC variant offshore.	G.
Indonesia	F, G.	PSC.	G.
Japan	F, G.	Exploration permits and production licenses.	F, P. 50% Japanese equity required. State assistance provided.
Korea, South	F, G.	Concessions.	F, P, G.
Malaysia	F, G.	PSC with royalty payments.	F, G.
New Zealand	F, P, G.	Prospecting and mining licenses. F, P, G.	
Philippines	F, P, G.	PSC variant (risk service).	F, P, G and joint F-G.
Thailand	F, P, G.	Concession.	F, P and joint F-P-G.

Sources: Siddayao (1984), Barrows (1983), *Oil and Gas Journal* (7 May 1984), p. 76,
Petroleum Economist/Petroleum Consultants (1981), *Petroleum News* (January 1984),
Resources Asia (December 1983), *World Oil* (1 August 1984).

[a] Legend:
  F = foreign companies, both private and state-owned.
  P = domestic private companies.
  G = domestic state-run agencies.
  PSC = production-sharing contract.

TABLE 4.5
Japan's Drilling Log

| Area | Includes Onshore and Offshore Wells | | | |
	1980	1981	1982	Total
Middle East				
Exploration	4	5	5	14
Development	8	14	5	27
Production	83	55	88	226
Total	94	74	98	267
North and South America				
Exploration	0	3	0	3
Development	0	1	0	1
Production	0	0	0	0
Total	0	4	0	4
Asia and Australia				
Exploration	37	31	24	92
Development	22	44	44	110
Production	74	94	101	269
Total	133	169	169	471
Africa				
Exploration	1	2	7	10
Development	2	3	1	6
Production	7	16	10	33
Total	10	21	18	49
GRAND TOTALS				
Exploration	423	41	36	119
Development	32	62	50	144
Production	164	165	199	528
Total	238	268	285	791

Source: *Offshore*, 20 July 1984, Vol. 44, No. 8.

the loss of processing arrangements with Indonesia and the influx of petroleum products from the Middle East, especially Kuwait. Term contracts later signed with China may offset the lost market. In any case, Singapore's refining industry is switching over from producing low-value fuel oils into higher-value middle distillates such as kerosene and diesel. The new hydrocracker will help the Singapore Refining Company, for one, compete with similar refineries recently completed in Indonesia. In Singapore's case, its economic stature provides it with relatively easy access to capital investments for its downstream operations.[31]

Capital investments are not generally as easily available domestically for petroleum projects. Except for Japan, which provides a significant amount of the capital flows within the region, most countries—including Australia and New Zealand—which seek the development of indigenous oil and gas (both for domestic consumption and for export) are aware that domestic capital sources are inadequate to meet current financing demands. Yet, as the discussion in the following sections show, certain aspects of the institutional frameworks in many of these countries suggest that policy planners do not appear to recognize the limitations of those frameworks in terms of achieving both national goals and overall allocative efficiency.

GOVERNMENT INVOLVEMENT IN OIL AND GAS IN THE REGION

Intervention levels vary by country and by industry stage. The country with the least amount of private sector involvement is Burma, where all types of foreign investment in the petroleum industry are allowed only according to specific targets set by the government with reference to a specific activity, upstream or downstream. All other countries have different (and sometimes parallel) types of intervention and involvement. The outline in Table 5.1 implies the degree of such intervention. The agency or agencies involved in supra-operational as well as in operational capacities are listed.[32]

To appreciate the degree of intervention by the state in the oil and gas sector of the western Pacific rim countries and to appreciate the arguments presented

TABLE 5.1

Western Pacific Rim: Government Involvement in the Petroleum Industry

Country	Agencie(s)	Areas of Involvement[a]
Australia	Various state governments. Federal: Department of National Development and Energy; Prices Justification Tribunal (PJT).	State: U, leases; D, pricing. Federal: U, taxation policies, ownership ratios, pricing, etc. PJT: D, on pricing.
Brunei	Brunei Petroleum Unit.	Policy only. New legislation reported which requires state partnership in ventures.
Burma	Ministry of Industry and Myanma Oil Corporation.	U, D.
China	State Energy Commission, Ministry of Petroleum Industry, National Oil and Gas Exploration and Development Corporation, and China National Oil Corporation, (CNOC).	U, D.

(continued)

TABLE 5.1 (Continued)

Western Pacific Rim: Government Involvement in the Petroleum Industry

Indonesia	Ministry of Mines and Energy; Pertamina.	Ministry: U Pertamina: U, D including petrochemicals and LNG.
Japan	Ministry of International Trade and Industry (MITI), Agency for Natural Resources (ANRE), Japan National Oil Company (JNOC).	U, D.
Korea, South	Ministry of Energy and Resources Korea Petroleum Development Corporation (PEDCO), Korean Oil Development Company (KODECO), Korean Electric Power Company (KEPCO).	PEDCO: U and overseas purchases. KODECO: D. KEPCO: D (LNG).
Malaysia	Ministry of Energy, Telecom, and Post Petroliam Nasional Bhd. (Petronas), Petronas Carigaloi, and Malaysian LNG Bhd. (MLNG).	Ministry: Policy only. Petronas et al.: U, D.
New Zealand	Ministry of Energy (MOE), Petroleum Corporation of New Zealand (Petrocorp), and Liquids Fuels Trust Board (LFTB).	MOE: U. Petrocorp: U, D. LFTB: gas.
Philippines	Ministry of Energy, Bureau of Energy Development, Philippine National Oil Company.	U, D.
Thailand	Department of Mineral Resources, Defense Energy Department (DED), Petroleum Authority of Thailand (PTT), and Thai LNG Company (TLNG, semi-govt.).	DED: U, northern onshore area. PTT: U, D. TLNG: D.

Sources: Siddayao (1984), *Petroleum News* (January 1984), *Oil and Gas Journal* (7 May 1984, 27 August 1984), *Petroleum Economist* (November 1984), U.S. Department of Energy (1981).

[a] U = upstream, d = downstream.

in this paper, however, a summary of the important features of such intervention is given below.[33]

Australia

The Australian government increased its role in the management of Australia's natural resources with the election into office of a new government in 1977. Legislation was enacted which, among other things, did the following: (1) Various exploration and development tax deductions and subsidies previously enjoyed by petroleum companies were eliminated. (2) Price controls on domestic crude oil were imposed. (3) Foreign equity ownership in energy development projects was restricted.

The government elected in 1975 attempted to restore some of the incentives that had been removed by the previous government, but maintained a policy of limiting foreign equity in new hydrocarbon ventures to 50 percent. It also adopted a "new oil" vs. "old oil" policy; it raised the domestic price of crude oil from new fields towards parity with the landed cost of crude oil imports. By 16 August 1978 several measures which had been adopted led to raising the price of oil supplied to refiners from Australian production to parity with imports; by August 1980 half of existing production was priced at import parity.

The Australian government influences petroleum prices through its taxation policies. Additionally, the Prices Justification Tribunal is empowered to inquire into and report on prices charged by companies.

A variety of new institutions were also set up after the 1977 election of a new government, including (1) the Department of National Development which has primary responsibility for energy policy, and (2) a National Petroleum Advisory Committee which would arrange for the equitable allocation of liquid fuels in supply emergencies. The new government also allowed expenditures on petroleum exploration and development to be deducted against total income.

A deviation from this trend occurred, which reversed some of the benefits from this policy when a new government entered in 1982. Current fiscal arrangements include the following: (1) Excise taxes on oil discovered before September 1975 continue. (2) A higher levy on "new oil" (discovered post-September 1975) onshore and offshore is in effect. (3) A "resource rent tax" (RRT) was introduced in 1984 that would apply to "greenfields" offshore which had not reached the development stage. (The RRT will be analyzed more closely in a later section, together with the cost-recovery allowance in the production-sharing type of contracts introduced by Indonesia.)

Brunei

Brunei's legislative council, which became an equal partner with Shell in 1975, is reported to have enacted new laws in April 1983 which would require this equity ratio in all future ventures. No details are available to this author at this writing.

China

The State Energy Commission, which was founded on 26 August 1980, is responsible for energy production and conversation in the People's Republic of China. It formulates and implements petroleum policies through the Ministry of Petroleum. Two other state enterprises are identified as part of the petroleum institutional framework; these are the China National Oil and Gas Exploration and Development Corporation and the China National Offshore Oil Corporation. Among their goals are (1) the improvement of secondary recovery techniques in China's older fields in order to maintain current production levels, and (2) the encouragement of Western investment in the Chinese oil industry, particularly in offshore areas, as part of its goal of importing foreign technology to improve its ability to discover and produce new fields.

Indonesia

The nucleus of the petroleum sector in Indonesia is Pertamina (which is short for Perushahaan Pertambangan Minyak dan Gas Bumi Negara). Formed in 1971 and merging three nationally-owned companies, Pertamina is responsible for all petroleum activities, including exploration, production, transportation, refining, and marketing. It also exercises supervisory control over the operations of foreign oil companies.

Indonesia has a Ministry of Mines and Energy, under which is the Directorate of Oil and Gas. The Directorate has responsibility for overseeing the basic activities of Pertamina, Contract of Work holders, and through Pertamina the operators with production sharing contracts. This office is also principally responsible for hydrocarbon development policy.

Pertamina is obligated to make available to the public unlimited quantities of eight fuel products at prices which are set by the government. If revenues from the sale of those products do not cover the costs (crude, refining, storage, transportation, and distribution), the government makes direct payment to Pertamina to cover the loss.

Korea

The Ministry of Energy and Resources (MER) was e' tablished in 1978 to coordinate overall energy policy in South Korea. The K' *ea* Petroleum Development Corporation (PEDCO) is a 100-percent government-funded state enterprise responsible for petroleum exploration/development and for the management of production and refining facilities. PEDCO is responsible for overseas purchases and is also in charge of the emergency petroleum reserve established by MER, intended to improve Korea's energy supply security. This includes efforts to engage in direct government-to-government deals with oil-producing nations. The Korean government also subsidizes the transportation of crude imports from Mexico, Ecuador, Libya, and Egypt—as part of its policy of diversifying its oil supply sources away from the Middle East. PEDCO is also heavily involved in providing the country with LPG.[34]

The Korea Oil Development Company (KODECO), formed in 1979, developed an offshore oilfield in Indonesia jointly with that country's NOC Pertamina, and the first shipment in exchange for development funds arrived in Korea in September 1984. With Asian Development Bank financing, the Korea Electric Power Company (KEPCO) has begun to implement the country's programme of utilizing gas more heavily. This involves an LNG contract signed by KEPCO with Pertamina, with plans to import LNG from Malaysia in the offing. The necessary infrastructure for receiving the LNG and distributing the gas is under development.[35]

Japan

Japan's Basic Petroleum Law of 1962 limits the role of foreign oil companies by curtailing their equity shares and the growth of refining and marketing operations. By the 1970s the refining sector was close to 50 percent Japanese-owned.

The law gave the Ministry of International Trade and Industry (MITI) the right to: (1) grant licenses for new refinery construction and permits for expansion or remodelling of older ones; (2) control refinery operation levels; (3) regulate the price of crude oil imports by reviewing refiners' operating plans; and (4) control petroleum product prices.

Government price regulation was initially felt in January 1974 when a ceiling was placed on the wholesale prices of kerosene and other oil products. "Administrative guidance" on petroleum product prices was removed towards the end of 1979.

In response to cutbacks on third-party sales by the majors in 1979, MITI (1) encouraged domestic oil companies to secure crude directly from oil-production states, and (2) raised the price ceiling for spot market purchases.

MITI also established the Agency for Natural Resources and Energy. This agency has direct jurisdiction over natural resources and responsibility for implementing the country's overall energy program and planning, including the review of foreign investment applications.

MITI's mandate includes providing assistance to independent Japanese companies in expanding their activities domestically and overseas by: (1) offering low-interest loans to both upstream and downstream operations, (2) giving these companies preferences in domestic refinery applications and favorable marketing quota allocations for service stations, (3) providing diplomatic assistance to enable these companies to obtain favorable foreign exploration agreements, and (4) providing them with assured access to the Japanese market for foreign petroleum developed under such arrangements.

The Japanese Petroleum Development Corporation (JPDC) was created in

1967 to serve as a catalyst for Japanese overseas petroleum exploration and development initiatives. Its functions were expanded in 1972 to include the provision of financial incentives (loans and equity capital) for stockpiling by both private companies and joint government/industry ventures. In 1978 JPDC's name was changed to the Japan National Oil Company (JNOC) with enabling legislation that gave it responsibility for developing Japan's strategic oil reserve. JNOC's scope includes the provision of loans for financing private projects as well as equity capital for both upstream and downstream ventures. JNOC furthermore guarantees the financial overseas projects of Japanese companies.

JNOC acts as an agent for the direct acquisition of overseas petroleum rights but this is predicated on the transfer of such rights to a private party. The government was reported to have increased its subsidy for domestic exploration in 1984 by 19 percent over the 1983 budget, for a total allocation of US$14.2 million. Higher taxes on crude oil imports and new taxes on LNG and LPG are also reported to have been imposed in 1984 to replenish the tax-based fund for the development of new energy sources that had been depleted as oil prices fell in the 1980s.[36]

Malaysia

Malaysia's Petroleum (Income Tax) Act of 1967 governing petroleum taxation provided for a 50/50 profit-sharing policy. Neither this law or the Petroleum Rules Act of 1968, which called for compulsory surrender of 50 percent of an original concession area, specified the rules for ownership or government participation.

The Petroleum Development Act of 1974 established the national oil company, Petronas (short for Petroliam Nasional Berhad), which was made directly responsible to the Prime Minister. It was envisioned that Petronas would eventually assume full ownership and exclusive rights to all of the oil and gas in the country, as well as to all processing and petrochemical operations.[37] Petronas is responsible for petroleum pricing.

Two other national companies are active in the oil and gas area. Petronas Carigali Sdn. Bhd., Petronas' exploration subsidiary, is responsible for government-funded exploration. The Malaysian LNG Berhard (MLNG) is a joint venture between Petronas (65 percent), Shell Gas BV (17.5), and Mitsubishi (17.5); it was formed to build and run an LNG plant, the output from which would be purchased by Japan's Tokyo Electric and Tokyo Gas. Production started in 1983.

The Malaysian government has also commissioned a methanol plant to use flared gas from Shell's operations; this plant was expected to start up in late 1984. Additionally, Esso Production Malaysia will provide flared gas from its operations off Peninsular Malaysia Natural Gas Utilization Project to supply 50 percent of the supply of a power plant on the east coast. Petronas Carigali will supply the balance from its own fields south of the Esso contract area.

While Petronas has the responsibility for implementing policies directly affecting the oil and gas sector, overall country energy policy-making is undertaken by a special energy unit in the Ministry of Energy, Telecommunications, and Post, which was set up in 1982.[38]

New Zealand

The Petroleum Corporation of New Zealand (Petrocorp), a government-owned enterprise, has sole or part interest in at least 19 of a total of about 50 permits, mostly offshore, to explore for oil and gas. The Ministry of Energy (which was a merger of the Ministry of Mines and Electricity with the Ministry of Energy Resources in 1978) is responsible for overall energy development programs. The Liquids Fuels Trust Board (LFTB), established in 1978, makes recommendations to the Ministry of Energy on matters pertaining to the use of indigenous natural gas in reducing the country's dependence on imported oil for transport fuels. An Energy Advisory Service under the Ministry of Works and Development advises companies and industries on the efficient use of energy.

The government sets the prices of natural gas and coal against that of oil. Its first pricing policy was established in 1976. Energy prices are set at levels that will allow recovery of the cost of production and encourage increased substitution of indigenous fuels for imported oil. With oil indexed at 100, gas was indexed in 1978 at 75, and coal at 73. Tax incentives are used to encourage the direct use of natural gas, with grants for 25 percent of capital expenditures related to LPG and interest-free loans for home insulation. Increased road-user taxes and progressive sales taxes related to automobile size were also expected to encourage oil conservation.

The state owns shares in petrochemical plants and will be joint owner of the natural gas plants with Mobil.

A tax policy change in 1979 was expected to stimulate hydrocarbon exploration by foreign and domestic investors.

As part of the policy shift, the role of Petrocorp has been reduced. The government is reported to be providing less funds for Petrocorp's operations. Petrocorp will have to fund its operations and the government's 51 percent share in development projects from retained earnings, borrowing in the open market, and farm out of some of its acreage interests. Interest payments and loan repayments are to be paid from government's share of revenues from output.[39]

The Philippines

The National Power Corporation was created in 1936 to develop energy resources; the Bureau of Mines administered petroleum exploration concessions. It was not until the 1973-74 price increases that national policy gave energy demand and supply programs a high priority. The present institutional structure evolved over the succeeding period. It currently consists of the Ministry of Energy and several state-owned companies, including the Philippine National Oil Company (PNOC) and its subsidiaries or affiliates. PNOC has special responsibilities in the country's petroleum refining, marketing, transportation, and development activities.

PNOC (which bought out the Esso marketing and refining subsidiary in the Philippines in the early 1970s) controls about 60 percent of the Bataan refinery; this refinery was jointly owned with Mobil until 1983, when Mobil sold its shares to Caltex (reportedly below book value).[40] PNOC controls about 40 percent of the domestic product market. Over half of Philippine oil imports are purchased on a government-to-government basis by PNOC and distributed to all refineries (including those privately-owned). It also has developed an ocean transport capability, owning as many as three tankers in 1981 and controlling 90 percent of product tanker lifting capability and all barge lifting capabilities.

The Bureau of Energy Development (BED) monitors and issues exploration service contracts to private contractors, both domestic and foreign. The Bureau of Energy Utilization (BEU) monitors the refining and marketing activities of the private companies. However, the distinction between the status of BED and BEU staff relative to those of PNOC is fuzzy at times. Whereas PNOC is run as a profit-making corporation and pays industry-competitive salaries, BED and BEU are technically government bureaus (which places them within the oversight of the government's Civil Service Commission). Some BED and BEU staff are, however, PNOC-appointees seconded to these government bureaus, and they move back and forth. The Minister of Energy, for example, is also the Chairman of PNOC, and one of the PNOC vice presidents is Deputy Minister. Hence, the boundary separating the policy-making and monitoring area from that of serving as a supplier of oil services (or the supra-operational versus the operational aspects of government intervention) is a gray area in this country.

Singapore

The Singapore government's involvement in the petroleum industry is mainly limited to equity ownership in two refining companies. The Singapore Refining Company (SRC) is 40-percent owned by the Singapore Petroleum Company (SPC) along with Caltex and British Petroleum, which own 30 percent each. SPC is, in turn, owned by three private companies and the Development Bank of Singapore, which has a 31⅓ percent share. The Singapore government established the Singapore National Oil Corporation (SNOC) in 1981, in partnership with Elf-Aquitaine and Total, to operate a sixth refinery. Currently, however, SNOC's responsibilities are limited to interacting with the oil companies and the Public Utilities Board to ensure adequacy of the country's oil supplies.[41] The Singapore government, through the companies in which it holds equity, owns some tankage. There were also reports that the Prime Minister had engaged in talks with Indonesia about the utilization of natural gas from the Natunas area in Singapore.

Petroleum prices at both the crude and the product level are, however, not controlled by the government.

Thailand

The Thai government has traditionally allowed the private sector to be principally responsible for oil and gas exploration, development, refining, and marketing. The Natural Gas Organization (NGOT) was formed in 1977 upon commercial discovery of natural gas in the Gulf of Thailand. The principal purpose of this agency was the management of gas transmission and distribution once production started. NGOT was also responsible for negotiating the transfer pricing terms between the petroleum companies and the users (principally the power sector).

In 1978 the Petroleum Authority of Thailand (PTT in short, according to Thai documents) was established to coordinate all oil and gas activities. It took over NGOT and the small government marketing outlet called Oil Fuel Organization, which had been formed earlier to complement private sector activities. PTT exercises control over crude purchases and product distribution.

PTT is under the Ministry of Industry. Within this Ministry is a Department of Mineral Resources, which oversees oil and gas exploration and the licensing of such activities. The Ministry also develops taxation policies and sets wholesale prices.

In December 1979 the government decided to take a 49 percent share in the Thai Oil Refinery Company Ltd. (TORC). Its other owners include Shell, Caltex, and other private companies. A semi-governmental enterprise called the Thai LNG Company was also reported to have been formed, with 60 percent capital provided by the Thai government and 40 percent by four major Japanese trading companies.[42]

The Thai government, through the PTT, is also reported to be arranging to set up a Petroleum Institute. This would be a non-profit academic organization designed to promote education in petroleum exploration and production.[43]

THE INSTITUTIONAL FRAMEWORK: SOME ALLOCATIVE IMPLICATIONS

The foregoing sections raise many allocative issues. It is not possible to discuss all of them in this paper.[44] It will be useful, therefore, to concentrate on a few topics, with emphasis on more recent developments; these are associated with (1) the role of national companies upstream and downstream, in domestic and foreign operations, and (2) the fiscal regime in the upstream stage.

State Intervention in the Form of National Oil Companies

Various explanations have been provided to justify the role of government in the petroleum sector and the formation of national oil companies.[45] This author's view of the roles of government and, where necessary, of a state-owned or national oil company was outlined in Section II of this paper. As Section V shows, however, the roles assumed by the state companies in the region vary. In the producting LDCs, the NOC can be both a regulator of other companies and an active participant in upstream and/or downstream activities (see, for example, Pertamina, Petronas, PNOC, and PTT). The reasons for their existence may have nothing to do with the conditions outlined in Section II. In the net-oil importers that also have financial capability, the NOC monitors other investors and also holds primary responsibility for achieving the energy supply security objectives of the country (see, for example, South Korea, and Japan). In the latter case, such responsibility includes investments overseas. In both the lower-income and higher-income oil importers, direct government-to-government deals and stockpiling are part of the NOC's responsibilities.

Active participation of the NOC raises no issue with regard to misallocation if the NOC does not draw upon a state's resources to survive in competition with other investors or if it does not hinder their efficient operation through unfair practices, such as undue preferences to markets where it would not otherwise survive. Since any economic activity involves the element of risk—in varying degrees—it is not clear that it is in a society's best interests that state resources be deployed in such activities, unless it can be shown that the private sector is not available to undertake activities that are considered socially necessary. Thus, the active involvement of NOCs in exploration—which is a highly risky, capital-intensive venture—may be questioned in terms of the efficient allocation of a state's resources where private investments are available. Yet, as proliferation of unorganized data will show, this occurs frequently in the region. It can thus be argued that, in the upstream stage of the industry, use of a state's limited resources to undertake the risks of exploring frontier areas raises allocative issues.

To reiterate that exploration is risky and that the discount rate for risk changes inversely with knowledge about an area is not to overstate one's case. The Mukluk "dry hole" was a US$1.6 billion loss, one of the biggest exploration investment losses in recent history. It is a timely reminder that, with all the advances in exploration technology, the only known method to date to establish the true potential of an area is by drilling.[46]

The overseas operations of NOCs is another area of interest. Section V noted that some NOCs actively engage in the upstream phases of the industry overseas or, at the minimum, provide assistance to private national firms attempting to invest in the upstream sector in producing countries. Where subsidies are involved to promote the home country's energy security goals, the premium paid may be justified by the state in terms of the future security of supply. It is not clear, however, whether the producing country or the rest of society is well served and that investments are, in fact, efficiently allocated in this manner. In other words, when an enterprise's funds are provided at interest below the opportunity costs of the normal investor or where "diplomatic assistance" is provided by the NOC to its nationals, effective competition for investment opportunities does not exist. Does this result in the optimal development of the region's petroleum resources? Is the receiving country truly benefitting from this exchange where inequality exists in bargaining positions among those competing for the right to develop the host country's petroleum? Are the investing country's taxpayer's well-served by the loss of revenue from such concessionary loans? The answer is not clearly negative or positive. All we know is that a significant amount of upstream and downstream investments are emanating from NOCs in the region, that these investments will eventually result in the movement of petroleum from the producing countries to the investing country, and that some investors are left out by the arrangement. At issue is imperfect information with respect to a "buyer's" alternatives.

Government investments in and control over refining or marketing facilities may be justified if private investors are not available within the country. Undue advantage in the domestic marketing of products can raise issues of efficiency in the use of state resources if no clear benefits result from such ownership or control, especially where the efficiency of such operations owing to lack of competition is impaired. Casual observation and some of the popular literature suggest this to be the case. Furthermore, where NOC investment in refineries precludes its taking advantage of the economies of scale in the home country or the region and, in the process, increases overall unused capacity, allocative efficiency issues on a global level are pertinent.

The desire of a home country to capture the value added in processing or the rents from the sale of petroleum products needs to be weighed against the costs of such investments. It is not clear that such trade-offs were the primary consideration in the construction of new refineries in producing countries or in new state investments in others. Because of the highly capital-intensive nature of the industry, a question could be raised with respect to the opportunity cost of reallocating those funds away from other industrial activities that might have larger proportions of domestic value added and a higher multiplier-accelerator effect on income and employment. The only thing that is clear is that trading and investment patterns are changing, and so are the relationships among the buying and selling countries. At this writing, it is also reported that refining capacity in the region significantly exceeds processing requirements.[47]

The proliferation of NOCs also exacerbates what has been identified as "lack of information" among the actors in the region. One of the conditions for efficiency of an economic activity is the existence of perfect information. That buyers and sellers must deal with uncertainty in real life is not arguable. To be partly responsible for increasing that uncertainty is another matter altogether. The multiplication of such uncertainty, given the complexity of petroleum trading in the region, and its implications for investment decisions may be gleaned from the following quotation from Fesharaki (1984): "All the actors . . . are fully aware of their own activities, but know little about other actors in the region or the changes outside the region which affect their operation. It is, therefore, often difficult to put together a whole picture and devise strategies to deal with impending change." (p. 3). It is tempting to suggest at this point that multinationals, having to address a larger scale picture, may be better able to deal with this problem; the evidence for a categorical statement is not available in this respect,[48] but again the overall efficiency implications and costs of the recent increase in refineries that are state-owned cannot be overlooked.

Section V also noted that NOCs engage in direct government-to-government deals to procure petroleum supplies: in many cases this means that the NOC then supplies other refineries the crude for their plants. This approach does not necessarily guarantee the best price for the country concerned. After all, NOCs are small buyers and, therefore, have relatively less bargaining power in dealing with a supplier than a large integrated company. Furthermore, a multinational's bargaining power is enhanced by its access to a variety of sources not necessarily open to small buyers. Again, however, the perceived security associated with such deals may outweigh the true social costs of such arrangements. There is no guarantee that large buyers will pass their savings on to their customers in pricing refined products. The low prices to customers preceding OPEC's dominance of the market would tend to suggest, however, that this is not unlikely.

The severity of the costs associated with errors in judgement associated with NOC purchasing may not be passed over lightly. Although not directly related to the trade of petroleum in the region, it may be useful to recall the issue of information and bargaining power. The Japan National Oil Company was created as a result of growing concern over the security of Japanese oil supplies if it continued to depend on the international companies. There was concern over the ability of these companies to deal with OPEC and a desire to have greater control over Japan's supply security. It is well known among petroleum analysts and market observers that spot market prices were partially driven up in 1979 by panic buying on the part of the Japanese government, which decided to increase its stockpile to levels far above its usual 90-day minimum (stockpiles were reported to have gone as high as 140-day levels). It is also public knowledge that they later had to sell some of these stocks at a loss (of about $4.00/bbl.) because of storage problems. What is the optimum social premium to be paid for energy security? Is this a luxury that Japan can afford? Can less affluent countries afford the costs of similar errors? What was the cost to the rest of the world of this error? For, indeed, the high prices were paid for not only by the Japanese but also by other oil importers, including the developing countries.

The move in the Western Pacific countries towards increased use of state resources for activities that are normally undertaken by private funds contrasts with the increasing commercialization in formerly non-market economies like Burma and China.

The Fiscal Regime

For the purposes of this paper, the fiscal regime will be defined as the deliberate choice of taxes and tax-type elements to influence economic activities in the petroleum sector. The usual intention is to raise revenues for the government, but in the extractive sector fiscal policy is also intended to capture rents that are associated with the production and supply of output. Thus, cost recovery allowances, royalties, general corporate taxes, output sharing ratios, bonuses, the pricing and marketing clauses, and—more recently—resource rent taxes form part of the fiscal regime. In this paper, only the cost-recovery clause in production sharing contracts (PSC) and the resource rent tax (RRT) introduced effective 1 July 1984 in Australia (which grants licenses to exploration companies) will be discussed.[49] These two features of two different fiscal regimes were chosen because of a clear similarity in their restrictive application. The cost-recovery clause of the PSC precludes recovery of losses by an operator from a contract area that turns out to be unsuccessful (or "dry") from the returns of a contract area that is successful. The RRT is to be applied separately to each individual project and not to aggregate company results.

The resource rent tax has been proposed as an optimal way of capturing the benefits from developing a resource while at the same time avoiding initial disincentives to investors.[50] This tax is collected only after a specified "threshold" discounted-cash-flow internal rate of return (IRR) on total cash flow has been realized. The "threshold" was defined by the Australian government as the "long term bond rate" (currently about 14 percent) plus 15 percentage points," and the RRT rate set at 40 percent.[51] The final version for initial implementation in late 1984 was expected to have a threshold still tied to the bond rate.[52] The RRT is levied prior to company tax and payments of RRT will be a deduction for company tax purposes.

The RRT's proponents suggest that this tax precludes the need to predict the inherently uncertain future profitability of a project, since the actual tax liability adjusts automatically and progressively to the outcome. It is claimed that risk in a project is actually shared by both investor and government when the RRT is adopted. Because the RRT starts only after the threshold IRR has been earned on the investment, the RRT is not expected to act as a deterrent to investments that are marginal in nature.[53] The strong interventionist nature of the RRT raises many related questions.

Assessing a rent tax based on the IRR of a company for a project assumes that such information is easily available. To assume this information is available for a project or even more for an investor's overall operations is to be highly optimistic. In Garnaut and Ross (1983) where the RTT approach is presented in detail, the authors implicitly assumed that cash flows represent economic rent. Since dividends do not represent the IRR where cash is set aside for reinvestment in expansion or in new ventures, then an RRT on cash flows would be taxing a portion of what the authors call "the supply price of capital" or part of what economists generally refer to as a "fair return on investment."

The Australian government has linked the threshold to the bond rate plus an additional charge. This is obviously an effort to deal with the heroic ideal of determining the appropriate threshold without knowing a company's IRR. There is no reason to believe that an exploration investor's IRR is close to the prevailing bond rate in a country. We only need to recall the notions of technical, economic, and "political" risks that are part of the foreign petroleum investor's discounting process to appreciate this.

The project-by-project basis for RRT suggests that the tax may be more conveniently tried in a small developing country, or a country with few petroleum projects. A problem arises in the application of this approach to a large country with many deposits, where a project-by-project calculation of a rent taxation scheme of the nature proposed would be administratively costly and could be socially counterproductive.

Even if such a scheme were inherently free of other problems, there remains the question of simplicity in administering the tax and monitoring it effectively and efficiently in a country where many projects exist. Consider the administrative costs of allocating resources to determining the resource rent tax for individual projects in Indonesia, for example, with its many fields. A new bureaucracy would be required to handle such a complex task. Proponents may implicitly assume—heroically—that bureaucracies can be designed to enhance a society's welfare; yet as Norgaard (1984) points out, to argue that this is so is mythology. It may further be argued that bureaucracies do not generally work well, whether in industrialized countries or in those less so.

Another principal problem with assessing a rent tax on a project basis rather than on an exploration company's overall operations within a country is similar to that identified for the cost-recovery clause of the Indonesian-type PSC. It is generally acknowledged that a significant proportion of capital investments for both upstream and downstream activities comes from internally generated corporate sources. Keenan (1981) estimated that even for downstream capital needs alone—where risks are relatively lower—as much as 73 percent normally comes from internal corporate sources. Even with the new schemes available (e.g., the "evergreen" hydrocarbon revolving credit already mentioned), one can expect that, in general, at least that proportion will come from internal funds for the riskier upstream operations, especially for oil and gas. By focusing on projects rather than on overall operations within a country, the RRT reduces that source of funds and can thus serve as a disincentive to risk-bearing.

Garnaut-Ross recognized that the RRT has a "bias towards under-investment under conditions of uncertainty . . . " (op. cit., p. 136). This shortcoming is, however, not sufficiently stressed in their book, nor is it treated at all in the *Outline* which served as the basis for its adoption in Australia. Petroleum exploration and development is perhaps one of the best examples of a venture involving a high degree of uncertainty with regard to outcome. As in the case of the Indonesian PSC, the RRT would influence risk-adverse investors to restrict search for new sources to areas where sufficient information exists to favor expectations of a higher probability of success than failure; this would result in under-investment in frontier areas. Game theoretic models have suggested that a government's share of economic rent increases in some direct proportion to the amount of information an interested investor has on a prospective exploration area.[54] Since definitive information on potential cannot be obtained without drilling, the RRT thus appears to have all the demerits associated with the U.S. "windfall profits tax" and more.[55] Observations in 1984 that the continued high levels of drilling activity in Australia suggest that the feared negative industry response had not materialized fail to specify the characteristics of the activities. The same popular observation was made of Indonesian activity in the late 1970s. Yet, the concentration of contracts in certain areas in Indonesia, especially those already known to be successful, is evidence of rational investor response to the risk element in the PSC.

The implications of the contractual framework for the behavioral response of profit-maximizing or cost-minimizing rationale firms may be gleaned from the number of operators in Indonesia and Malaysia, for example, that bear the names of the majors such as Shell and Exxon (e.g., Sabah Shell and Sarawak Shell in Malaysia). One might well ask if this multiplication of subsidiary companies is an efficient way of organizing economic activity and if the costs that might accrue to society as a result could very well have been spent more effectively on another economic activity.

It will be useful at this point to review some basic concepts in taxation.[56]

a. The economics of taxation bears not only on the financing aspect but on the level and allocation of resource use as well as on the distribution of income among consumers. The public sector operates interactively with the private sector. Not only do the effects of expenditure and tax policies depend upon the reaction of the private sector, but the need for fiscal measures is determined by how the private sector would perform in their absence.

b. Obviously, an economy cannot operate without a public sector. And the operation of a public new sector requires the financing of such operations. The issue at hand, then, is what the best approach might be to raising such revenues without adversely affecting the performance of the private sector or worsening the distribution of income. There are several fiscal devices. Whatever approach is chosen, it is important to consider not only the resulting gain in revenues or improved income distribution, but also the possible effects on the efficiency of the economy. In the final analysis, the productivity of the various inputs in the production function of the economy will be the ultimate criterion of the effectiveness of a chosen approach.

c. Economists and social philosophers, from Adam Smith on, have propounded what the requirements of a "good tax structure" are. One of those is that taxes should be chosen so as to minimize interference with economic decisions in otherwise efficient markets. At the same time, taxes may be used to correct inefficiencies in the private sector provided they are a suitable instrument for doing so. Another criterion is that the tax system should permit efficient administration. Proponents of a fiscal regime in the petroleum sector are not exempt from these criteria.

CONCLUDING REMARKS

Several inferences may be drawn from the preceding sections:

— The countries of the region may be grouped into four: (1) those that produce oil sufficient to meet most of their requirements, (2) those that produce all of or slightly more than they want to use, (3) those that produce more than they can use, and (4) those that produce negligible amounts relative to their total energy requirements. This diversity has resulted in a significant flow of oil among these groups of countries.

— Geologically, although no one thinks of the region in terms of its potential for giant discoveries, the region's oil and gas resources are still far from fully developed. Hence, in addition to direct state involvement, the region is still seen by investors as a growth area for exploration, development, and production. The flow of capital into the projects comes from both within and outside the region.

— Security of petroleum supply is a priority in the agenda of most net-oil-importers. Their responses to the instabilities created by the 1973-74 and 1979-80 threats to petroleum supply have varied according to their own geological endowments and financial capabilities for reducing the degree of such insecurity. Such responses have sometimes appeared to be socially costly, especially where the impacts of errors extend beyond national borders.

— Among the responses to the market upheavals has been the creation of new institutions to deal with the problem. In addition to strictly policy-making and implementing bodies, national oil companies have sprouted. Such national companies occasionally serve as both competitor and regulator in the industry. They also engage in international activities in competition with private foreign investment. The social value of this competition with respect to societal efficiency is not immediately clear, because of special privileges accorded national companies that are not available to private investors.

— Recognition of the changing structure of the relationship between investors and resource owners plus the desire to capture as much of the associated rent from such ownership have given rise to new fiscal regimes and shifts in investment and trading patterns.

— Although most countries are not capable of tapping domestic capital sources for the development and marketing of indigenous petroleum resources, the institutional framework does not always appear to recognize this need. Directives affecting the way business is conducted, price controls, and the like affect the investment climate.

— The existence of some elasticity is observed in the demand and supply of hydrocarbons, even that of the critical liquid commodity; this elasticity is reflected in the behavior of all actors involved, both on the buying and selling sides. Responses vary according to differing attitudes toward risk, whether private or national.

Overall, a general assessment suggests that present arrangements are far from optimal. To date this situation has not been aggravated by potential conflicts that could arise from boundary problems in the process of developing these trade resources. There is no guarantee, however, that the present amicable situation, or at worst dormant hostility, will prevail and that countries will always see the benefits of settling disputes amicably.[57]

REFERENCES

Albers, J. P., M. D. Carter, A. L. Clark, A. B. Coury, and S. P. Sweinfurth (1973). *Summary Petroleum and Selected Mineral Statistics for 120 Countries, Including Offshore Areas. Geological Survey Professional Paper 817. Washington, D.C.: U.S. Government Printing Office.*

American Association of Petroleum Geologists (1984). AAPG Bulletin. "World Energy Developments, 1983" issue. Vol. 68, No. 10.

American Embassy (1984). "Indonesia's Petroleum Sector." Jakarta.

Asian Oil and Gas (April 1984). "Energy Update." pp. 5-6.

Asian Wall Street Journal (23 September 1983). "Mobil signs accord to sell its Manila unit." p. 14.

Asian Wall Street Journal (11 May 1984). "Asia is called a reasonable risk for firms." pp. 1, 14.

Barrows, G. H. (1983). *Worldwide Concession Contracts and Petroleum Legislation.* Tulsa, Oklahoma: Penn Well Publishing Company.

Australian Government (1984). "Statement by the Treasurer the Hon. P.J. Keating, MP and the Minister for Resources and Energy Senator The Hon Peter Walsh—27 June 1984." Canberra, Australia.

Bangkok Post (1984). "Thailand signs oil deal. 8 May p. 1.

Bell, J. (1983). "Government oil companies: 'Quo vadis'?" In P. Nemetz (ed.), *Energy: Ethics, Power and Policy. The Journal of Business Administration,* Vol. 13, Nos. 1 and 2. (Vancouver: University of British Columbia).

British Petroleum Company (1984). *BP Statistical Review of World Energy.* London.

Chase Manhattan Bank (1979, 1984). *Capital Investments of the World Petroleum Industry.* New York.

Eck, T. R. (1983). "Energy economics and taxation." *Journal of Energy and Development,* Vol. 8, No. 2 (Spring), pp. 293-304.

152 Economic and Political Incentives to Petroleum Exploration

Far Eastern Economic Review (1984). *Asia Yearbook*. "Asia-Pacific Principal Energy Financings," pp. 96-97.

Fesharai, F. (1984). "The Singapore Story: A Refining Center in a Transitory Oil Market," Manuscript, OPEC Downstream Project, Resource Systems Institute. Honolulu: The East-West Center.

Garnaut, R. and Ross, A. C. (1983). *Taxation of Mineral Rents*. Oxford: Clarendon Press.

Hoffman, S. L. (1984). "The ASEAN Refining Industry: A Preliminary Survey and Analysis." Draft manuscript for the OPEC Downstream Project, Resource Systems Institute. Honolulu: The East-West Center, April.

Ibrahim, Y. (1984). "China pushing oil on Asian markets at cut-rate prices." *Wall Street Journal* (15 October), p. 34.

International Monetary Fund (1983). *Government Finance Statistics Yearbook*. Washington, D.C.

Keenan, P. J. (1981). "Financing the petroleum industry 1980-1990: $3.17 trillion," *Ocean Industry* (October).

Mooradian, A. H. (1984). "Asian oil production outside China is expected to decline after 1986," in *Asian Wall Street Journal* (9 April 1984), p. 3.

Musgrave, R. A. and P. B. Musgrave (1973). *Public Finance in Theory and Practice*. McGraw-Hill Book Company.

Norgaard, R. B. (1977). "Uncertainty, competition, and leasing." Manuscript, Energy Resources Group, University of California, Berkeley.

Norgaard, R. B. (1984). "Bureaucracy, systems management, and the mythology of science." Giannini Foundation of Agricultural Economics Working Paper No. 297. May (first draft).

Offshore (January 1984). "Drillers seek Alaska supergiant." Vol. 44, No. 1. pp. 29-39.

Offshore (May 1984). "Offshore China offers great potential." Vol. 44, No. 5. p. 122.

Offshore (20 July 1984). "Japan provides funds, encourages worldwide search." Vol. 44, No. 8, pp. 90-94.

Offshore (20 July 1984). "Offshore crude, gas production increases."

Oil and Gas Journal (18 December 1981 and 26 December 1983).

Oil and Gas Journal (5 September 1983). "Australia approves crude oil exports," Vol. 81, No. 36, p. 54.

Oil and Gas Journal (12 December 1983). "Mukluk test appears to be dry hole." Vol. 81, No. 50, pp. 66-67.

Oil and Gas Journal (16 January 1984). "Apparent Mukluk wildcat failure doesn't dim North Slope outlook." Vol. 81, No. 3. pp. 45-48.

Oil and Gas Journal (30 January 1984). "Beaufort lists strike; Mukluk plugged." Vol. 82, No. 5. pp. 74-75.

Oil and Gas Journal (26 March 1984). "LPG international trade seen rising." Vol. 82, No. 13. pp. 58-59.

Oil and Gas Journal (7 May 1984). "Changing times alter the way state oil firms do business." Vol. 82, No. 19, pp. 73-78.

Oil and Gas Journal (27 August 1984). "Asia/Pacific oil flow up, exploration down." Vol. 82, No. 5. pp. 55-62.

Oil and Gas Journal (3 September 1984). "Thai concessions carry revamped terms." Vol. 82, No. 36. pp. 50-51.

Oil and Gas Journal (10 December 1984). "Indonesia presses oil companies to use its ports." Vol. 82, No. 50, p. 54.

Oil and Gas Journal (10 December 1984). "New Zealand energy changes to open acreage." Vol. 82, No. 50, p. 55.

Petroleum Economist (August 1983). "World survey: Natural gas." Vol. 50, No. 8, pp. 293-296.

Petroleum Economist (August 1984). "News in brief: Taiwan." Vol. 51, No. 8. p. 39.

Petroleum Economist (August 1984). "World survey: Natural gas." Vol. 51, No. 8, pp. 286-288.

Petroleum Economist (August 1984). "South Korea: Economic boom continues." Vol. 51, No. 11, pp. 413-415.

Petroleum Economist (August 1984). "News in Brief: Burma." p. 428.

Petroleum Economist and Petroconsultants (1981). *Far East Oil and Energy Survey,* London.

Petroleum News (March 1982). "Asia's finance business: how does energy tap in?" Vol. 12, No. 12, pp. 14-15.

Petroleum News (July 1983). News Supplement: "Philippines." Vol. 14, No. 4.

Petroleum News (January 1984). *Exploration Annual.* Vol. 14, No. 10.

Petroleum News (March 1984). "Tracking energy demand: Malaysia sets up new unit." Vol. 14, No. 12. p. 26.

Petroleum News (March 1984). "Map of the month." Vol. 14, No. 12. pp. 60-61.

Petroleum News (May 1984). "Map of the Month: Major crude flows to East Asian countries." Vol. 15, No. 2. pp. 24-25.

Petroleum News (July 1984). "Compromise reached on Australia's RRT." Vol. 15, No. 4, p. 61.

Petroleum News (August 1984). "NW shelf gas flows to Perth." Vol. 15, No. 5. pp. 29-30.

Petroleum News (September 1984). "Taiwan moves to total import reliance." Vol. 15, No. 6, p. 17.

Resources Asia (December 1983). "Outlook for 1984."

Siddayao, C. M. (1978). *The Off-shore Petroleum Resources of South-East Asia: Potential Conflict Situations and Related Economic Considerations:* Kuala Lumpur: Oxford University Press.

Siddayao, C. M. (1980). *The Supply of Petroleum Reserves in South-East Asia: Economic Implications of Evolving Property Rights Arrangements.* Oxford University Press.

Siddayao, C. M. (1981). "Petroleum resource development policies: Implications of the Southeast Asian contractual framework," *Energy, Vol. 6, No. 8 (August).*

Siddayao, C. M. (1984). "Oil and gas on the continental shelf: Potentials and constraints in the Asia-Pacific Region." *Ocean Management,* Vol. 9, pp. 7-100.

Siddayao, C. M. (forthcoming 1985). "Capital investment requirements for oil and gas development: Constraints in developing countries." In R. K. Pachauri (ed.), *Proceedings* of the International Conference on "Global Interactions" of the International Association of Energy Economists, Delhi, India, 4-6 January 1984. Delhi: M/s. Allied Publishers.

Siddayao, C. M. ed. (forthcoming 1985). *Criteria for Energy Pricing Policy:* A Collection of Papers Commissioned for the Energy Pricing Policy Workshop, Bangkok 8-11 May 1984. London: Graham & Trotman Ltd.

Thailand Government, National Energy Administration (1983). *Thailand Energy Master Plan,* Bangkok.

Toner, A. J. (1984). "Iran's crude oil floods East Asia as prices plunge." *Wall Street Journal* (26 June), pp. 1, 3.

Turvey, R. (ed., 1968). *Public Enterprise* Baltimore, Md.: Penguin Books, Inc.

U.S. Department of Energy (1981). *Energy Industries Abroad.* Prepared by the Office of International Affairs. Doc. No. DOE.IA-0012. September.

United Nations (1976, 1979). *World Energy Supplies.* Statistical Series J, Nos. 19, 22.

United Nations (1984). *Yearbook of World Energy Statistics.* New York.

Wall Street Journal (19 April 1984). "After Mukluk fiasco, Sohio strives to find, or perhaps to buy, oil." pp. 1, 24.

World Bank (1983). *World Tables.* Washington, D.C.

World Oil (1 August 1984). "Offshore China: High risk, potential." Vol. 199, No. 2, pp. 59-60.

Footnotes

[1] For purposes of this paper, the term "petroleum" will be used in the accepted industry terminology that includes both liquid and gaseous hydrocarbons. The terms "oil" and "gas" will be used where a distinction is necessary.

[2] The *upstream* stage involves exploration (or the location of producible reserves), development (or the delineation of the discovered resources), and production (or the actual lifting of the resources from the traps). The *downstream* stage includes transporting, refining, and marketing of the discovered resource in crude or processed form.

[3] *Petroleum News* (May 1984), p. 25.

[4] See Table 2 in Hoffman (1984).

[5] *Petroleum Economist* (August 1984), p. 39.

[6] *Bangkok Post* (8 May 1984).

[7] Se: Table 10 in Hoffman (1984).

[8] LPG is the generic term for propane, butane, and mixtures of both. It is produced from two sources: (1) as a by-product in refineries and chemical plants, and (2) as a result of the extraction of such liquids from natural gas streams or crude oil at or close to the point of production.

9 *Oil and Gas Journal* (26 March 1984), p. 58.

10 Thailand Government, National Energy Administration (1983).

11 Government source, as reported in *Petroleum News* (January 1984), p. 85.

12 Mooradian (1984) and *Offshore* (May 1984).

13 Ibrahim (1984) and Toner (1984).

14 See *Oil and Gas Journal* (5 September 1983).

15 See *Petroleum News* (January 1984), p. 83, and (August 1984), pp. 29-30. *Asian Wall Street Journal* (22 May 1984), p. 3, *Petroleum Economists (November 1984), p. 415.*

16 *Asian Oil and Gas* (April 1984), p. 5.

17 See Fesharaki (1984) for a more detailed discussion of the situation.

18 Chase Manhattan does not specify the countries covered, but one assumes that this includes the traditional group of Asian and Australasian countries.

19 Some loans by India in April 1983 shown in the reference material were for exploration and development, and two short-term loans were shown for Bangladesh for the payment of oil imports.

20 Oil companies sometimes want to refer to themselves in this era as management companies in the upstream stage because of the nature of the current contractual arrangements.

21 *Petroleum News* (May 1984), pp. 61-63.

22 The Indonesian version of the 85/15 split—and presumably of the 88/12 split, for which no details are available to this author at this writing —includes corporate and other taxes due the government in the 85 percent share of "profit oil." The true split after cost-recovery, therefore, may be close to or even better than the 70/30 split of Malaysia and the Philippines. See pages, 65, 89, and 105 in Siddayao (1980) for a detailed explanation.

23 See Table 5.5 in Siddayao (1890) which shows how these variables affect the net "take" of governments and companies.

24 The interested reader may find a perusal of the annual exploration issues of the *Petroleum News* informative.

25 *Petroleum News* (January 1984), Supplement.

26 *Petroleum News* (September 1984), p. 17.

27 *Petroleum Economist* (November 1984), p. 428.

28 *Offshore* (20 July 1984).

29 *Petroleum News* (March 1982), p. 14.

30 See Appendix C in Siddayao (1984) for a summary of the details of some of these loans.

31 *Asian Oil and Gas* (April 1984).

32 Supra-operational activities are defined, for the purposes of this paper, as policy interventions (licensing procedures, contract determinations, price setting, etc.) and government activities that are of a general oversight type. Operational involvement is defined as engaging in actual exploration, production, refining, purchasing, and marketing activities.

33 The summary that follows draws from the references cited in Table 5.1., except where otherwise noted. The author has also provided additional insights from personal knowledge of the framework in the Philippines.

34 *Petroleum Economist* (November 1984), p. 413.

35 *Petroleum Economist* (November 1984), pp. 413-415.

36 *Oil and Gas Journal* (26 March 1984), p. 58, and *ibid.* (27 August 1984), p. 58.

[37] Details with regard to the issues and events related to petroleum exploration are found in Siddayao (1980) and some insights into the refining area in Fesharaki (1984).

[38] *Petroleum News* (March 1984), p. 26.

[39] *Oil and Gas Journal* (10 December 1984), p. 55.

[40] *Asian Wall Street Journal,* 23 September 1983, and *Petroleum News* (July 1984). Mobil reportedly also sold its retail outlets and distribution system for industrial customers to Caltex.

[41] *Asian Oil and Gas* (April 1984), p. 5, and Fesharaki (1984).

[42] *Asian Wall Street Journal* (22 May 1984), p. 3.

[43] *Asian Oil and Gas* (April 1984), p. 6.

[44] Furthermore, some of the issues peculiar to the region's upstream and downstream institutional framework (including the contractual framework, subsidies, and pricing policies) have already been discussed by this author in depth elsewhere. See, for example, Siddayao (1980, 1981, 1985 forthcoming), Siddayao, ed. (1985, forthcoming).

[45] See, for example, Bell (1983).

[46] Those interested in the historical details of this loss may consult *Oil and Gas Journal* (12 December 1983, 16 January 1984, 30 January 1984), *Offshore* (January 1984), and *Wall Street Journal* (19 April 1984, 23 August 1984).

[47] The *Economist* (28 July 1984) and map in *Petroleum News* (March 1984), pp. 60-61.

[48] This author's personal experience in the industry and in dealing with Singapore marketers in the late 1970s provides an impression that conflicts with those suggested by Fesharaki (1984).

[49] The interested reader is referred to Siddayao (1980, 1981, and forthcoming 1985) for an analysis of the allocative implications of the other elements of the fiscal regime in Asia.

[50] For details on this tax, see Garnaut and Ross (1983) and *Outline of a "Greenfields" Resource Rent Tax in the Petroleum Sector* (April 1984) prepared for the Office of the Prime Minister, Canberra, Australia.

[51] Australian Government (1984).

[52] *Petroleum News* (July 1984), p. 61.

[53] See Garnaut and Ross (1983).

[54] Norgaard (1977).

[55] See Eck (1983).

[56] See Musgrave and Musgrave (1973) for an expanded discussion of the general aspects of taxation.

[57] These issues are discussed by the author elsewhere. See Siddayao (1978 and 1984).

Impact of Lower Oil Prices

by Joseph A. Yager

The uncertainty of future oil prices has significantly affected government planning in the Asia-Pacific region. The fundamental energy policy dilemma facing oil-importing countries today is balancing the short-term opportunities offered by lower oil prices against the need to reduce dependence on imports as a means of hedging against the possibility of another oil supply crisis. The author's paper addresses the impact of lower oil prices on oil-importing countries in the region and discusses a variety of possible policy responses.

The era of high international energy prices came to at least a temporary end in the mid-1980s. Oil prices peaked at $32.60 a barrel in 1981 and declined to $26.70 in 1985.[1] The fall of oil prices accelerated in early 1986. In July, some spot prices fell below $10 a barrel. In August, oil prices rebounded on news of an OPEC agreement to limit production. For most of the oil remainder of 1986, spot prices averaged $13-14 a barrel. In late December, a new OPEC agreement to limit production pushed average oil prices up to about $16 a barrel. As the year ended, the oil market remained volatile, and prospects for OPEC's achieving and maintaining its proclaimed goal of $18 a barrel by February 1987 were uncertain.[2]

From 1981 to early 1985, the appreciation of the U.S. dollar (in which crude oil prices are quoted) wiped out all or most of the decline in crude oil prices in terms of the national currencies of many oil-importing countries.

During this period, the weighted average of crude oil prices paid by European members of the International Energy Agency (IEA), expressed in national currencies, actually increased 30 percent.[3] Beginning in April 1985, however, the depreciation of the U.S. dollar in terms of many currencies has magnified the effect of decreases in international prices of crude oil. From April 1985 to January 1986, crude oil prices paid by European members of IEA dropped 25.7 percent. During the same period, the cost of oil imported into the United States (in U.S. dollars) decreased only 11.2 percent.[4]

Note: An earlier version of this paper was prepared as background for the Regional meeting on Energy Policy convened by the Asian Development Bank at its headquarters in Manila, December 11–12, 1986.

POSSIBLE FUTURE DEVELOPMENTS

The future of international oil prices is obscured by many uncertainties. On the supply side of the oil market, the uncertainties include developments in the war between Iran and Iraq, and the success or failure of OPEC in restricting production on the basis of agreed market shares for its members. On the demand side of the market, uncertainties include changes in oil stocks, the level of economic activity in major oil-importing countries, and changes in exchange rates between the U.S. dollar and other currencies.

Further uncertainties result from the effects that oil prices have on future supply and demand. If oil prices remain at or near recent levels, exploration for oil in some areas will be discouraged, expenditures to enhance the output of existing wells will in many cases not be made, and some wells with high operating costs per barrel of output will be plugged. Incentives for energy conservation are being weakened, and some of the substitution of other fuels for oil may be reversed. These effects of lower oil prices on supply and demand are to some extent already being felt.

By increasing demand and decreasing supply, low oil prices will in time create conditions favorable to higher oil prices. Rising requirements of consumers could simply outpace the ability and willingness of producers to increase oil supplies. In an expanding oil market, the members of OPEC might be able to agree to restrict oil exports enough to push prices up substantially. Such an agreement would be more likely, if Saudi Arabia decided that market conditions favored its resuming the role of residual supplier.

Predicting how long international oil prices will remain low and how rapidly and how far they may subsequently rise is virtually impossible. In developing country members of the Bank, however, there is a widely shared perception that real oil prices will rise only gradually and will not regain their 1985 level until the late 1990s.[5] This perception is of course not necessarily correct, and an alternative possibility is considered later in this paper.

EFFECTS OF LOWER OIL PRICES[6]

The effects of a sharp drop in international oil prices are roughly the reverse of the effects of a sharp increase in those prices. The two cases are not likely to be symmetrical, however, and lower oil prices will not simply re-enact the oil crisis of 1973–74 or 1979–80 in reverse. As was the case with past increases in oil prices, the effects of lower oil prices will vary greatly from country to country.

General Effects

Lower international oil prices alter the terms of trade between oil-exporting and oil-importing countries and shift income from the exporters to the importers. Average oil prices in 1986 were about $15 a barrel lower than they were in 1985, and the total volume of oil imports was almost five percent larger. The income transferred in 1986 as roughly $115 billion of which oil-imported developing countries gained about $24 billion.[7]

Just as past large increases in international oil prices raised the rate of inflation, a substantial fall in oil prices would reduce the general price level[8] and lower interest rates. A fall in international oil prices would also probably bring about a temporary increase in the rate of world economic growth.[9] How large this increase, if any, would be would depend on whether those who gained from the income transfer caused by the drop in oil prices adjusted their expenditures more rapidly than those who lost. The answer to this question would in turn depend on:

- The extent to which oil-exporting countries borrowed or drew down foreign exchange reserves to avoid reductions in imports.

- The distribution of terms-of-trade induced income gains within oil-importing countries and the effect of the fall in energy prices on investments by domestic energy industries.[10]

- The extent to which fiscal and monetary policies of governments of oil-importing countries happened to counter or reinforce the stimulating effects of lower oil prices.

Effects on Individual Countries

Since the price elasticity of demand for oil is quite low, especially in the short run, lower oil prices mean lower oil import bills for oil-importing countries. As was noted above, lower oil prices probably stimulate international economic activity and improve the markets for the exports of many countries. Exports of goods and services to oil-exporting countries, however, can be expected to decline.

Data on several oil-importing developing countries indicate that through 1985 declining international oil prices caused them to suffer losses in both worker remittances from oil-exporting countries and exports to those countries. For example, from 1985 to 1986, worker remittance (in current U.S. dollars) fell 37.0 percent in Korea, 23.4 percent in Bangladesh, 6.2 percent in Pakistan, and 1.8 percent in Thailand.[11] Over the same two-year period, exports to oil-exporting countries decreased 58.6 percent in Pakistan, 36.0 percent in Korea, and 31.9 percent in Thailand.[12]

Despite the decline in receipts from oil-exporting countries, the balance of payments on current account of oil-importing countries as a group has undoubtedly been improved by the recent fall in international oil prices.[13] The ability of such countries to service international debt has been increased, and their credit standings improved. Lower oil prices have had the reverse effects on most, if not all, net oil-exporting countries.

Lower oil prices can stimulate increased rates of economic activity within individual oil-importing countries both by improving their balances of payments on current account and by shifting disposable income from energy producers to energy consumers. The latter effect depends on energy consumers increasing expenditures more rapidly than energy producers reduce investments. The fiscal and monetary policies of governments can influence the magnitude of both stimuli, as can government policies on passing reductions in international oil prices on to domestic consumers.

A policy of passing on reductions in international oil prices fully would maximize the shift of income from domestic energy producers to energy consumers. Such a policy would also result in larger oil imports and lower production costs for export industries than a policy of blocking the pass-through of all or part of the oil price reductions. Changes in the exchange rate on the U.S. dollar could increase or decrease the effect of any pass-through policy.

Passing oil price reductions on to domestic consumers in whole or in part would affect both energy consumption and the choice between oil and other sources of energy. Sympathetic reductions in the prices of other fuels would reinforce the stimulus to energy consumption provided by lower oil prices. Sympathetic price reductions would, however, weaken incentives to switch from other fuels to oil. Even if none of the decrease in international oil prices was passed on to domestic consumers, some increase in energy consumption would result from the positive effects of lower oil prices on world economic growth.

In the short run, lower energy prices will probably cause only limited increases in energy consumption. Cars will be driven more, houses will be kept at more comfortable temperatures, and the enforcement of energy conservation rules in industry may slacken. The energy efficiency of the stock of industrial and household equipment will, however, decrease only slowly, if at all. Many plans to buy more energy-efficient equipment will probably be carried out despite the fall in oil prices.

Similarly, only a small part of the substitution of other sources of energy for oil that took place during the period of high oil prices will be reversed in the short run, even if oil maintains a substantial price advantage over other fuels. Electric utilities with excess thermal generating capacity will run oil-burning power plants at higher percentage of capacity than coal-burning plants, and more oil may be used in plants that burn a mixture of oil and coal. Power plants and industrial boilers that are equipped to burn either oil or coal will shift to oil as long as it is cheaper. Investments in new oil-burning electric power plants or industrial boilers, or even in the conversion of coal-burning facilities to oil, do not appear to be likely, unless lower oil prices continue for more than a few years.

EFFECTS OF AN INCREASE IN OIL PRICES IN THE EARLY 1990s

In the late 1980s, a tight oil market with rising prices and limited excess productive capacity would be vulnerable to the kind of external shocks that set off the oil crises in 1973–74 and 1979–80. Without predicting that this will in fact occur, it is instructive to assume that real international oil prices will regain their 1985 level of about $27 a barrel by 1990 and that, because of a new international crisis, they will increase another 50 percent in the following two years to about $41 a barrel. Understanding the possible effects of this assumed sharp increase in oil prices can be helped by comparing it in general terms with the oil crisis of 1979–80.[14]

The assumed increase in international oil prices in the late 1980s would at first progressively reduce the transfer of income from oil-exporting countries to oil-importing countries caused by the earlier drop in oil prices. This phase would end in 1990, and a continued sleeper rise in oil prices would cause larger and larger income transfers in the opposite direction. The assumed rise in oil prices in 1991–92 would be about 30 percent as large as the increase in 1979–80. In absolute terms, however, the difference is not as great. In 1979–80, oil prices rose about $17 a barrel, compared with the $14 a barrel increase assumed for 1991–92.

In both 1980 and 1981, higher oil prices transferred about 1.75 percent of the GNP of OECD countries to oil-exporting countries.[15] The assumed increase in oil prices might transfer about 1.0 percent of the GNP of OECD countries to oil exporting countries in 1992 and declining shares of rising GNP in subsequent years.[16]

In addition to the transfer of income to the oil-exporting countries, the OECD countries lost GNP in 1980 and 1981, because not all of the transferred income was spent and because of their own efforts to counter the inflationary effects of the increase in oil prices. Losses from OPEC-induced extra saving have been estimated at 3.0 percent of the GNP of OECD countries in 1980 and 4.25 percent in 1981. Losses from OECD counterinflationary policies have been estimated at 0.25 percent of GNP in 1980 and 1.75 percent in 1981.[17] Losses from these two causes would probably be less serious in the circumstances assumed for 1991 and 1992, if only because both the amount of income transferred and the percentage rise in oil prices would be smaller than during the second oil crisis. Losses from OPEC-induced saving would be further curtailed, if the oil-exporting countries spent their increased revenues fairly quickly to make up for the years of low oil prices. Moreover, benefitting from the experience gained in two oil crises, the international financial system might recycle new OPEC savings more efficiently than after the earlier crises. Losses from OECD counterinflationary policies might be held down, if, as appears possible, the effects of low oil prices in the late 1980s continued to moderate inflationary pressures in the early 1990s.

Oil-importing developing countries would experience similar losses of GNP as a result of the assumed sharp increase in international oil prices. These losses would be smaller quantitatively than the losses of the OECD countries, but they might involve a larger percentage loss in GNP. The developing countries would suffer further temporary losses in GNP because of the reduced ability of the industrialized countries to buy their exports. Exports of goods and services to oil-exporting countries would, however, probably increase.

Oil Prices and Structural Change

Changes in oil and other energy prices initially stimulate changes in energy consumption that can be made fairly easily. If increases or decreases in energy prices appear to be lasting, investments are made that can substantially change the amount of energy used per unit of output. Investments made on the basis of incorrect estimates of future energy prices may not only fail to yield the expected returns, but also make the economy less efficient. Lags between trends in energy prices and the resultant trends in structural changes are unfortunately inevitable. Reversals in energy price trends may impose heavy costs in terms of economic efficiency.

The higher energy prices caused by the oil crises of 1973–74 and 1979–80 stimulated investments in more energy-efficient production processes and shifts in the relative importance of various industries. To some extent, capital and labor were substituted for energy. In some activities, other fuels displaced oil. These changes were presumably retarded by the declining oil prices that began in 1981. Low oil prices in 1986 followed by several years of rising, but still relatively low, oil prices could initiate structural change in the opposite direction. At some point, however, further increases in oil prices would reactivate the move toward lower energy intensity and reduced dependence on oil.

Policy Issues for Oil-Importing Countries

The above review of past and possible future developments with respect to international oil prices raised several policy issues for oil-importing countries. Oil-exporting countries face a different set of policy issues that will not be considered here.

The most fundamental problem facing the governments of oil-importing countries is determining the optimum path for domestic oil and other energy prices. In theory, these prices should be set at long-run marginal cost to facilitate the structural changes that will maximize the efficiency of the economy. There is no assurance that either market forces or the calculations of government regulators can keep energy prices on the right path. At a minimum, however, governments should be aware of the structural consequences of actions that affect energy prices.

If international oil prices go up or down, the governments of oil-importing countries must decide whether, and to what extent, the price changes should be passed on to domestic consumers. In establishing pass-through policies, governments must strike a balance among partially competing goals of price stability, economic growth, and energy security. In the case of an increase in international oil prices, a policy of passing all of the increase on to consumers both depresses total demand and adds to inflationary pressures. Such a policy, however, increases energy security by encouraging energy conservation and the substitution of other fuels for oil. To the extent that energy conservation reduces costs, the competitiveness of the economy in export markets is improved. In the case of a decrease in international oil prices, a policy of passing on the decrease fully has favorable effects on total demand and inflation, but weakens incentives for conservation and fuel switching.

In the cases of both increasing and decreasing international oil prices, the balance among various policy goals can be altered by adjusting the percentage of the price change passed on to consumers and by applying more or less expansionary macroeconomic policies. In determining the right mix of policies, governments must also take into account the impact of their actions on the distribution of income between the energy sector and the rest of the economy.

The recent fall in international oil prices poses major problems in two areas:

a. How should the windfall created by lower oil prices be used? Should it be appropriated to supplement government revenues? Or should it be passed on to stimulate economic activity and, in some countries, ease austerity measures imposed to deal with foreign debt problems?

b. What should be done about energy investments made when oil prices were much higher? Should facilities created by such investments be shut down as soon as the prices of their products fall below variable costs? What price assumptions should be used in planning future energy investments?

Early Reactions of Oil-Importing Countries to Lower Oil Prices

On the basis of recent reports from ten countries, the developing countries are only beginning to deal with the policy issues posed by lower international oil prices. The decline in oil prices from 1982 to 1985 was too gradual to stimulate substantial changes in energy policies, and in an atmosphere of great uncertainty concerning future developments, there has not been time to react fully to the sharp drop of oil prices in 1986.

None of the ten countries has made important revisions in current energy plans. These plans still give priority to objectives such as energy security, energy conservation, and reduced dependence on imported oil that were adopted when international oil prices were much higher. Since (as was noted earlier in this paper) oil prices are expected to rise again, the validity of these objectives over the long run has not been seriously questioned.

Tension inevitably exists between these long-run objectives and new questions requiring immediate attention, such as: Should lower oil prices be passed on to domestic consumers at the risk of weakening incentives to conserve energy? Should the phasing-out of oil-burning electric power plants be delayed? Are emergency oil stocks less necessary at a time of oil glut, or should more oil be bought and stored while it is cheap?

The most difficult energy policy problem facing the oil-importing developing countries may be what to do about domestic energy prices. The most common solution to this problem has been to pass on only part of the reduction in international oil prices to domestic consumers. For example, Korea, the Philippines, Sri Lanka, and Taiwan, have lowered petroleum product prices substantially (20–30 percent). Bangladesh cut domestic oil prices 10 percent, but raised the price of natural gas (which was believed to be underpriced) 20 percent. India has thus far not reacted to lower international oil prices and raised the prices of both petroleum products and coal at the beginning of 1986. The price of coal was increased to cover higher production costs. Prices of petroleum products were raised principally to curtail the rate of increase in their consumption.

The fundamental problem of energy policy facing the oil-importing countries today is balancing the short-term opportunities offered by lower oil prices against the need to prepare for the possibility of a third oil crisis.

Footnotes

[1] D. Mitchell, Acting Chief, EPDCS, *Primary Commodity Price Forecasts,* World Bank Office Memorandum, August 18, 1986, p. 2. These prices are weighted averages of official sales prices of members of the Organization of Petroleum Exporting Countries (OPEC).

[2] *Wall Street Journal* and *New York Times,* various issues.

[3] International Energy Agency, *Energy Prices and Taxes,* Fourth Quarter 1985, p. 39.

[4] *Energy Prices and Taxes,* First Quarter 1986, p. 45.

[5] Asian Development Bank, "Energy Policy Concerns and Responses to Falling Oil Prices," background paper for Regional Meeting on Energy Policy, Manila, December 11–12, 1986.

[6] This section relies heavily on Flemming Larsen and John Llewellyn, "Simulated Macroeconomic Effects of a Large Fall in Oil Prices," Working Paper No. 8, OECD Economics and Statistics Department, June 1983, and Edward R. Fried, "Economic and Security Implications of a Collapse in Oil Prices," unpublished paper, Brookings Institution, May 1985.

[7] Extrapolated from Fried's estimate of the effect of a hypothetical $10 a barrel fall in oil prices in 1985.

[8] One of the simulations by Larsen and Llewellyn estimates that, in the third year after a 25 percent drop in the price of oil, GDP inflators in OECD countries would on the average be about three percent lower than they would be if the real price of oil had remained unchanged.

[9] Fried estimates this increase at one percent in each of the two years following a decrease of $10 a barrel in the price of oil. He assumes that after two years the adjustment to lower oil prices will have been completed and trend growth resumed.

[10] The drop in oil prices could be expected to cause sympathetic declines in the prices of other forms of energy.

[11] Data collected by Asian Development Bank.

[12] International Monetary Fund, *Direction of Trade Statistics, 1986 Yearbook.*

[13] There may be a few exceptions to this generalization. Countries that import relatively little oil, but have enjoyed large exports of goods and services to oil-exporting countries, could experience a worsening of their balances of payments on current account.

[14] This comparison draws on the analysis of the effects of the 1979–80 oil crisis in Sylvia Ostry, John Llewellyn, and Lee Samuelson, "The Cost of OPEC II," *OECD Observer,* March 1982, pp. 37–39.

[15] Ostry, Llewellyn, and Samuelson, p. 38.

[16] This estimate assumes that the GNP of OECD countries will grow at an average annual rate of 2.5 percent from 1985 to 1992, the GNP elasticity of demand for oil during this period will be 0.5, and domestic oil production of oil in OECD countries in 1992 will be 15.0 million barrels a day (compared with 17.1 mbd in 1985).

[17] Ostry, Llewellyn, and Samuelson, p. 38.

[18] This section draws upon the background paper, "Energy Policy Concerns and Responses to Falling Oil Prices," Asian Development Bank, December 1986. This paper is based on reports from Bangladesh, China, India, Indonesia, Malaysia, Korea, Pakistan, Philippines, Sri Lanka, and Taiwan.

World Oil Markets—Back to the Future: The Evolution of the Meganationals

by Paul Mlotok

In the petroleum industry, the demise of one cartel has always been followed by the emergence of a new and more comprehensive one. Current volatility in the world oil market is a reflection of fundamental change in the influence of OPEC and, the author suggests, could result in the creation of a new partnership that will act as the principal determinant and regulator of world oil markets. The author believes that this partnership might include OPEC nations and certain major international oil companies, which together would constitute integrated "meganational" units functioning from wellhead to pump.

"The dear people, if they had produced less oil than they wanted, would have got their full price; no combination in the world could have prevented that, if they had produced less oil than the world required."

John D. Rockefeller (1888)

Summary

World oil markets are currently undergoing a fundamental change paralleled only by the breakup of the Standard Oil Trust in 1911. That breakup was followed by 20 years of extreme volatility in world oil markets, which was brought to an end by the establishment of the Texas Railroad Commission in 1933. The end of the OPEC era (1973–85) could lead to a period of similarly high volatility, although we expect that it will last for only two to four years—instead of two decades. We anticipate that the disorder in world oil markets will generate a new and more comprehensive mechanism for regulating world oil markets. Although no cartel has ever lasted, in the case of oil, the breakdown of one cartel has always been followed by the creation of a new and more comprehensive one. This might now take the form of an amalgam of the key OPEC nations with the major international oil companies to form a small group of powerful, fully integrated "meganationals."

Back to the Future—Rockefeller and the Texas Railroad Commission

To better understand the current situation, it is useful to review the history of the oil industry. Oil was first discovered in the United States in 1859 by Colo-

Figure 1. Real Price of U.S. Oil, 1901–85 (In 1972 Dollars)

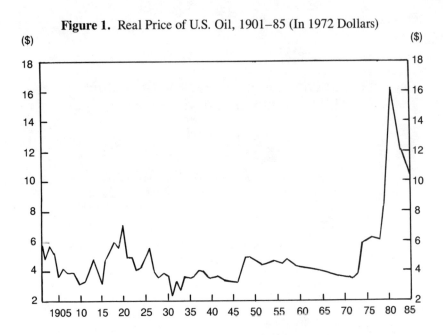

nel Drake, who was drilling in Titusville, Pennsylvania. By 1875, John D. Rockefeller had established the Standard Oil Trust, which dominated and regulated oil markets until it was broken up in 1911. Oil prices were extremely volatile before the Standard Oil Trust. Rockefeller took control of the transportation network, which gave him the ability to balance supply with demand and smooth out the boom-bust cycle. From 1901–11 (earlier data is unavailable), the average year-to-year fluctuation in the price of oil was held to 12%.

In 1911, the U.S. Government broke up the Standard Oil Trust, and a 20-year period followed in which oil markets were virtually unregulated. The year-to-year fluctuation in oil prices averaged 25%. For example, from 1916–20, the price of oil rose by 479%; by 1928, it had fallen by 62%. During five of these 20 years, the price changed by 40% year to year. This instability led to demands in Texas and Oklahoma for development of some regulatory mechanism to protect the local economy from such violent price changes. The Texas Railroad Commission was established in 1933 to regulate production levels, and it still functions today. This organization was effective in controlling prices through the 1930s, but it probably would have become ineffective after World War II when the industry became truly international. However, in a seamless transition, the "Seven Sisters"[1] rose to ascendancy by extending a

---

[1] British Petroleum Exxon, Gulf, Mobil, Shell Group, Texaco, and Standard Oil of California.

Texas Railroad Commission pricing scheme on a worldwide basis. They regulated world oil markets until OPEC wrested away control in 1973. During the 1933–72 period, the average year-to-year fluctuation in world oil prices was only 6%.

OPEC was "effective" in controlling world oil markets in that it pushed the price of oil up well above an equilibrium level and kept it there for a surprisingly long period of time. OPEC achieved this through production restraints (not always voluntary); its output dropped from 32 million barrels per day in 1979 to 16 million barrels per day in 1985.

Such extreme production curtailment has pressed the organization beyond its limits, and OPEC's ability to regulate oil markets is now breaking down. During the OPEC era (1973–85) year-to-year price changes averaged 24%. (The change occurring in 1986 will raise this figure substantially.)

Thus, four distinct periods have occurred during this century. From 1901–11, markets were reasonably stable under the Standard Oil Trust. From 1912–32, they were extremely volatile in an unregulated market. During the 1933–72 period, prices were the most stable under the Texas Railroad Commission and then under the Seven Sisters. During the OPEC years, prices have again been volatile, initially mostly on the upside, but now on the downside (see Figure 2).

Figure 2. Year-to-Year Percentage Change in Price of U.S. Crude Oil, 1901–85

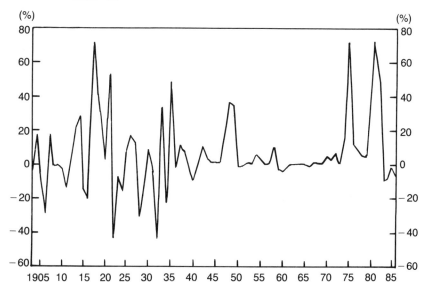

Ahead to the Future—The Meganationals

While OPEC may periodically be able to forge temporary arrangements for controlling output and prices, we do not believe that it can control oil markets on an ongoing basis. For this reason, we expect that the current period will be similar to 1912–32, when markets were virtually unregulated. We expect oil prices to be extremely volatile, centering in the range of $12–$16 per barrel, but sometimes spiking out in either direction. This will set fundamental forces in motion that will reduce supplies, increase demand and bring markets to a point at which market regulation becomes feasible again within two to four years.

At that time, we expect a new type of cartel to emerge. No cartel has ever lasted; however, in the case of oil, the breakdown of one cartel has always been followed by the formation of another, more comprehensive cartel. OPEC is trying to extend this record by reshaping itself into a larger cartel that would include as many as 20 members, up from 13 currently. However, the problems of achieving a consensus among that many parties with disparate interests condemn such an effort to failure.

Instead, we expect an arrangement of several large, integrated units to emerge, functioning from wellhead to pump, and amalgamating the core OPEC nations with the major international oil companies. Elements of this arrangement are already in place. In some cases, these meganationals may consist of producer nations that have integrated downstream, such as Kuwait and Venezuela are doing. In other cases, it may consist of a major oil company that works closely with a major producer and serves as a distributor and marketer. (In some cases, the oil companies may also operate the fields.) The Aramco arrangement was along these lines, but it left the Saudi Arabians with little actual control over and understanding of the downstream. Evolving arrangements would need to give the oil company a financial interest in the upstream and the producing nation a financial interest in the downstream in order to create a clear community of interest. Netback arrangements hint at such accommodation by giving the producing nations an interest in the state of product markets and giving the oil companies protection from noneconomic crude pricing.

Such fully integrated meganationals would solve some of the problems that led to the breakdown of the previous two cartels—the Seven Sisters and OPEC. The Seven Sisters did not appreciate the revenue needs of the producing nations, and they kept the price of oil too low. This increased demand and also set political forces in motion within the producing nations, which eventually led to OPEC's ascendancy. OPEC, in turn, did not understand the distribution end of the business or the consumer. So, it emphasized revenue needs and set the price too high, which has led to OPEC's shrinking market share and breakdown. Meganationals, working at both the supply and the demand ends of the business, would have a better chance of achieving a sustainable balance.

One necessary element to the survival of a meganational cartel is that there be a limited number of players (perhaps seven). In several years, it should be feasible for such a small number of players to maintain control of the oil markets. Low prices near term will reduce the production potential in the non-OPEC nations and the smaller OPEC nations and will also lead to increased demand. By 1988–90, the gap between demand and potential supply could be small enough that the major producers alone (Saudi Arabia, Iran, Iraq, Kuwait, and Venezuela) working with certain of the major oil companies (Exxon, Shell Group and others) could vary their production within acceptable limits to balance markets at a sustainable price level.

What is the Real Price of Oil?

One of the questions that the recent decline in oil prices has raised is, what is the "equilibrium price" or "correct price" for oil. One approach to this is to review the historical record. We have assembled data on the nominal and real prices of oil from 1901–85. During most of the 1901–72 time frame, the real price was surprisingly constant, fluctuating within a range of $3.00–$5.00 per barrel in all but nine of those years, and averaging $4.03 per barrel over the period. Over the full period 1901–85, the real price averaged $4.80 per barrel. In 1985, the real price was $10.41 per barrel (in 1972 dollars), and the nominal price was $24.03 per barrel. Thus, to adjust back to a real price of $5.00 per barrel, the nominal price would have to fall by about one half, to $12 per barrel. As the cost of finding oil is higher today, the equilibrium price is probably above this level. However, the exercise shows that current "low" oil prices are not really an anomaly; rather, they are in line with historical real prices.

Is History a Guide?

An argument can be made that oil should cost more today, because it is more expensive to find and produce: The "easy finds" were developed first, and we are now exploring more difficult frontier regions. Two factors moderate this argument.

- Advances in technology continually reduce the real cost of finding oil. While locating and drilling a 5,000-foot well in West Texas seems to be easy to us today, it may not have been so simple or "cheap" in 1900, using the primitive tools of the time.

- We tend to think of the marginal barrel available today as being from a frontier region such as the Beaufort Sea, where costs are high. However, this reflects a curious inversion through which we shut in the world's cheap oil (in Saudi Arabia) and then look for expensive oil in the Beaufort Sea. Politics aside, the marginal barrel would come from the Middle East, where much oil is yet to be found and developed at extremely low costs.

Figure 3. U.S. Oil Prices — Nominal and Real (In 1972 Dollars), 1901–85

	Nominal Dollars	Yr.-Yr. Pct. Chg.	Real Dollars	Yr.-Yr. Pct. Chg.
1901	$0.96		$6.15	
1902	0.80	(17)%	4.94	(19.7)%
1903	0.94	18	5.77	16.8
1904	0.86	(9)	5.21	(9.7)
1905	0.62	(28)	3.66	(29.8)
1906	0.73	18	4.21	15.0
1907	0.72	(1)	3.98	(5.5)
1908	0.72	—	4.01	0.8
1909	0.70	(3)	3.77	(6.0)
1910	0.61	(13)	3.20	(15.1)
1911	0.61	—	3.23	0.9
1912	$0.74	21%	$3.77	16.7%
1913	0.95	28	4.86	28.9
1914	0.81	(15)	4.06	(16.5)
1915	0.64	(21)	3.07	(24.4)
1916	1.10	72	4.71	53.4
1917	1.56	42	5.38	14.2
1918	1.98	27	6.06	12.6
1919	2.01	2	5.40	(10.9)
1920	3.07	53	7.24	34.1

	Nominal Dollars	Yr.-Yr. Pct. Chg.	Real Dollars	Yr.-Yr. Pct. Chg.
1944	$1.21	1%	$3.27	(1.5)%
1945	1.22	1	3.22	(1.5)
1946	1.41	16	3.20	(0.6)
1947	1.93	37	3.90	21.9
1948	2.60	35	4.91	25.9
1949	2.54	(2)	4.84	(1.4)
1950	2.51	(1)	4.68	(3.3)
1951	2.53	1	4.43	(5.3)
1952	2.53	—	4.37	(1.4)
1953	2.68	6	4.56	4.3
1954	2.78	4	4.66	2.2
1955	$2.77	—	$4.55	(2.4)%
1956	2.79	1%	4.44	(2.4)
1957	3.09	11	4.75	7.0
1958	3.01	(3)	4.56	(4.0)
1959	2.90	(4)	4.29	(5.9)
1960	2.88	(1)	4.19	(2.3)
1961	2.89	—	4.17	(0.5)
1962	2.90	—	4.11	(1.4)
1963	2.89	—	4.03	(1.9)

Year				
1921	1.73	(44)	4.90	(32.3)
1922	1.61	(7)	4.96	1.2
1923	$1.34	(17)%	$4.03	(18.7)%
1924	1.43	7	4.31	6.9
1925	1.68	17	4.99	15.8
1926	1.88	12	5.67	13.6
1927	1.30	(31)	4.01	(29.3)
1928	1.17	(10)	3.55	(11.5)
1929	1.27	9	3.86	8.7
1930	1.19	(6)	3.74	(3.1)
1931	0.65	(45)	2.25	(39.8)
1932	0.87	34	3.39	50.7
1933	0.67	(23)	2.67	(21.2)
1934	$1.00	49%	$3.66	37.1%
1935	0.97	(3)	3.49	(4.6)
1936	1.09	12	3.63	4.0
1937	1.18	8	4.03	11.0
1938	1.13	(4)	3.94	(2.2)
1939	1.02	(10)	3.59	(8.9)
1940	1.02	—	3.51	(2.2)
1941	1.14	11	3.65	4.0
1942	1.19	4	3.46	(5.2)
1943	1.20	1	3.32	(4.0)

Year				
1964	2.88	—	3.96	(1.7)
1965	2.86	(1)	3.84	(3.0)
1966	$2.88	1%	$3.75	(2.3)%
1967	2.92	1	3.69	(1.6)
1968	2.94	1	3.56	(3.5)
1969	3.09	5	3.56	0.0
1970	3.18	3	3.48	(2.2)
1971	3.39	7	3.53	1.4
1972	3.39	—	3.39	(4.0)
1973	3.89	15	3.68	8.6
1974	6.74	73	5.87	59.5
1975	7.56	12	6.02	2.6
1976	8.14	8	6.16	2.3
1977	$8.57	5%	$6.12	(0.6)%
1978	8.96	5	5.96	(2.6)
1979	12.51	40	7.66	28.5
1980	21.59	73	12.10	58.0
1981	31.77	47	16.24	34.2
1982	28.52	(10)	13.62	(16.1)
1983	26.19	(8)	12.16	(10.72)
1984	25.88	(1)	11.58	(4.8)
1985	24.03	(7)	10.41	(10.1)

Figure 4. Real Price of U.S. Oil—Five-Year Moving Average, 1905–85 (1972 Dollars Per Barrel)

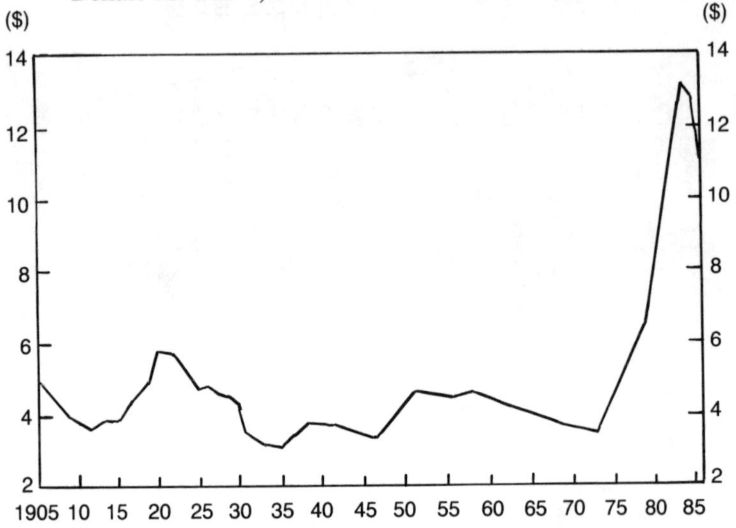

Hence, in a truly free market environment, the current real price of oil might not be too far above the historical level. Even assuming an increase of 50% over the 1901–72 range, this only brings the real price to $6.00 per barrel and the nominal price to $14.00.

Politics do affect the market, however, and foreign oil will not be the United State's first choice; therefore, in order to generate adequate supplies, a nominal price of more than $14.00 per barrel will be necessary. It is important to be aware that this level will not be based purely on economics.

BS

Y/011 PF
LAMBERT